INSTITUTIONAL SETTINGS
IN CHILDREN'S LIVES

Institutional Settings in Children's Lives

Leanne G. Rivlin

Maxine Wolfe

Environmental Psychology Doctoral Program
City University of New York Graduate School

A WILEY-INTERSCIENCE PUBLICATION

JOHN WILEY & SONS

New York • Chichester • Brisbane • Toronto • Singapore

Library of Congress Cataloging in Publication Data

Rivlin, Leanne G.
 Institutional settings in children's lives.

 (Wiley series on personality processes)
 Includes indexes.
 "Wiley-Interscience publication."
 1. Children—Institutional care.   2. Environmental
psychology.   3. Architecture and children.   4. Child
development.   I. Wolfe, Maxine.   II. Title.   III. Series.

HV715.R58   1985   155.4   85-3235
ISBN 0-471-08313-5

Printed in the United States of America

10 9 8 7 6 5 4 3 2 1

To

Ben   Marc
Karen   Amy

for years of patience and support.

Preface

After writing many individual reports and journal articles, limited by space requirements and focused on detail, we wanted the opportunity to examine our fifteen years of work in a comprehensive way, with some distance and a perspective that would enable us to look for broader generalizations. This book gave us that opportunity, the chance to reflect on what we had done in our various research efforts and consider what it all meant.

The work emerged out of our professional interests as environmental psychologists. Despite its name, Environmental Psychology is a multi-disciplinary field, concerned with the relationship between the physical environment and people's lives. It grew out of the desire to make psychology relevant to real world problems and to have an impact on changing the conditions of people's lives. Its basic assumption, broadly described, was that if we understood the relationships between people and the environment, we could help create places that would be an improvement over existing ones, places that would speak to the needs of people. As the field developed, varied approaches emerged. Some environmental psychologists, following a traditional psychology paradigm, applied existing constructs and research approaches to the work, studying, for example, people's perception of environments. Others focused on the physical environment in a deterministic way in the belief that constructing what they considered to be the best possible physical environment would ensure the best lives for people. Our own experiences have shown that neither of these approaches provides adequate grounds for understanding people–environment relationships, nor do they provide a sound basis for helping to bring about constructive change. As we and our colleagues in the Environmental Psychology Program of the City University of New York define problems in this area, the physical environment and people's understanding of it are not viewed as separate from each other or from the social, political, and economic contexts of which they are a part. Defining the problem is as important as attempting a solution if change is to have the possibility of being positive rather than undertaken for its own sake.

For those with humanistic intentions the conditions of children's lives evoke the desire to alleviate suffering and to create positive and supportive experiences.

As our work will show, this is not a new attitude. Yet today, as in the past, the best intentions often lead us to ignore the outcomes of our work and do not necessarily guarantee that what we are helping to create is an improvement over what previously existed.

Upon reflection, we found that the three children's environments that we had studied most intensively—schools, psychiatric hosptials, and day-care centers—were no less ridden with problems today than they had been when we began our work. In fact, one could argue that the crises have exacerbated over the years with prospects for alternatives less clear now than they were earlier. From our perspective, the amount of information available about the problems in these settings should have warranted serious and fundamental changes. Yet this has not occurred. The same issues are being debated as in the past: institutionalization vs. deinstitutionalization, back to basics vs. humanistic education, the family vs. social agents as caretakers for children. Despite the basic maxim of the scientific community, that the availability of information will lead to rational planning, decisions being made in the present political context remind us that this is not necessarily what happens. It appears to be an appropriate time for reflection.

This book summarizes our critical analysis of some of the environments for children that we have studied. In reviewing our work we found it essential to place the findings in a historical context and to examine the political and economic influences. This required extensive additional reading on the history of the creation of settings, a stage that proved to be a laborious but rewarding one in understanding the meaning of our work. Recognizing the powerful shaping force of the heritage of the past—obvious to historians but largely neglected in other social sciences, especially psychology—has been an important learning experience. This implied the use of the past as another source, a focus rather than introductory color, a factor that will shape the questions posed as well as the interpretation of findings. Throughout the analysis and the writing, we have made an effort to point out the role of the physical environment, but not in isolation from the social, political, and economic context.

Although the three kinds of settings we have studied intensively deal with what may appear to be different aspects of children's lives, our reading and research uncovered the continuity of values, institutional qualities, and patterns of behaviors that proved to be overriding forces on development, often constraining the potentials of the children involved. It also made us aware of the connections between settings. We believe that it is essential to be aware of these forces before any attempts at positive changes can be undertaken, and the book documents this argument.

This book should be of interest to a wide range of persons concerned with children and their development from those involved in child psychology and environmental psychology to people responsible for policies and physical designs for the education, nurturance, health, and development of children. We also feel that there are messages for administrators of children's environments, people in charge of the day-to-day operation of places that children inhabit, people who may not be aware of the powerful and long-range implications of their decisions.

Wherever possible, we have let the children speak for themselves.

LEANNE G. RIVLIN
MAXINE WOLFE

Brooklyn, New York
June 1985

Acknowledgments

Over the years many people have been part of the work on which this book is based. The book is the result of a team effort and comes out of the contributions of many members of our program. We were fortunate to work with Carol Baldassari, Arza Churchman, Marian Beyda-Golan, Sheila Lehman, Mimi Leibman, Marilyn Rothenberg, Alan Sommerman, Linda Lewin, Dennis McCarthy, Allan Wallis, Jeff Weiland, Susan Fox, Fred Wheeler, Francine Justa, Mary Schearer, Joan Lester, Carol Seavey, Nathan Altschuler, Nora Rubinstein, Richard Olsen, Vincent Bogert, Jack Bailey, Sheree West, Pat Dandonoli, Bill Hilton, Wendy Gaynor, Julio Montalvo Del Valle, and Charles Cook. The research on which this book is based was funded by the National Institute of Mental Health, the National Endowment for the Arts, and the Faculty Research Awards of the City University of New York. We want to thank Sheila Lehman for being there when we needed her. Thanks also to D'Ahlborn Slater, Evelyn Crowell, Mary Boyd, and Glenda Sullivan for typing sections of the manuscript.

Leanne
Maxine

Contents

CHAPTER 1

An Environmental Perspective on Children's Lives

INFLUENCES ON OUR WORK

For many years, looking at the child development literature meant considering a child suspended in mid-air, surrounded by meaningful people and the objects necessary for the development of such concepts as object existence, permanence, and differentiation. The richness of descriptions and data about family relationships, peer relationships, motoric, cognitive, and linguistic development, play behavior, emotional problems, learning difficulties, and the like were in sharp contrast to the lack of information about the places in which these occur, settings such as homes, schools, play areas, hospitals, the countryside, and city streets. It was not simply the physical environment that was absent in such work. The economic and political realities of children's lives were equally absent. To a large extent the kind of perspective taken reflected the development of psychology as a discipline during this century—an atomistic view that focused on individual variables. It was the science of the individual and individual stimuli, devoid of context. The laboratory and experimental approach was the logical translation of this perspective and served to perpetuate its basic premises. Even social categories such as class, race, and sex were treated as individual variables with little attempt to understand the subtle ways in which they played a role in the development of individual consciousness.

The work in this volume has roots that are quite different from much of the developmental literature. The beginnings of our work were imbedded in the complex changes of the late 1950s and the 1960s, the counterculture and urban crises, which communicated a humanistic perspective at the same time heightening awareness of environmental issues ranging from the effects on ecosystems of DDT and other pollutants to the failure of urban renewal to provide decent living conditions for most people. It was a time of new programs and much new building, often eliciting dissatisfaction with the results.

Emerging from this *Zeitgeist* were changes in the conception of psychiatric treatment, part of which involved seeking out new therapies, new approaches, and new ways of "housing" them. A very popular treatment modality of the time was milieu therapy, an approach that attempted to use all components of a patient's hospital life as part of the treatment plan. In the momentum of this perspective we and our colleagues were asked by the National Institute of Mental Health (NIMH) to study the "effect" of the psychiatric hospital environment on patients.*

The thinking behind this request was very simplistic—suggesting that if psychiatric patients perceive the physical world differently from other people, and if the available psychiatric settings were built without recognizing this fact, then these settings could not be successful in reaching their goals. The logical conclusion was that by recognizing the perceptual problems of patients, one could design or redesign facilities that would not interfere with treatment and might even help it.

Perhaps it was our lack of extensive clinical training at that time that made it important to see for ourselves the nature of the problems that had been described to us. This led us to examine the history of psychiatric care and to spend time in psychiatric settings, approaching them with few preconceived ideas about "patients" and their "treatment." After a good deal of reading, looking, and listening in order to familiarize ourselves with what was going on, we discovered that the issues were neither as simple nor as deterministic as had been outlined.

While not denying that some people in the hospital had perceptual difficulties or symptoms, or that the physical environment could be improved upon, it seemed to us that both the definition of the research problem and its level of analysis needed serious reconsideration. The simplistic view that specific physical environmental details were directly related to specific perceptual problems was untenable. It was equally apparent that the pathology people evidenced within the psychiatric setting could not be attributed solely to their ability or inability to deal with personal problems in their lives. The literature on institutionalization such as Goffman's *Asylums* (1961) had documented this as well.

The environment emerged not as a "stimulus" in the traditional psychological sense but as a complex system. Recognition of a series of interdependent factors, physical, social, political, and economic, was necessary in order to understand the relationship between the psychiatric hospital environment and the behavior of patients and staff. These factors together came to constitute the core of our conception of the "environment" or "setting," terms we use interchangeably to include far more than the physical details alone. The physical environment was one element, albeit a neglected one, in the treatment setting—a system that had a conceptual history, a social history, as well as an architectural history within

---

* Some of the early work is reflected in the edited book of readings *Environmental Psychology: Man and His Physical Setting* (H. E. Proshansky, W. H. Ittelson, & L. G. Rivlin, Eds., New York: Holt, Rinehart & Winston) published in 1970 and revised in 1976.

our culture. As an element in the system, the physical environment both provided possibilities and created potential barriers for defining what people were, who they should be, and how they were valued.

Our work not only gave us a different view of psychiatric patients and so-called treatment settings; it also led to the understanding that the issues involved were not unique to the psychiatric treatment setting but were much broader in scope. The psychiatric hospital, in its physical as well as social embodiment, is only one of a series of environments within our society that has a significant impact on all our lives. Factories, offices, schools, day-care centers, train stations, post offices, shopping centers, high-rise apartment buildings are sociophysical systems shaping much of our behavior as well as defining what our world is and should be like.

The physical environment appears to us as a given. Both as lay people and as professionals we come to assume its existence and hence to ignore its importance. Yet there is no way in which we can be without being some "place"—except in the most metaphysical sense. As the Goodmans (1947) have written:

> A child accepts the manmade background itself as the inevitable nature of things; he does not realize that somebody once drew some lines on a piece of paper who might have drawn otherwise. But now as engineer and architect once drew, people have to walk and live. (p. 3)

CHILDHOOD SOCIALIZATION

Children are, by definition, in a subordinate power relation to all adults within a society. Most individual caretakers are not themselves ultimately responsible for the conditions under which they and their children are forced to live. Beginning with the birth environment, adults create and control the physical as well as social conditions in which children learn about the world. The development of a sense of object permanence by the child of a migrant worker must differ from that of the child whose family has owned the same home for generations (Coles, 1970). To be more specific, there is no structure without content and in this sense all of child development, including cognitive development, is socialization (Ingelby, 1974). Part of that socialization involves learning to use the physical environment in specific ways and to understand its social, personal, and symbolic meanings.

We use the term socialization to refer to a set of processes, having many components and occurring on many levels of life, by which we are taught to understand the world and the patterns of behavior that will enable us to fit into the places assigned to us within the dominant culture (Magaro, Gripp, & McDowell, 1978). Some aspects of socialization processes are overt; others are not. Often the goals are implicit rather than explicit. Some of the people within a society are aware of, accept, and shape these implicit and unstated goals. Others are aware of the goals even if they do not always accept or shape them and, indeed, may see their role as changing them. The vast majority of people are aware neither of these implicit goals nor that what they do on a day-to-day basis heavily reflects them. The overall goal of the process of socialization is the shaping of consciousness, the internalization of dominant norms, which then become so "natural" that they are largely unquestioned as they govern our behavior and attitudes (Bem, 1970).

The work presented in this volume grows out of an attempt to understand the physical environment as one of the factors that shapes consciousness within society. Even if one accepts the notions of progressive, partially genetically based cognitive development, the physical environment, its attendant social structure and symbolic meanings, allow or limit the kinds of activities in which children can engage and hence what they learn about the world. And since it is through learning about the world that children learn about themselves, it is important to understand that the physical environments in which children grow up give them a message about who they are and who they can be within this society. To have "grown up on the wrong side of the tracks" implies, via a spatial/physical referent, a whole set of images about a particular person or set of persons and the continuing impact of the environment on their growth and development. But it also reflects an *actual* difference in the material reality of the daily lives of children depending on which side of the tracks they live.

Through the various mechanisms of socialization, children are expected to internalize the normative social order, both its social and physical aspects. Yet the socialization process is far from "perfect." Various explanations have been offered for its imperfection, ranging from the contradictions inherent in any social system (Marx, 1977) to the existence of a collective memory which transmits the history of alternatives even when they no longer exist (Halbwachs, 1980). It seems clear that under all but the most repressive circumstances some people will gain access to a range of attitudes, roles, and behaviors especially in a heterogeneous society. These existing alternatives provide some support for deviation from the expected or acceptable. The goal of those in power to reproduce the social order is often met with resistance and the outcome is generally the result of both (Giroux, 1983). Resistance can take many forms and has varying consequences depending on the nature of the historical period, the power of those resisting in relation to those supporting the status quo, and the general possibilities for material and social support.

However, since children have no control over the material and social conditions of their lives, their access to alternatives is severely constrained and often serendipitous. Therefore, their understanding of the world, their sense of themselves and their competence will largely reflect the relationship between the dominant values and the extent to which they can realize these values within the reality of their lives. Their resistance, given their limited power, often has severe consequences.

OUR GENERAL PERSPECTIVE

We will be discussing children's environments, how they influence what children do and how they feel about themselves. Age-related behavior is not the major focus. Rather, by examining human behavior in a period of time when shaping is strongest we can consider the physical environment as a factor in that process while understanding other factors such as the structure of social relations. We believe that children more than adults are shaped and formed by a whole range of experiences in the material world, a perspective that is not typical of much of the existing work on growth.

Several other aspects of our approach should be clarified. First, we do not see the socialization of children at this point in historical time as a discrete break from the past, in the larger sense of the development of society and the role of children within it. Although we were trained as psychologists, we found it necessary to understand the present context within which we view individual human behavior in relation to the history of that context. In *The Sociological Imagination* (1959), C. Wright Mills outlines a compelling argument for historical analysis but warns against using history as a "ritual," as "dull little padding" provided with little purpose. In the case of children's institutions, the history of these settings in relation to their political and economic contexts over time adds more than color and background to the picture. We believe it is central to understanding the behavior of children and staff in institutions because their behavior is not solely individual. It reflects the structure and intent of the institutions. A historical analysis also reveals the resistance of institutions to change, something that cannot be identified without a longitudinal perspective.

Second, culturally specific settings (hospitals, schools, public parks) also have a history behind their present form and their functional and cultural roles. We are writing about institutions in the United States, how they have fit into, reflected, and created the role of children within our society. Though many of the conceptions behind American institutions were affected by those in other societies and cultures, and granting the power of the United States at the present time to influence the same institutions in other places, we do not generalize about other cultures.

Each individual environment, whether it is Central Park or the Sears Tower or the local public school, has a history of its own development, starting with the basis for its construction and the early occupancy and continuing over its years of use. After discussing the history of particular institutions in the United States, we will present some specific present day examples. Even within one society, these can and do differ and the processes by which they operate and change vary over time. Within a particular place what happens from one day to another and over the years may change. Furthermore, each person in a setting has his or her own history in places which influences every successive environmental experience. Yet the central thesis of our work suggests that there is a systemic nature to the institutions for children within our society and a dominant ethos that affects their form and functioning at any one time despite differences between settings and among the persons experiencing them.

In the fifteen years that we have been doing research in settings for children, we have used the physical environment as a way of entering complex systems, of organizing the varied elements that contribute to their functioning, and of assessing their impact on the lives of children. (For a list of references which describe the research in detail see p. 12.) We have worked in a variety of different kinds of setting for children, including medical hospitals, schools, day-care centers, community residences for delinquents, and psychiatric facilities.

These settings have been large and small, public and private, long-term and transitional. They have had innovative and traditional programs and designs, some a mix of types. Administratively, some have been bureaucratic, some anarchistic, others cooperatives. In these places, some of which could be described as shabby and neglected, others cared-for and pristine, there have been young people ranging in age from infancy to teenage. We have observed, interviewed, photographed, and attended staff meetings. We have conducted workshops for children and adults, implemented environmental changes, and evaluated and documented the results. We have helped to develop standards for children's psychiatric hospitals, consulted with community groups on the design of day-care centers and with teachers on planning their rooms. Although most of our work has centered in New York City, our research and consultation have covered a wide range of settings in this country and abroad.

Out of this work, a general framework has emerged for understanding the role of the physical environment in people's lives, the relationship between the physical environment and the political, social, and economic environments, as well as its specific role in the lives of children. Before we turn to the discussion of institutions we will present this framework.

THE ROLE OF THE PHYSICAL ENVIRONMENT

Understanding the role of the physical environment in people's lives is a complex task. On the one hand, we must explain the power of the physical environment, in both its material reality and its symbolic meaning, to affect people's actual behavior as well as their understanding of themselves and the world. Yet we must also account for the fact that people are active agents in the creation of their own worlds. They attempt in some way to exert control over their own lives and the physical environment as part of that life. In light of this perspective, we believe that the physical environment plays a role in the lives of people in a number of ways.

To begin with, people's attempts to exert control over their lives take place within a culture in which there are dominant values concerning the possession and use of physical environments and their elements. At the same time the rules on acceptable and taboo behavior presuppose given personal characteristics as well as the existence of physical and environmental support systems. Individuals' senses of themselves and their competence, as well as how they are perceived by others, reflect the relation between the dominant norms and the extent to which the reality of people's lives allows them to be fulfilled. Until recently, little has been done to make the physical environment reflect the reality of people's lives or to give them the support systems they require, even when the requirements have been obvious. Most Western physical environments assume that one can walk, see, and hear. In fact, even without considering persons who are severely physically handicapped, existing environments function only moderately well for average-sized people roughly within the ages of 12 to 30. Before and after those ages environments are often difficult to negotiate: chairs may be too big or too small, stairs set too high, doors too heavy, print too small for clear visibility.

Thus, what should be most obvious about the physical environment in relation to people's lives is its *functional component that can facilitate or inhibit the range and quality* of potential behaviors. It is, in this sense, that *the physical environment can also have a powerful and possibly determining impact on the user, if only to delimit the boundaries of potential action*. If a room or a building has only one door and no windows, one's entry and exit can be said to be determined by its location. If all the chairs in a classroom are lined up in rows, bolted to the floor, and face one direction, the range of social interactions is severely restricted. The availability of adequate public transportation more or less controls the degree to which so-called public beaches are actually available as recreational space for those who do not own a car. Yet, because of the normative social order which these *physical-environmental experiences* reflect and create, they are internalized and are partially or completely accepted as the normal order of things.

It is rare for a person to move a chair once it has been placed—even in one's own living room. In public places such as libraries, waiting rooms, and workplaces this passivity is even more pronounced as people inflict the most uncomfortable positions upon themselves in order to avoid disturbing the existing physical arrangements. Part of this hesitation may result from the lack of clarity as to the responsibility for a particular place, and part may be based on fear of reprisal or punishment for taking control of someone else's property, but equally *powerful is the fact that early in life the physical environment ceases to be conceived of as playing a role in shaping the course of events.* Any problem in our society becomes interpreted as an individual one. The role of the physical environment in supporting the social order fades quickly as we focus on *people* as being deviant. This attitude is pervasive in a society which holds people responsible for their endeavors while giving them limited control over the mechanisms that would enable them to do as they see fit. Thus, the child is labeled as a "chronic latecomer" because he or she must rely on erratic public transportation to get to school or labeled "fidgety" when unable to sit still on a wooden chair for a long period of time.

It is essential, then, to understand that the *environment is part of a totality* rather than a backdrop for behavior. In the same way that it may limit or support action, it also reflects and helps to define a system of social relations and the person as part of that system. The environments in which we live out our lives were, and are, planned by a specific group of persons with a specific set of priorities at a specific point in time. The shape of cities, the amount of land cultivated or uncultivated, the number and type of school buildings, the presence or absence of highways as opposed to mass transportation, the design of factories and mass production processes—all have a priority system embedded within them, a philosophy, whether apparent or not. The desk at the head of a classroom, decisions regarding who does and who does not have windows in their offices, the allocation of single-bed hospital rooms, and ability to pay also demonstrate this principle.

Furthermore, users, especially children, are generally not the initial environmental decision makers, nor do they have formal influence on the decision-making process. Yet environmental decisions most often have the greatest impact on those with the least power. Low-income families do not design their housing nor do they control where it is located. Yet design and siting strongly influence the nature of the style of life of occupants. For example, the size of the kitchen determines whether it can be used for eating meals; location determines access to transportation and mobility within and outside of the neighborhood.

It is because the physical environment reflects and helps to define a system of social relationships and the person as part of that system that *people–environment transactions have symbolic as well as personal meanings.* The physical environment conveys what is expected, what is normative, what is acceptable and taboo, defining in the end the individual's sense of self and competence as well as how that individual is perceived by others. In some cases the symbolic and personal meanings are consciously understood. Residents in low-income projects know that closets without doors are *not* what most people have. Most workers know that there is a priority system in the allocation of offices with windows. In other cases, especially where children are involved, the social basis for these decisions may not be understood and instead taken as an individual responsibility. For example, the ease with which a door can be opened, relative to the age, size, or physical ability of a child creates an experience of success or failure. The need to rely on an adult to negotiate the door can make children feel that they are incompetent rather than that the door is inappropriate to the setting.

These people–environment transactions will have different implications depending on the objective conditions of people's lives and on the possibilities people perceive for effecting change. On the one hand, it can lessen people's sense of themselves and their ability to effect change in this system especially if they have no social validation for their experiences and therefore interpret their problems as individual ones. On the other hand, the experiences themselves form the material basis for seeking to create change if the social validation and support can be found. It is for this reason that we must understand more about the role and the limits of power of environmental decision makers and people's attempts to create change.

It would be simplistic to assume either that environmental decision makers, whether politicians, teachers, designers, principals, or researchers, are a monolithic group with a single common goal that they are always aware of and that they are in control of the consequences of their decisions or that users, because of their limited *formal* power, can have no impact. Frequently, there is competition among environmental decision makers. The narrow perspectives of decision makers, focused on their particular goals, can limit their perception of the consequences of their plans. The desire to cut costs which was one basis for much open-plan school construction failed to anticipate a range of pedagogical problems and subsequent teacher dissatisfaction due to the conflict between educational style and physical context. The problems necessitated the further outlay of funds for physical changes to reduce the openness.

The active role that users can have despite their lack of formal decision-making power can be seen in the unwillingness of low-income families to reside in many high-rise projects despite their dire need for better housing, the existence of squatter settlements in many parts of the world including the centers of London and Amsterdam, the unauthorized creation of nude bathing at public beaches as well as the strong protests of local residents concerning environmental decisions they perceive as unwise. Thus it must also be recognized that *most people attempt, in some way, to exert control over their own environments*. These attempts have differing consequences depending on the power of the person as well as the individual in contrast with group nature of the action. The individual child who is seeking privacy within a school environment devoid of real possibilities may achieve this privacy by daydreaming. Yet the teacher has the power to label the child accordingly. Goffman's (1962) description of the "Catch-22" for psychiatric patients' expression of their ego is a similar phenomenon. On the other hand, group attempts to exert control, while not necessarily guaranteeing success provide social validation for action. If the outcome of the action is unsuccessful, due to the arbitrary exercise of another's power, at least the cause can be labeled as external to the self. Therefore, it is not only the success or failure of the endeavor to control that is significant in defining people to themselves and to others, it is also the act of having attempted to exert control and the context in which that action is understood that gives meaning to experience.

SUMMARY

What this book will consider, through an analysis of children's environments, are the ways in which the physical aspects of these places are parts of the socialization to the normative social order. At the same time we will show how these environments provide experiences that can become the basis for attempts at change and the meaning of these attempts for the participants as well as for the settings in which they are found.

In reading the material in this book, then, a number of principles should be kept in mind.

1. A series of interdependent factors, including physical, social, political, and economic variables must be addressed in order to understand people's behavior, attitudes, and feelings.
2. As part of a totality, the physical environment reflects and helps to define a system of social relations and the person as part of that system.
3. Within any given culture, environments have a conceptual history, a social-political-economic history as well as an architectural history.
4. At any given time, within a culture, there are dominant values concerning the possession, uses, and meanings of physical environments and their elements.
5. The individuals' sense of themselves and their competence as well as how they are perceived by others reflect the relation between the dominant norms and the extent to which the reality of people's lives allows them to be fulfilled.
6. Yet, early in life, in our society, the physical environment as well as the social, political, and economic environments cease to be conceived of as playing a role in the course of events. Events are explained in terms of people's qualities instead of environmental qualities or some combination of the two.
7. This enables people to be held responsible for their behavior while giving them limited control over the mechanisms that would enable them to do as they see fit.

8. Physical environments have priority systems embedded within them. Users generally are not the initial environmental decision makers, nor do they have formal influence on the decision process. Yet environmental decisions most often have the greatest impact on those with the least power.

9. In fact, physical environments can have a powerful and possibly determining impact on the user simply in terms of their functional components — their potential for delimiting the boundaries of potential action.

10. However, because environmental decision makers are not a monolithic group with a single common goal and because they are not always aware of or in control of the consequences of their decisions, users can have an impact despite their limited formal power.

11. People without power still attempt in some way to exert control over their environments. The act of attempting to exert control and its individual or social context is a meaningful experience in the development of consciousness whether or not the results are successful.

In understanding the role of the physical environment in the lives of *children* it is important to understand a number of principles.

12. The physical environment, while virtually eliminated from the developmental literature, is one of the factors that shapes consciousness within a society.

13. Part of socialization involves learning to use the physical environment in specific ways and to understand its social and personal meanings.

14. Adults create and control the physical as well as the social conditions under which children learn about the world.

15. Children, by virtue of their limited power, are as greatly impacted by the physical environmental qualities of the settings in which they are placed as by the social organization of those settings.

16. To understand the role of settings in the lives of children, we must utilize historical and developmental perspectives. We must address the dynamic qualities of the physical and social environments and understand that they are at one and the same time products of their own pasts and contributors to the future development of children.

The following list represents publications by the authors and their colleagues that form the research foundations for this book. These publications will not be cited in the text, although data from them will be broadly applied in our analyses.

Baldassari, C. Lehman S., & Wolfe, M. (In press). Imaging and creating alternative environments with children. In C. S. Weinstein & T. G. David (Eds.), *Spaces for children: The built environment and child development*. New York: Plenum.

Golan, M. B. (1978). *Children in institutional settings: Privacy, social interaction, and self-esteem*. Doctoral dissertation, City University of New York.

Laufer, R., & Wolfe, M. (1977). Privacy as a concept and a social issue: A multidimensional developmental theory. *Journal of Social Issues*, *33*, 22–42.

Proshansky, E., & Wolfe, M. (1974). The physical setting and open education: Philosophy and practice. *School Review*, *82* (4), 557–574.

Rivlin, L. G., Bogert, V., & Cirillo, R. (1981). Uncoupling institutional indicators. In A. E. Osterberg, C. P. Tiernan, & R. A. Findlay (Eds.), *Design research interactions: Proceedings of the Twelfth International Conference of the Environmental Design Research Association*. Washington, D.C.: Environmental Design Research Association.

Rivlin, L. G., & Rothenberg, M. (1976). The use of space in open classrooms. In H. M. Proshansky, W. H. Ittelson, & L. G. Rivlin (Eds.). *Environmental psychology: People and their physical settings*. New York: Holt, Rinehart & Winston.

Rivlin, L. G., & Weinstein, C. S. (In press). Educational issues, school settings and environmental psychology. *Journal of Environmental Psychology*.

Rivlin, L. G., & Wolfe, M. (1972). The early history of a psychiatric hospital for children: Expectations and reality. *Environment and Behavior*, *4*, 33–72.

Rivlin, L. G., & Wolfe, M. (1979). Understanding and evaluating therapeutic environments for children. In D. Canter & S. Canter (Eds.), *Designing for therapeutic environments: A review of research*. London: Wiley.

Wolfe, M. (1974a). Behavioral effects of group size, room size, and density in a children's psychiatric hospital. *Environment and Behavior*, *7*, 199–224.

Wolfe, M. (1974b). Environmental stimulation and design: For the "different who are not so different." In M. J. Bednar (Ed.), *Barrier free environments*. Stroudsberg, PA: Dowden, Hutchinson & Ross.

Wolfe, M. Childhood and privacy (1974c). In I. Altman & J. Wohwill (Eds.), *Children and environment: Advances in theory and research*. New York: Plenum.

Wolfe, M., & Golan, M. B. (1976). Privacy and institutionalization. Presented at Environmental Design Research Association Meetings, Vancouver, B.C., City University of New York, Center for Human Environments, Publication #76–4.

Wolfe, M., & Rivlin, L. G. (In press). Institutions in children's lives. In C. S. Weinstein & T. G. David (Eds.), *Spaces for children: The built environment and child development*. New York: Plenum.

REFERENCES

Bem, D. (1970). *Beliefs, attitudes, and human affairs*. Monterey, CA: Brooks/Cole.

Coles, R. (1970). *Uprooted children: The early life of migrant farm workers*. Pittsburgh, PA: University of Pittsburgh Press.

Giroux, H. A. (1983). Theories of reproduction and resistance in the new sociology of education: A critical analysis. *Harvard Educational Review, 53*, 257–293.

Goffman, E. (1961). *Asylums*. Garden City, NY: Doubleday.

Goodman, P. and Goodman P. (1947). *Communitas*. New York: Random House.

Halbwachs, M. (1980). *The collective memory* (F. J. Ditter, Jr. & V. Y. Ditter, Trans.). New York: Harper & Row.

Ingelby, D. (1974). The psychology of child psychology. In M. P. M. Richards (Ed.), *The integration of a child into a social world*. London: Cambridge University Press.

Magaro, P. A., Gripp, R., & McDowell, D. J. (1978). *The mental health industry: A cultural phenomenon*. New York: Wiley.

Marx, K. (1977). *Capital: A critique of political economy* (Ben Fowkes, Trans.). New York: Vintage.

Mills, C. W. (1978). *The sociological imagination*. New York: Oxford University Press.

CHAPTER 2

A Historical Perspective
on Conceptions of Children

Despite the fact that many aspects of development are common to all children, concepts of children have varied considerably over time. That a child *physically matures* over time says little about his or her place in society and the economic and social structure, the values and attitudes that shape the course of social development, and physical development, as well. Whether children live in poverty or plenty, whether they are seen as valuable or a burden, whether there is sufficient food to support their physical growth and nurturance to support their emotional development, are time-bound, place-bound, and value-laden alternatives, and all center around the notion of what the years of development contribute to individuals, to families, and to the social community group in which they live.

Conceptions of childhood are social constructions (Beuf, 1979), reflecting changes in the status of families, their livelihoods, their functions, and in the nature of their social relationships over the years. The way the child is perceived dictates what the growing years are like, whether they are a time of work, play, submission, or inspiration. Concurrently, these perceptions determine the degree and kind of nurturance and support given by parents, siblings, and other relatives. In his social history of family life, Phillippe Aries (1962) documented the evolution of childhood and families as we know them. Prior to the fifteenth century, with the termination of the years that we generally call the preschool period—by the age of six or seven—children were considered to be adults with all the responsibilities, rights, and independent initiative accorded to grown persons (Aries, 1962). This view is reflected in paintings of the period where the young appear as miniature adults, dressed in clothing similar in style to that of fully grown persons. Prior to six, the child was, according to Aries, largely ignored or, at the very least, not catered to. One must recall the high rate of infant mortality. With more infants dying than surviving, they did not really count (Plumb, 1973). Little was expected of children but neither were they seen as having special needs in clothing, toys, or in any other aspects of their material existence. When the child reached the end of infancy, somewhere between five and seven, full participation in adult society was expected as they were integrated into the economic life of the family, which might be work in the fields, in the kitchen, in crafts, or in court affairs. At that point they were generally presumed to be competent citizens (Beuf, 1979). The term "child" now used to designate a stage of development formerly expressed kinship (Plumb, 1973). Clearly, a radical series of changes has altered this image into the much different perspective of today.

Industrialization and urbanization were the major forces in this transformation, although by the sixteenth century in Europe the conception of the child as "innocent" had emerged (Takanishi, 1978). Influenced by the church and by education the child took on a different image from that of adults. This process continued into the eighteenth century, although it was largely a phenomenon of the middle and upper classes (Plumb, 1972; Takanishi, 1978). For children of the working class the nature of the labor merely changed from farm or shop to factory.

With industrialization came dramatic impacts on home life. As economic and family functions became separated, there were profound consequences on the control that adults had over their own lives and the lives of their children.

> . . . the child, once viewed as a blessed economic asset in the European agricultural family system, became a consumer—an economic liability. (Beuf, 1979)

By the end of the nineteenth century legislation limiting children's participation in the labor market was proposed.

Women's roles had altered as well, as their lives were reshaped to meet a changing economy. The work available to them was no longer centered around the family, farm, or crafts. Rather, they were relegated to low-status jobs outside the family unit. At the same time the new emphasis on childhood defined another set of domestic functions for them, major functions, whatever else they had to do for their families' survival.

The conceptions of children and family responsibility in the United States reflected the impact of these European conceptions and experiences filtered through the Puritan morality of early settlers. They reveal an interesting interplay between ethical concerns for bringing up children and attitudes toward human nature. In colonial times much of the ethical concern regarding children came from Puritan morality. It was based on the conviction that the child must be led down the path of good deeds and that the major responsibility for this rested on the family. Two predominant perspectives evolved, one taking for granted the basic immorality of children, the other—drawing on the work of Europeans Rousseau and Locke—viewed children as more innocent and malleable.

By the late nineteenth century, and in the years that followed, in the U.S. immigration joined industrialization and urbanization as major influences on conceptions of children and changes in family structure. Children moved from the position of needing to be redeemed to that of redeemer (Wishy, 1968) and the twentieth century was characterized as the "century of the child" (Takanishi, 1978). This new view had implications for child care, social reform, education, and, most basically, for the role of parents, especially women. Takanishi quotes Isabel Simeral, who wrote in 1916:

> As women have come to participate more fully in the rights, privileges, and labors of men, a new conception of childhood has developed—a conception for which men and women together are mutually responsible. It is the vision of all children . . . as the torch bearers to the civilization of the future, as the links in the chain of human endeavor. With this vision before mankind, the child has in our own day entered into his rights. For the first time . . . he has become an entity in himself: his physical needs, his mental requirements, his moral training as considerations to be studied entirely apart from the adult. His life has become an autonomous world set within that of maternity.

These new views of childhood had many consequences including the development of major social reform movements. There was a conviction that problems could be prevented—that forming a child is easier than reform (Takanishi, 1978). The emphasis on social reform approaches paralleled the stress on nurturing techniques, techniques that would avoid the need for remedial care later. Basic to this approach was the recognition of children's rights to a childhood (Takanishi, 1978)—but one that would lead them down the path of self-control and good citizenship, qualities essential to the new industrial work force. Toward this goal there was an emphasis on activities likely to make for healthy and productive lives, and social reform programs directed to clean milk, parent education, improved housing, regulation of the employment of mothers, and education of children. Play was also seen as a right (Takanishi, 1978) and the movement to establish playgrounds was an attempt to provide play areas where adequate and safe sites had been absent, especially in dense urban areas.

In the period referred to as post-industrial America beginning in the 1920s, perhaps most conspicuous is the prolongation of the years of childhood. A concrete example can be seen in the rise in age for compulsory school attendance as well as an increase in the length of the school year and the numbers of youth in post-secondary education. Held up at least as a middle-class ideal, is the notion of this protracted period as one which provides opportunity for creativity and self-development. For the most part there is little expectation that the adolescent will be a productive member of society and, as a result, there are few opportunities for this to occur. And, in reality large segments of our young population, such as the children who share their families' lives as migrant laborers or who are poor U.S. minority youths, are unable to obtain either entrance into a steady school experience or employment, again pointing to the discrepancy between concepts and realities in the lives of many children.

Yet part of recent conceptions of childhood has been the acknowledgement, due largely to the existence of the civil rights movement, the women's movement, and even earlier, the Depression, that all American childhoods are not the same. Beginning with these movements and embodied legally in the *Brown* v. *Board of Education* decision in 1954, was the recognition that children were not being treated equally and that regardless of race, sex, or class they were entitled to equal opportunities. During that period and up to the present, there has been an emphasis on the idea that children are the products of their environments, defined in the larger social sense, and that by providing compensatory education, whether through Head Start programs, bilingual schools, or nonracist, nonsexist materials, each child could be helped to develop to his or her maximal potential. Whether these programs can or do eliminate inequality is questionable (Bowles & Gintes, 1978), but nevertheless the idea persists and both reflects and creates a conception of childhood that is different from earlier ones.

During these last 50 years, the focus of the late 1920s and the 1930s on the child's physical health and physical development was supplemented by the 1940s with an emphasis on mental and/or emotional health, placing even greater responsibility on the family unit. It was now not enough for parents to provide for the physical well-being of their children, it became necessary for them to assure the psychological well-being of their children as well. In the wake of the flower children, huge increases in the number of runaway children and drug users in the middle class, followed by the anti-war militancy and the anti-nuclear and anti-technology back-to-the-land-movements, the 1960s as well as the 1970s saw the rise of a variety of attempts to make people "effective" parents. This perspective laid blame for the "unrest" of youth, including "riots" in the ghettos and takeovers of schools, on the excessive permissiveness of post World War II childrearing practices and stressed the need for more effective communication between parents and children.

Yet, while the period since World War II has been characterized as an era of "permissiveness" in childrearing, we feel it would be more accurate to say that the post-war period, culminating in the civil rights, anti-war, and women's movements of the 1960s and early 1970s, was a period in which broadened alternatives were made available to American youth. These were largely due to their own demands, the demands of their parents, as well as institutional and governmental attempts to, once again, create a stable polity. Conspicuous in this period, in addition to the ideas described earlier, which place the problem in the environment rather than in the child, was the acknowledgement of children and youth as having rights, including the right to a sexual life. The availability of contraceptives, sex counseling, and abortions for minors without parental consent all reflect the dramatic changes in the reality of the lives of younger people as well as society's conceptions of them. An embodiment of this perspective can be found in the 1971 White House Conference on Youth which asserted "the right of the individual to do his/her own thing so [sic] long as it does not interfere with the rights of another" (Takanishi, 1978). The notion that children are people in their own right and not merely the property of parents has led to the public acknowledgement of the extent of child battering and sexual abuse and to laws and programs which protect children living in these circumstances.

It is difficult to have a perspective on the role that such conceptions have in the process of permanent change. This is especially true when we are writing about a period in which we are living and when it is also clear that there is much pressure from conservative political groups to eliminate the alternatives which have evolved during the last 50 years. The so-called economic crises of the mid-1970s witnessed the contraction of open admissions to colleges, the elimination of many compensatory education programs, and an extraordinarily high rate of unemployment among youth in general and especially among U.S. minority youth. At the same time that child battering and sexual abuse are being acknowledged and legislated against, the Supreme Court in 1977 upheld the constitutionality of corporal punishment in public schools. Recently introduced legislation such as the Family Protection Act (1979, 1980) and the Chastity Bill (1980) make it clear that some segments of the population are anxious to remove alternatives by eliminating school busing, seeking restrictions on school attendance, limiting younger people's access to sex education, contraception, abortions, counseling for venereal disease, help with abuse by parents, and by limiting the images available to children in textbooks to the "traditional sex roles as historically defined in the United States of America" (Family Protection Act, 1979, 1980). Yet even the appearance of such bills acknowledges the reality to which they are a reaction, a reality vastly different than it was earlier in this century.

Throughout the history of this country, as in other countries, conceptions of the nature of children and childhood, whether held by the government, professionals, or by adults in general, have influenced the types of settings demanded and provided to support or change these characteristics, while the settings themselves have influenced the way that children and childhood have come to be viewed.

In the chapters which follow we will examine specific examples of this process by a critical analysis of past and present settings for deviance, for learning and for nurturance, highlighting their relationship to conceptions of children and childhood.

REFERENCES

Aries, P. (1962). *Centuries of childhood: A source history of family life*. New York: Knopf.

Beuf, A. H. (1979). *Biting off the bracelet: A study of children in hospitals*. Philadelphia: University of Pennsylvania Press.

Bowles, S., & Gintes, H. (1976). *Schooling in capitalist America*. New York: Basic Books.

Plumb, J. H. (1973). Children: The victims of time. In J. H. Plumb, *In the light of history*. Boston: Houghton Mifflin.

Takanishi, R. (1978). Childhood as a social issue: Historical roots of contemporary child advocacy movements. *Journal of Social Issues*, *34* (2), 8–28.

Wishy, B. (1968). *The child and the republic*. Philadelphia: University of Pennsylvania Press.

CHAPTER 3

Settings for Childhood Deviance: A Historical Perspective

In his book *In the Light of History* (1973) the historian J. H. Plumb describes a monastic hospital, Our Lady of Bethlehem, "the leading repository for the luckier of London's lunatics" (p. 29) and its evolution into the infamous Bedlam. Although this hospital became one of the largest and the most impressive of facilities, with the remnants of its earlier religious relics removed or destroyed and the monks replaced by secular staff, there was never enough room. When it moved from its original medieval setting to Moorefields, the new building, designed by Robert Hook specifically for "lunatics," was the first specialized architecture for the "insane." It became more than a hospital, for it was a showpiece for foreign visitors and entertainment for local residents of all classes. Visitors paid admission to walk through various parts of the building—cells for the violent, sweeping galleries containing the "gentle insane" (Plumb, 1973). Plumb indicates that according to physicians of the time, what we regard as a strange form of amusement was beneficial to the disordered. As mainstream society came into close contact with patients they were possibly offered a relief from their days of confinement. Over time this practice ended, but many inhumanities continued and others were added.

We begin with this small vignette on early institutional life not because we are about to describe an identical situation, nor to contrast it with a more modern alternative. Rather, we want to emphasize the evolutionary aspect of institutional care, as well as its roots in the history and practices of the time.

One of the most dramatic changes in settings that encompass the lives of children in the United States and elsewhere has been the removal of much of a child's life from the home. Reasons why children were moved outside the family realm and the types of settings that evolved for them are embedded in the existing social climate. A complex mixture of the structure of the family, the economy, the community, and the political context of the times shaped the conceptions of the child, attitudes toward child care and responsibility, and the settings accommodating children.

CONCEPTIONS OF DEVIANCE

If the conceptions of children and childhood have varied over the years, so have the definitions of deviance. Society's views of a normal member of a group have had an extraordinarily inconsistent history, and this is as true for its judgment of children as that of adults. Poverty, mental retardation, physical disabilities, emotional problems—each has been the subject of pity, contempt, ridicule, concern, scorn, awe, fear—often in succession. The persons involved have been ignored, punished, worshipped, assisted, or neglected. They have lived at home, in religious residences, in hospitals, in workhouses, in prisons, in almshouses, or on the street. They have been integrated into their social group or kept as far apart as possible. They have been segregated into separate kinds of facilities for different kinds of conditions, or lumped together and held in common places.

In any context, and at any point in time, most disorders or perceptions of disorders take time to develop. Although some cultures have stigmatized particular kinds of children at birth (the child of an unmarried or "adulterous" woman, a redhaired child, a physically disabled child, or the child of poor parents), most signs of deviance take time to appear. How these will be judged and whether they will be seen as remediable is a matter of the social context for, as Plumb expressed it, children are "the victims of time" (1973). Although we could say this for all people, as we have seen in our earlier discussion, the position of children and their dependent status, at the very least through infancy, make them especially vulnerable.

The conception of deviance forms the basis for the model of care which is provided, and whether, indeed, the individual will receive any attention. For neglect is one outcome of particular diagnoses or judgments. The conceptions covered a range of conditions often applied indiscriminately to people that we would consider to be the poor, the physically disabled, the mentally retarded, the emotionally disturbed. We might suggest that children were most vulnerable in this respect, with judgments that often have not stood the test of time. Some examples of conceptions and care are useful to consider.

One of the earliest models that can be found in history stemmed from a religious or spiritual sphere. It viewed deviance in two major and differing ways. One way considered the deviance to be a divine process, and the individuals as possessing special powers. For these persons, the care was based on regard, if not awe. They were either kept at home and considered to be "special," or placed in the religious edifices of the time (the temple, the monastery, or shrine) and integrated into the religious ceremony. Release from duties and the order of religious life may, in fact, have had therapeutic value. It might be added that religious places (the temples of ancient Greece, the monasteries through the Middle Ages) were frequent residences for a range of special persons, including children.

The alternative supernatural or religious view was that of fear and contempt. The deviant was seen as being possessed—by devils, spirits, or whatever evil forces were components of the belief. In this case the treatment could be as mild as ridicule and shunning or as extreme as putting the individual to death. Cases of children hanged as witches have been documented in our colonial history (Bremner, 1970).

Another conception embodies principles of work as therapy. The workhouse was a particular institution of the eighteenth century, aimed at solving problems of poverty, "insanity," and crime, often in a single setting. Based on principles of Puritan morality, work was provided as a means for salvation, and children often followed their penniless parents into workhouses and almshouses. It might be added that work as therapy, or at least as part of the therapeutic program of a facility, was often a central component of a facility, whether for the deaf, the physically disabled, or the delinquent. (Bremner, 1970).

In other periods, the family served as the model for care with persons defined as deviants accommodated within the home. Use of the actual home for care presumed that families had both the responsibility and capability of providing their members with support. But the institutional form of family care had a very different perspective. Based on the assumption that the family was inadequate or unavailable, surrogate or simulated care was provided. Surrogate care might be the foster home, or the family care movement as seen in the community of Gheel, in Belgium. Gheel's tradition of offering the disabled a place within the community goes back to the Middle Ages and has been tried out periodically by other places with little success. To some degree foster care and community-based treatment and residential programs, often part of deinstitutionalization efforts, represent that kind of model which follows a surrogate or simulated family plan.

A model of care especially significant in the context of children is that of education. From the time of the Greeks to the present, education has been seen as the medium for shaping people, for teaching them how to live properly, and for giving them the skills needed to move them into the society of the times. It has also been seen as the shaper of the character, of citizenship. For those without character, skills, or ideas on a proper life, reeducation would be the medium of correction. From ancient times to the current fashion for behavior modification, one can see the learning model underlying a range of care types. In truth, for years facilities for children defined as retarded, delinquent, disturbed, or disabled have been classified as schools—and the treatment, where it existed, was very much shaped by current educational philosophies and techniques. Their names often included "school," and the scheduling of time and activities was derived from the model, often communicating a profound sense that the total existence of children should be consumed by formal education.

Finally, the origins of a medical or physiological orientation to care derive from the fine line between mind and body and the ambiguity of the signs that constitute symptoms of disorder. The particular indicators of deviance, behavior appearance that is "different," extreme fatigue, depression, anxiety, often have passed through medical review, only to have physicians prescribe the remedy of the moment—rest, activity, a specific diet, bleeding, purges, surgery, shocks, or the like. Based on the assumption of an underlying physical condition, treatment might be pursued at home, in a spa or retreat, or in a hospital.

As we review the history of concepts of care for the deviant, we find that these models cut across the plane of time, sadly with little cumulative benefit to the individual, especially so if we are concerned with children.

CONCEPTIONS OF CARE

A critical period in the early history of this country, where care of the deviant is concerned, came in the surge of nationalism and reform following the American Revolution and the War of 1812. It culminated in Jackson's translation of the principles of democracy formulated by Jefferson (Magaro et al., 1978). One of the results was the development of the asylum as a solution for a range of human problems (Rothman, 1971) which included care of the "insane," orphans, the poor, criminals, and delinquent youth. In many cases these were individuals who had been incorporated into a rural farm life, but a change in the nature of the economy and the moral structure underlying it led to very different concepts of deviance.

According to Rothman (1971) the origin of the asylum was neither the result of extensive experimentation nor a broad search for reform, since many kinds of models could have been selected. It reflected the spirit of the time, less a logical culmination or product of the accumulation of medical and social knowledge and more a result of social change.

> The response in the Jacksonian period to the deviant and the dependent was first and foremost a vigorous attempt to promote the stability of the society at the moment when traditional ideas and practices appeared outmoded, constricted, and ineffective. The almshouse and the orphan asylum all represented an effort to insure the cohesion of the community in new and changing circumstances. (p. xviii)

A form of care developed, over the years, that has been identified as "moral treatment." The anti-slavery movement, social reformers such as Dorothea Dix, various women's rights movements, and the reform spirit of the times led to the period of 1776 to 1861 being identified as one of "Romantic Exuberance" (Magaro et al., 1978).

Embodying principles used by the Greeks and derived from English examples, the asylum became a durable fixture in the American scene. Despite changes in conceptions of deviance and treatment prescriptions, it has continued until today. It originally was conceived of as a place where shelter and security would be provided for the poor, the orphaned, or the disturbed. A tranquil setting (often in the country), a regular schedule of activity, an adequate but light diet, and recreational activities were all prescribed in order to restore the patient to active citizenship (Magaro et al., 1978). In a certain sense the asylum was undermined by its own perceived success. Although originally designed for middle- and upper-class patients, the reforms of the 1840s found huge numbers of the poor taken from prisons and other institutions and placed in asylums (Magaro et al., 1978). As the asylum grew in size it lost both its original mission and any semblance of humanity as it turned to custodial care. However, the form itself has proved difficult to eliminate.

The Civil War and its wake brought another period of reflection, including reflection on the growing asylums and their mandates. With the tremendous increase in their size, questions developed over their failure to rehabilitate inmates and the curability of the "insane." Science became the hope as the moral treatment programs were perceived as failures. Therapy was largely turned over to medical practitioners: the psychiatrists (Magaro et al., 1978). Physical medicine became the model of institutional care and extensive hospitalization the remedy. These stays continued to be more custodial than therapeutic. Magaro and his associates (1978) describe the functions of the institution as "something of a clearing house where diseased people came to be shelved while awaiting classification." In this process "it was forced to accept all kinds of chronic conditions, including a variety of social misfits" (p. 40). Given the official stamp of approval by state legislatures, this form became an integral part of the governmental social service structure. Where do children fit into this history?

SETTINGS FOR DEVIANT CHILDREN

Since the late 1950s and the early 1960s, books and articles have been published which provide critical analyses of the institutional psychiatric treatment of *adults* (Goffman, 1961; Braginsky, Braginsky, & Ring, 1969; Stanton & Schwartz, 1954; Caudill, 1958; Rothman, 1971, to name a few). "Anti-psychiatric" concepts of mental illness argue for the idea of the political and social nature of the definition and incarceration and treatment of adult "mental patients," challenging the traditional conceptions of a medical model of disease (Laing, 1967; Braginsky et al., 1969; Szasz, 1961; Scheff, 1966). Social and political movements such as "Mental Health Liberation" have evolved and fought for the right to treatment, the end to involuntary commitment of adults and for other aspects of patients' rights, including the right for people to live in their communities.

Surprisingly, for a country considered to be child-centered and for a century noted as "the century of the child," little of the same attention or level of analysis has been available in relation to *children* in psychiatric institutions. Some writing has documented the treatment of mentally retarded children, analyzed the roots and consequences of their labeling and exposed the myths of their incompetence (Kugel & Wolfensberger, 1973; Mercer, 1973; Braginsky & Braginsky, 1971), tracing their historical developments and criticizing the present situation—again accompanied by a social movement for change. The treatment of children called "delinquent" has also received some limited discussion (Rothman, 1971, 1980; Platt, 1977) though there is little analysis of present-day policies or institutions.

It is primarily in relation to the topic of children considered "emotionally disturbed" enough to "require residential treatment" that the absence of literature is glaringly evident—especially literature challenging the reasons for the commitment, their labeling, or providing a critical analysis of the conditions of their treatment. Some work details the historical treatment of children considered emotionally troubled (Whittaker, 1979; Despert, 1965) but with minor exceptions (Rothman, 1971, 1980; Koocher, 1976) generally accepts the idea that their problems are validly defined, though perhaps wrongly labeled. These views accept the necessity of a residential setting while acknowledging that these settings have problems which can be solved. Small, mostly private, residential treatment settings are described as the type of care that should be available (Whitaker, 1979). Few have totally challenged the concept of the "emotionally disturbed" child in need of residential treatment or analyzed who these children are and how they get into institutions. We have few accounts of the day-to-day life of these children in existing institutions and no attempt to connect these experiences to our conceptions of children and their problems.

It would be inaccurate to claim that this lack of critical attitude grows totally out of conscious intent. However, Koocher's (1976) position that "children who are different or who are considered defective in some way have long been institutionalized as a kind of 'sanitizing' service for society" (p. 7) definitely would seem an appropriate characterization of present as well as historical trends. In other instances the position taken by recent childrens' rights advocates, such as Apter (1976), provide another partial explanation:

We do not see children as people with all the rights and duties thereof. All the recent work on children's liberation points to our denial of rights to children. Politically, economically, legally and sexually we have double standards for adults and children. . . . Why are children being incarcerated today for offenses that would not be considered crimes if they were committed by adults? (p. 104)

This conception of children as non-people (a term Goffman [1961] uses to describe the status of adults in psychiatric institutions) is based partly on the *material* reality that at very young ages children are physically and economically dependent on adults, partly on the *legal* reality that parents (and/or guardians, including the school) can be held responsible for the behavior of minor children, and partly on a *paternalistic yet obviously false pride* which Beyer and Wilson (1976) ascribe to Americans:

> Americans pride themselves on the care they provide their children. That care encompasses childrens' spiritual, intellectual, and physical needs; it is demonstrated by superb schooling and medical attention for many, and it extends to psychological benefits. As evidence of their concern, some might point to the number of children in mental hospitals. The statistics are incomplete and sometimes in conflict but they indicate that the number of institutionalized adults has decreased in recent years while the number of children in mental hospitals has apparently continued to grow. (p. 133)

That the majority of children in such institutions are now, and have historically been, the children of the poor, the immigrant, and the U.S. racial minorities (Rothman, 1971, 1980; Magaro et al., 1978; Platt, 1977) makes it clear that such treatment may be done in the name of the "child's best interests" but truthfully it may not be "for the child's own good."

As our own experience will show, we must take a serious and critical look at the institutions we assume are "therapeutic" for our "children." A first step is to ask: what is the conceptual and concrete nature of the "therapeutic settings" we provide for children, who are "the children" ending up in these settings, and what is the real nature of their problems? To begin we will review the historic development of psychiatric settings for children and the development of the concept of the "emotionally disturbed child."

Contemporary residential treatment settings, whether for children or adults are usually called "therapeutic environments." This term began emerging in the 1950s. Usual definitions of "therapeutic" focus on a specific group of people who are identified as requiring "therapy." Their names define their problem: emotionally disturbed, physically disabled, mentally retarded. Their common experience is one of being designated as different and singled out for a specific form of care.

The isolation inherent in the definition of someone as having a problem has an environmental component as well. The physical isolation of people who are "different" in places specifically designed for special care enhances their stigmatization. The names of the places parallel the definition of the problem— psychiatric hospital, center for the developmentally disabled. Beginning with the nineteenth century, the combined social and physical designation of groups of people with a specific problem and a type of place to treat the problem produced the modern structure we call an "institution." The type and extent of care as well as the physical environment closely follows the rationale for defining the particular group.

Historically, the goals of psychiatric institutions, their physical environments, and treatment programs have varied depending on the changing definitions of the people and the explanation of the etiology of their problems. The definitions changed with the social, political, and economic context. Wolfensberger (1972) in describing the evolution of institutions for the mentally retarded and Magaro et al. (1978) in detailing the history of the treatment of "madness" in institutions, demonstrate the relationship between the general conceptions of the deviant and the methods and places of treatment. The definers of the acceptable and the unacceptable are generally the middle and upper classes. The less powerful members of the society—the poor—are seen to be deviant when they do not share the goals, values, genes, and life-style of the power class. The distinction between the powerful and the less powerful, between the definer and the defined, means that methods of treatment and places for treatment vary for different groups (Magaro et al., 1978). We would add that conceptions of deviance also vary with the age, race, religion, sex, and sexuality of the "deviant" and that the standards for acceptable behavior within American society have been set by white Christian middle- and upper-class male heterosexual adults.

If we focus on age, we see that children are in a less powerful position than adults, and it is adults who define acceptable and unacceptable childhood behavior. Adults were labeled "insane" and were treated as such during the nineteenth century. They were considered "incurable" by the late 1800s and the institutions for them had reached a period of stagnation and custodial care by 1918 which has continued, in most instances, up to the present day. Yet the first inpatient psychiatric treatment facility for children did not open until 1923. Where were troubled children prior to 1923? Did childhood "madness" not exist?

> Children affected with what we would describe today as neurotic and psychotic illness were (prior to this century) variously labeled through the ages as "possessed," "wicked," "guilty," "insubordinate," "incorrigible," "unstable," "maladjusted," and "problem children," roughly in this order. (Despert, 1965, p. 28)

Disobedient Children and Houses of Refuge*

Prior to the late 1800s, the predominant child-caring institutions in the United States were orphan asylums. By 1850, the shift of children out of almshouses,

---

* For much of this information and analyses we have relied on Rothman's book, *The Discovery of the Asylum, Social Order and Disorder in the New Republic* (Boston: Little, Brown, 1971), and Bremner's collection of original documents, *Children and Youth in America. A Documentary History*, vols. 1–3, (Cambridge, MA: Harvard University Press, 1970–1974).

into the 15 or so privately sponsored orphan asylums that opened between 1800 and 1830, had grown into a systematic program. New York State alone had 27 public and private child-care institutions. "Within two decades they had become common structures, widespread and popular, with their own unique and important attributes, not just a last resort when apprenticeship was impossible" (Rothman, 1971, p. 207).

The children these institutions "cared for" were not limited to the abandoned and orphaned, but included children from single parent families and two parent families who, because of either their poverty or their morality, were thought to be incompetent in caring for their children.

The House of Refuge—a reformatory for disobedient children—emerged at the same time and was intended for the child convicted of a petty crime or picked up for wandering the streets. But it also was used for the "willfully disobedient child, turned over by distraught parents" (Rothman, 1971, p. 209).

> Taken together, the admissions policies of child-care institutions were a catalogue of practically every misfortune that could befall a minor. The abject, the vagrant, the delinquent, the child of poverty-stricken or intemperate parents were all proper candidates for one or another asylum or refuge. . . . The asylum and refuge were two more bricks in the wall that Americans built to confine and reform the dangerous classes. (Rothman, 1971, p. 209)

Wolfensberger (1972) describes the treatment of the mentally retarded during this period as "making the deviant non-deviant." The approach to the children we are describing had a similar focus in that children were believed to be malleable. They were to be trained and rehabilitated and brought back into mainstream society. However, their treatment differed from the mentally retarded at this time in that it also rested on protecting them from the temptations of a corrupt community, that is, "protecting the deviant from the non-deviant" (Wolfensberger, 1972). Their problems were seen to lay in a faulty environment. By placing them in an appropriate environment—defined as one which would teach respect for authority through order—they would return to the society and function as intended. A report of success with such treatment from the 1827 Annual Report of the New York House of Refuge is cited by Rothman (1971):

> . . . "it was found necessary to apply severe and continued punishments, in order to break the obstinacy of his spirit. The discipline enforced had a most happy effect. He became submissive and obedient." (p. 215)

The treatment also reflected the contemporary opinions of childrearing techniques. Childrearing literature contained the same ideas as reports from refuges and asylums; "the same critique of society; the same fears of the future; the same criteria for reform" (Rothman, 1971, p. 217). "At the root of this popular insistence on the primacy of obedience was a conception of individual respect for authority as the cornerstone of an orderly society" (Rothman, 1971, p. 220). There was such a strong relationship between the concept of the problem, the type of institutional program, and the type of environment that it is worth focusing on it in detail because of its legacies to the present.

To remove and protect the inmates from corrupting influences the asylum was built outside the community in a physically isolated place. Parents and other members of the immediate social environment were seen to be part of the problem and many institutions required parents to transfer to the institution all legal rights to their children—sometimes forever, sometimes over the course of the child's stay (in loco parentis)—which could be indeterminate. Visiting schedules reflected the same attitude: in some it was limited to once a month or once every three months, and in others visiting could occur only at the discretion of a committee. Houses of Refuge were more stringent than asylums. Since the children were presumed to be more "degenerate," their isolation had to be more complete.

The isolation was not thought to be problematic because the child's length of stay was to be "short"—one month to two years. There was faith that the "treatment" would work. After short periods the successful children were apprenticed to respectable families in the country or to relatives. The focus on a short length of stay and faith in their work meant that the place of discharge was related to a grading system such that delinquents who did not do well might be sent on whaling voyages to take them away from the community altogether. Little attention was paid to aftercare—nor was there a careful assessment of the families to whom children were apprenticed.

The focus on order, obedience, and routine as the "cure" defined the type of program that was used. At the New York House of Refuge, for example, bells rang to announce periods and changes of activity, beginning with sunrise wakeup (as early as 5 A.M.) and followed by unlocking the cell doors. Children then "proceed, in perfect order, to the Wash Room. Thence they are marched to parade in the yard, and undergo an examination as to their dress and cleanliness; after which they attend morning prayer." School followed and ended at 7 A.M. (in summer) when breakfast began (A routine day in the New York House of Refuge, from the Tenth Annual Report, 1835, pp. 6–7, cited in Bremner, 1970, p. 688). After breakfast, boys worked in shops while girls cooked, cleaned, and mended. After lunch at noon, work resumed, followed by washing, eating dinner, two and one-half hours of evening classes and evening prayer and return to cells into which they were locked, "when perfect silence reigns throughout the establishment." In some refuges verbal communication was not allowed at all during work times; in others it was kept to a minimum, and no communication was allowed between boys and girls. All of these settings had a distinct military quality—relying on drill and activities in unison whether in reciting or in marching. The physical environments were also strikingly similar:

> Managers typically followed what they called the congregate system. Rather than divide the children into small groups and supply each of them with a cottage and a caretaker, they lodged the inmates together, either in wings where cells followed upon cells or in one central building, where dormitories stretched along either side of the length of hallways. (Rothman, 1971, p. 228)

The description Rothman offers of the New York House of Refuge gives further detail:

> The institution's architecture was as monotonous as its time-table. Boys and girls occupied separate buildings, each structure of bare brick and unvarying design; as the refuge expanded, adding more wings, the repetition and uniformity increased. The buildings were usually four stories high, with two long hallways running along either side of a row of cells. The rooms, following one after another, were all five by eight feet wide, seven feet high, windowless, with an iron-lattice slab for a door and flues for ventilation near the ceiling. Each group of eleven cells could be locked or unlocked simultaneously with one master key; every aperature within an inmate's reach was guarded by iron sashes, every exit door from the asylum was made of iron. On the first floor of each wing was a huge tub for bathing, sizeable enough to hold fifteen to twenty boys; on the fourth floor were ten special punishment cells. In keeping with the external design, all inmates wore uniforms of coarse and solid-colored material. No sooner did they enter the institution than they were stripped, washed, their hair cut to standard length, and put into common dress. (p. 226)

In summing up the uniformity among these institutions, Rothman comments: "From all indications, a visitor to one house of refuge could be confident of having seen them all" (p. 228).*

Order and organization were followed through in systems of classification and punishment. Grading systems prevailed, especially at houses of refuge. Entering children were placed in the lowest category and advanced to the top level by proving their worthiness. Each staff person, from the guard to the teacher, filed reports that were used in ranking. Those in the bottom grades could be prevented from joining sports activities, denied the right to speak or be spoken to by other inmates, had to go to bed early, or be isolated physically. Those in the top rank would get extra recreation time. The ranking was also connected

---

* Rothman adds that the major difference between asylums and houses of refuge was that cells were not that usual in asylums and more time was devoted to classroom instruction as opposed to work. But they also used the congregate system with large dormitories of approximately 20 children each.

to release: those top ranked would be released to parents, friends, or an apprenticeship while those staying at the bottom would be sent to a ship captain.

Punishment was central to this system. Elijah Devoe, assistant superintendent of the New York House of Refuge from 1845 to 1848, described the types of punishments that were usual but which he opposed:

> For every trifling commission or omission which it is deemed wrong to do or to omit to do, they are "cut" with ratan. Every day they experience a series of painful excitements. The endurance of the whip, or the loss of a meal—deprivation of play or the solitary cell. On every hand their walk is bounded; while Restriction and Constraint are their most intimate companions. (Devoe, excerpted by Bremner, 1970, p. 689)

Other punishments described in existing documents include increased work load, reduction of food to bread and water, wearing a ball and chain, or the "shower bath," a much dreaded punishment especially in cold weather. The number and diversity of punishments given to each child varied with the severity and repetitiveness of their wrongdoings.

All of these procedures and routines were openly admitted and defended on the grounds of teaching obedience and retraining the child to fit into society. And, while there was "great range in the personalities of refuge managers, with some tending to be overbearing and cruel, others considerate and gentle . . . the institutional norms maintained a strict and severe discipline" (Rothman, 1971, p. 233).

The "family" was often used as a metaphor to describe the program being offered even though the reality of family life and the reality of institutional life had little in common. Rothman believes that institutional managers could use the term without contradiction because they felt that "the family" was in need of strengthening and should use the refuge as a model for carrying its purposes (obedience, respect for authority) into reality:

> As long as the desideratum was order and discipline, as long as the virtues most in demand in child rearing were regularity and respect for authority, then the asylum was at least as effective a training center as the home. To the extent that the family neglected or overindulged or corrupted its members, the institution was a distinctly preferable setting. (Rothman, 1971, p. 236)

Juvenile Delinquency, Individuality, and State Training Schools

Enchantment with houses of refuge was soon to disappear and was transferred during the "Progressive Era"* to the development and support of the juvenile

---

* Some authors date this period from 1865 to 1930. Others begin it later at 1900 and end it later at 1940.

court system, state training schools, child-guidance clinics, inpatient psychiatric clinics and, eventually, the children's residential psychiatric center we know today. The "family" analogy has been maintained to the present day as well as the emphasis on control, the segments of society needing control, and the identifiable institutional atmosphere. What shifted were the concepts of problems and explanations for their origin, the labels attached to these problems, the concepts of new institutions and the ways in which the "family" analogy has been applied to them.

Changes in children's institutions which occured during the Progressive Era "were part of a much larger movement to readjust institutions to conform to the requirements of corporate capitalism" (Platt, 1977, p. xix). The late nineteenth century witnessed strikes, violent episodes (including the Haymarket Riot of 1886), and economic depression as well as the development of militant movements demanding economic and social justice, such as the anti-lynching crusade, the Socialist Party, and the International Workers of the World. Platt sees the Progressive Era child-saving movement as a social parallel to the attempts at economic regulation. Both, growing out of the earlier period, wanted to achieve "order, stability, and control, while preserving the existing class system and distribution of wealth" (Platt, 1977, p. xxii).

The sweeping changes in the view and treatment of children during the Progressive Era, ranging from the implementation of new laws to the building of new institutions and covering a multitude of aspects of daily life, was made possible by a broad coalition of people whose interests merged. Middle class activists, supporters, and professionals were backed up financially and politically by the wealthiest and most powerful sectors of society who saw these changes as being to their benefit.

Yet the reformers, Platt cautions, while working closely with corporate interests were not simply their "lackeys." But the eventual failures of their reforms, despite the good intentions of many and genuine concerns with the lives of the poor, must be viewed in light of their belief in the status quo and their bigoted and class-biased view of the poor.

The Progressive Era embodied a reaction against the gross failures of the Jacksonian institutions. Knowledge of the horrors of these institutions, according to Rothman (1980) was not, in and of itself, sufficient to fuel the development of the Progressive program. Indeed, despite this knowledge and exposés from time to time, the institutions continued and consolidated up to 1900 (Wolfensberger, 1972). At least four factors sustained them: (1) bigotry: "The aliens had only themselves to blame for the decline of the system, for they were untreatable and unmanageable" (Rothman, 1980, p. 25); (2) economics: the states received considerable income by selling the labor of prisoners, manufacturers had a source of cheap labor, and because the costs of asylums were taken over by the state as opposed to local financing of almshouses these costs were not immediately apparent on a local level; (3) do-goodism: the institutions were believed to be better than the "barbarian" institutions of the past; and (4) vested interests: certain professional groups (especially from the new field of neurology) criticized existing institutions and made minor suggestions for reform (e.g., establishing research laboratories) although they had no new scheme for replacement. Medical superintendents supported these changes because, at least, their positions remained unchallenged. The institution was unquestioned as the caretaking model agency, only its form was subject to criticism.

In addition to the social and economic factors discussed earlier, the development of the social sciences was a turning point for the Progressive Era in relation to dealing with "deviancy" (Rothman, 1980; Rosen, 1968). The reformers came from colleges and universities where they had studied the new field of "criminality" including public and private systems for dealing with these social problems. An emphasis was placed on the gathering of "objective facts" to find the cause of a problem and to discover the solution. Rational arguments based on these facts would be used for persuading legislatures to change laws (Rothman, 1980).

With this attitude they set out to examine and find solutions to the problems of "deviant" behavior. They were optimistic, despite their findings of the extreme poverty and circumstances of the people they were to help. They believed that societal interest went hand in hand with the reform necessary to enable every citizen to reap the benefits of the American system, giving all a high standard of living through enlarged opportunities to become truly "American." And they believed that state intervention (through laws) was necessary to ensure success.

While Progressives varied in their explanation of problems, they agreed on their approach—a case-by-case approach (Taylor, 1973; Rothman, 1980). Their critique of the Jacksonian institution was that it lumped together all deviancy in terms of causality (social disorder) and therefore only had one remedy for all— the structure and discipline of the asylum or house of refuge. Arguing that it was necessary to deal with each offender as an individual, the Progressives covered each life history and based on this information suggested a remedy particular to the case. The Progressive program reflected the search for a diversity of solutions each suited to the individual involved. It was felt that some people should remain at home and probation seemed appropriate; some needed short-term help while in the community—outpatient clinics were the solution; others needed long-term treatment—the psychopathic hospital seemed applicable, and so on.

Progressives were not opposed to the institution, per se. Rather they believed, as many still do (see Whittaker, 1979) that the institution could and should coexist with other programs. The other programs, however, would insure that treatment was individualized and that the institution would indeed be a last resort.

Despite similarities in approach, the Progressives had differences in ideology. The environmental ideology was dominant, especially during the early years.

Instead of society as a whole being seen as "corrupting," the problems were attributed to specific economic and social causes. Most of American society was doing very well, indeed. "The problem was manageable; it could be located *spatially* in the ghetto and it could be solved, given the right programs" (Rothman, 1980, p. 52). Opportunities available in American life had simply not yet reached these people. By bringing the benefits of middle-class life to the inhabitants of the "slums," the immigrant poor could be taught to be like the "native born." Reformers would change the material conditions of people's lives through a combination of legislation and action around housing and workplaces and would rehabilitate deviants with their case-by-case approach.

In the 1920s and 1930s the psychological approach gained ground. The social conditions of daily life were perceived to be a necessary but not sufficient cause for individual deviancy. Only specific individuals were affected by such conditions. G. S. Hall's work in child development, the emerging field of psychological testing, and Freud's ideas all led to the notion that *problems were located within the individual* and that they could be diagnosed and subsequently treated. In the end, however, they put forward the same solutions as the environmentalists, since they came up with no other remedies. Rothman asserts that the psychological interpretations of deviancy also fit in well with the belief in the American system. "If mental conflict was the root of the problem then social conflict was not. It was sex, not capitalism; it was images, not reality" (Rothman, 1980, p. 57). And, again, investigations would yield solutions.

Each of these approaches existed along with the eugenicists who mainly focused on those "deviants" where the heredity argument fit a deviance behavior they could more easily ascribe to biological causes—the case of the mentally retarded or "incurably" insane (Wolfensberger, 1972). Their program focused on marriage and sterilization laws. The coexistence and alliances of the other groups with the eugenicists is understandable since reformers argued for acknowledging a range of reasons for individual problems and obviously did not shed their class, race, or nationalistic biases in their analyses of these problems.

While reforms were sought and implemented in adult institutions (concepts of parole, probation, indeterminate sentencing, medical treatment, the psychopathic hospital), the main thrust of the Progressive program focused on children. There were suggested reforms for the adult insane asylum, but generally the inmates were regarded as "incurable" until such time as medical science could find the cure for their "illness." This attitude was inspired by the growing field of medicine and the finding that paresis was caused by syphilis (Rosen, 1968). Middle-class clients could reap the benefits of psychoanalysis but institutions would provide more humane custodial care and experiment with medical remedies for the adult poor.

Rothman asserts that it was most disturbing for reformers to see immigrant children "following in the footsteps" of their parents. Their assumptions, that the system was fine for the most part and that children were malleable in a way that adults were not, led them to develop a range of experiences that would encourage the proper development of the children. Hall's work spread the idea that there were stages of child development, each stage having certain goals and requiring certain experiences. In the early stages children had to learn proper habits for it was then that they were susceptible to drill and discipline. Adolescence, a concept Hall introduced, was the time for developing "individuality" and required different experiences. Mothers were instructed to learn about childhood, since proper training could not be left to "maternal instinct" in the face of such a complicated phenomenon. While most of the ideas were aimed at *voluntary* implementation by the middle class, the reformers translated them into *legislated programming* for the immigrants and the poor, because these parents were believed to be too ignorant or incapable of implementing such training (a consequence of the reformers' moralistic and environmentalist perspectives).

Kindergartens and settlement-house clubs would help children and their parents (but particularly their mothers) develop the right attitudes for a middle-class life-style and for developing a love of country. "They would teach the newcomers such mottos as 'the clock helps us to be good' and patriotic songs and stories of the great men who have made America what she is" (Rothman, 1980, p. 206). Clinics would focus on preventative medicine and good nutrition. Compulsory schooling would take them from unhealthy conditions of the factory and give them the opportunities to develop skills ensuring economic success. The National Congress of Mothers, a middle-class group organized in 1897, had 190,000 members by 1917 in 36 state chapters. It was a major lobbying force for Progressive child-welfare legislation including kindergartens, playgrounds, compulsory schooling, and widow's pensions. They wanted to substitute family care for asylum care.

The first strong thrust of dealing directly with childhood "deviancy" was the reform of the juvenile justice system. The work of social scientists and psychiatrists such as G. Stanley Hall, Adolph Meyer, and William Healy was instrumental in the eventual creation of the concept of "emotional disturbance" and institutions for its treatment. Before their work, children had been believed to be either "delinquent" or "dependent." They argued that existing institutions used rigidity, uniformity, and conformity because problems had been misunderstood as disobedience and lack of respect for authority. From their view, the problem was that children and adolescents lacked confidence in themselves and their abilities and needed to develop their individuality in constructive ways.

Arguing that the bases of the problems of the criminality of youth were different from that of adults, the creation of a separate juvenile court system was the first step.

These courts were dressed by their architects in a cloak of benign concern for children's welfare, a concern soon raised to an ideology termed, variously and seriatim, "parents patriae," "the best interests of the child," and the search for "individualized" treatment. Forever banned from the lexicon of juvenile court personnel would be such terms as "punishment" and "retribution." From this treatment and rehabilitative ideology sprang the assertion that the state legitimately could institutionalize children who "habitually associate with immoral and vicious persons" or "habituate railway yards or bucket shops" as some early statutes phrased it. Clearly, to these early thinkers, such conduct indicated a propensity to commit crime if it remained untreated, particularly because the affluent, educated and troubled youth they knew did not do such things (or, it might be suggested, were not apprehended doing such things). . . . The early statutes . . . empowered them to rule on every conceivable form of conduct by the young, ranging from the truancy and rebelliousness of the stubborn child to acts that would be crimes if committed by adults. (Taylor, 1973, p. 182)

Sexism as well as classism and racism were evident in the application of statutes (Platt, 1977; Rothman, 1980). Boys could be charged with "acts of carelessness or mischief," being "ungovernable" or "beyond parental control." "Such nebulous complaints were even more commonplace in the case of girls. . . . Exactly what constituted one of the most popular charges leveled against girls (but not boys), 'sex offenses' was rarely spelled out; it might include dating a young man whom parents disliked to outright prostitution" (Rothman, 1980, p. 252).

The major concepts of the court were to focus on the individual and not on the act; on rehabilitation, not punishment; on the needs of the child and not on guilt or innocence.

Of course the court does not confine its attention to just the particular offense which brought the child to its notice. For example, a boy who comes to court for some such trifle as failing to wear his badge when selling papers may be held on probation for months because of difficulties at school; and a boy who comes in for playing ball in the street may (after the court has caused more serious charges to be preferred against him) be committed to a reform school because he is found to have habits of loafing, stealing or gambling which cannot be corrected outside. (as excerpted in Bremner, 1970, p. 520)

By providing a hearing, rather than a trial, all types of information about the child including school records, health, family situation, and home environment could be brought to bear on a solution that would be in the "best interests of the child." The court procedures were, therefore, unlike those for their adult counterparts. There were relaxed rules: attorneys were allowed but seen as unnecessary, there was no jury, and the judge had the authority to pressure the child into confessing (Rothman, 1980; Platt, 1977; Taylor, 1977).

To truly separate the young person and support their ideology, the reformers even urged the construction of totally separate judicial facilities, although these appeared mainly in larger cities. The physical make-up of the courtroom mirrored the professed ideology:

> The court room . . . should not be a court room at all, just a room, with a table and two chairs, where the judge and the child, the probation officer and the parents, as occasion arises, come into close contact, and where in a more or less formal way the whole story may be talked over. The judge should sit at a desk rather than a bench so as to "evoke a sympathetic spirit" from the child. (Platt, 1977, p. 144)

Few questioned the state's right to usurp the privacy, liberty, and due process of the child since the child, then, as now, was seen to be already subjected to the unlimited authority of the parents. The state was simply substituting itself for parents.

There were obviously no set solutions, such as "sentences," for the varied problems of youth. As noted earlier, the reformers were not opposed to institutionalization. Indeed, as we shall see, they created *special* institutions to match their rhetoric. But the newer concept they employed was "probation," a concept which ultimately spread the net of the states' control outside the institution and was the basis for the total invasion, by the state, into the lives of the poor. In order to have a hearing on which to base the solution, a probation officer was supposed to supply the judge with all pertinent information.

The court gave the officers extreme latitude in securing the information which could be obtained from the parents, people in the neighborhood, teachers, police department records, the child, and any agencies dealing with the child, including their local religious institution. Court officers could also go to experts in child psychology and psychiatry. In fact, many reformers suggested that the courts employ a staff of such experts, and/or work closely with clinics who already had a staff of these professionals (Rothman, 1980).

It was anticipated that institutionalization would be avoided as much as possible and so the duties of the probation officer extended to the period after the hearing as well. He was supposed to supervise not only the offender but the family and he could use any tactic, including threats, to do his job with no legal restrictions. The idea was to retrain the family so that the child in question and any others would never become problems again.

While the implementation of special courts, special judges, and probation officers was not totally uniform across the country, the juvenile court system and the concept of probation tenaciously took hold in an extremely short period of time. The first court opened in Illinois in 1898, by 1909 they had been created in twenty states and the District of Columbia (Glasscote et al., 1972); by 1920 they existed in all but three states (Rothman, 1980). There was some opposition from police officers and lower-level municipal judges who defended their purview and their previous handling of cases. Some legal scholars and lawyers, spurred on by parents who wanted to contend court commitments, brought cases challenging the lack of due process. But Progressive judges overrode earlier decisions with tautological arguments: a trial was not necessary because these were not criminal proceedings and the child was not being punished (Rothman, 1980).

The swift acceptance and lack of success of the opposition is attributed by both Rothman and Platt to the power of the rhetoric but primarily to the range of groups that allied to push the program, including wealthy philanthropists, charitable organizations, women's clubs, social scientists, superintendents of juvenile institutions, legislators, district attorneys, psychologists, psychiatrists, and social workers. Obviously many people had a vested interest of their own in supporting the creation of such a *system*.

What eventually distinguished the era and has remained as a legacy both materially and ideologically to the present day, was not its progressivism but the creation of a *system* rather than a piecemeal approach for dealing with children presumed to be delinquent or dependent—a system which did not eliminate institutions nor prevent institutionalization. Indeed, Rothman cites statistics showing that in Pennsylvania, during one year, the regular court system dealing with adults disposed of 71% of its cases by dismissing them and/or imposing a fine while in only 12% of the cases was probation *or* incarceration the sentence. In the juvenile court only 30% of the cases were dismissed while probation accounted for 28% and incarceration for 28% of the remainder.

The net expanded to include children who would not previously have come under jurisdiction of the state but whose actions would have been "ignored or handled informally . . . [including] drinking, begging, roaming the streets, frequenting dance-halls and movies, fighting, sexuality, staying out late at night and incorrigibility" (Platt, 1977, p. 139).

Some of these offenders might be placed on probation but the institution remained the major solution for the same group of people it always had accommodated—the recidivists. And the sexism of the system combined with a concept of "major" offenders meant that "the more serious offender, especially with a prior record, was a prime candidate for institutionalization and so was an ungovernable boy and a sexually active girl" (Rothman, 1980, p. 259).

The institution was seen as having two purposes. It would act as a back-up sanction so that the child offender and his or her family would take probation seriously and it was seen to be appropriate in many cases including the circumstances in which "the child's parents are hopelessly weak or morally bad, or if he has no home. . . ." (Rothman, 1980, p. 220). According to Platt (1977) it blurred the distinction between "delinquent" and "dependent" children and served to make a "social fact out of the norm of adolescent dependence."

The first institutions which appeared were the state training schools. Indeed, very early on—in December 1904—the new Illinois State School at St. Charles opened. Existing institutions were seen as unfit in terms of location, physical environment, philosophy, and program.

It was important that institutions for children be located in the country far from the "noisy, bustling, dirty city" with its "saloons, low dives, and gangs of bad boys." Rural purity as opposed to urban corruption was a recurring theme . . . it was impossible to reform children in the city where there were temptations all around and children were not taught by their parents to respect the rights and property of others . . . a change of environment was the only proper remedy . . . "from the crowded slum life of a noisy, disorderly settlement," where seventy percent of the population is of foreign parentage, these boys should be sent to the open country, where a regular methodical existence and a training and education that will develop and promote habits of industry. (Platt, 1977, p. 66)

While new institutions were part of the Progressive Era, existing refuges and reformatories had already begun to make changes in the direction of existing Progressive sentiments (Platt, 1977). Exposés condemned the non-homelike qualities of the institutions and suggested, in a reversal of Jacksonian era thinking, that the worst home was better than the best reformatory. Thus, changes were begun in the late 1800s (Platt, 1977) such as the introduction of cottages and dormitories and vocational training based on a Deweyan philosophy as well as some amenities.

But Progressives wanted even more. Again the rhetoric of "family" and "the home" entered and was augmented by the notion of "normal" (a phrase which was resurrected in the 1960s). According to Rothman, the routines of the schools were supposed to be as much like outside as possible and also "intimate," approximating families (Rothman, 1980).

Names of institutions were changed to reflect the ideology, an action which, ironically, continues to be a reform suggestion of today (Whittaker, 1978). Houses of refuge and reformatories became state "training schools" or "industrial schools," replacing the idea of a moral or discipline problem.

The idea of a training school carried very different associations: an environmental cause of crime (no training for an occupation); a parental failure (in G. Stanley Hall's terms inadequate habit training, or in the later terminology inspired by John Watson, a failure to "train the child to happiness"). (Rothman, 1980, p. 264)

Incorporating the Deweyan philosophy, there was academic as well as vocational training, and the vocational training was not supposed to be simply floor scrubbing or maintenance.

The physical environment would also be changed to reflect and promote the ideology. Living arrangements were to follow a cottage, not a cell block or even dormitory, design. To this idea, first begun in the 1880s

. . . the Progressives added their own interpretation. The new cottage plan, echoing the essential themes of child-rearing tracts . . . was to provide the setting in which highly trained and insightful surrogate parents would shape the development of the child, always meeting individual needs. (Rothman, 1980, p. 265)

According to Rothman, Carrie Smith suggested that to support individuality children needed their own rooms and a place for their possessions, a position echoed in physical design suggestions as a solution to the institutional qualities of children's psychiatric facilities today. As the statement in Rothman suggests, Smith held a view that could even be deemed "radical" for the present: without these provisions "we give *humane* treatment, as we do with dogs and cats, the while they are yearning for *human* treatment. Eliminate the "e" from humane and you have helped to eliminate the reformatory" (Rothman, 1980, p. 265).

Cottages would also make the institution into a "normal community." Since the environment was like the "usual" community, with home, school, and recreational facilities, it was assumed that the child who made a good adjustment there would also make a good adjustment to the community upon release. One school even attempted a form of self-government, but that component did not survive (Rothman, 1980).

The reality of institutional life did not match the rhetoric. Academic training failed and vocational training focused on children serving as unskilled assistants, doing repair and construction work around the institution. Platt (1977) asserts that the children were taught "middle-class values and lower-class skills." They mended clothing and shoes and washed in the laundry. Girls "learned" cooking, laundering, and ironing to prepare them for domestic service.

The cottages were a far cry from "home." Part of the blame was laid upon incompetent staff (paid wages far below a decent living standard) but Rothman and Platt also describe the overcrowding—64 boys in a cottage designed for 50. We can even question the thinking that accepted a concept of a "family" of 40—an obvious abuse of an analogy. In many cases, in order to make supervision easier, the cottages used dormitories as opposed to individual rooms. They could hardly be considered to have a "homelike" atmosphere. Rothman gives this account of a visitor to the Illinois Training School for Girls:

> "The typical cottage has on the first floor a day room, which is fairly large and with a sufficient number of windows, but with a distinctly institutional air. All the chairs, for instance, are placed in straight rows, and there are the most unhomelike lockers along one side of the room." The girls had their own bedrooms, "but the single window is barred and the doors of all rooms are locked when the girls go to bed, usually around 8:30." . . . Perhaps most institutional of all: "Although it was a very beautiful day and quite warm when we visited the institution, not a single child was outside." The matron quickly explained the fact: "There were not enough people to look after the girls, and they would simply run away." (1980, p. 273)

Descriptions gleaned from other institutions attest to the prisonlike quality of cottages, where children could not go outdoors, where the glass of cottage windows was painted so inmates could not look out, where girls were seen constantly scrubbing the floors. Boys institutions had a military quality with drills and dress parades on Sundays. The use of silence and mechanical routines continued. Punishment remained prevalent and one list of infractions, cited by Rothman, included: writing notes, lying, stealing, disobedience, negligence, talking in the dormitory, talking on line, communication between cottages, and running away. Almost all institutions had a merit and demerit system that was supposedly related to parole. Besides the denial of privilege, punishments included standing or sitting still for hours and the segregation cottages, the training school variation on prison solitary confinement. At Kansas Industrial Training School for Girls:

> There are two places where the girls are put in solitary confinement. One is a small dark room in the cottage. The window is painted to make the room dark and a mattress is laid on the floor for a bed, and the culprit is fed bread and milk. The other is a cell-like place located in a dairy room. The walls and floors are of cement and the only piece of furniture is a small iron bed. One wall is covered with iron bars. (Rothman, 1980, p. 279)

In some institutions, those in the disciplinary cottage wore special clothing . . . "a thin khaki coverall (with no underwear) and lived under a rule of total silence" (Rothman, 1980, p. 281). Some inmates could end up in segregation cottages for a year, especially if they continued to attempt to escape or repeated other infractions. And, corporal punishment was also used even where it was officially prohibited.

Rothman discussed why such conditions could come to exist despite the progressives' rhetoric and why no one challenged the discrepancy between rhetoric and reality. For example,

> Why was it that the cottages were anything but homelike? Because the inmates had to be kept under firm control, because the fear of disorder and escape was the nightmare that dominated the institution. The rules of silence, the dormitory with the light on, the general rigid tone of daily life, were not just random preferences on the part of the staff, but a way of keeping guard, of insuring control, of fulfilling the ultimate requirement of the training school, that is to confine its charges securely. (Rothman, 1980, p. 283)

The "incompatibility of custody and rehabilitation, of guarding and helping" was obvious in that custody and guarding won out. The institution itself was a back-up sanction for another system. Inmates left either when they reached the maximum age or when the institution was so crowded that one had to be released to make room for another.

Rothman believes that the absence of fundamental challenge from within the system was based on the vested interests of each group involved. Neither the judges nor the superintendents would admit failure; the private child-care agencies did not want to get rid of the "dumping grounds" for their most difficult cases. Investigations from outsiders, mostly social scientists, while describing the failures and horrors continually reached the conclusion that the institution had a vital role to play and could be made better. Rothman opines that reformers became partisans, unable to examine the outcome of their efforts and afraid that alternatives could be worse. They could always say that the reforms were never given enough of a chance. Platt (1977) has another point of view. Based on his historical survey of the development of the child-saving movement as well as the failure of recent reforms designed to allow for due process for children, he questions our belief that the juvenile court and its training schools are or were designed for or are capable of reducing crime, rehabilitating delinquents and enhancing justice:

> If, on the other hand, the juvenile court system is viewed as an instrument of class and racial oppression, emerging in a specific period of this society's historical development to regulate the children of the urban working class and attune them to the realities and discipline of industrial life under advanced capitalism, then its "failures" are not surprising. To put it another way, it is impossible to conceive of the juvenile court system as an agency of "rehabilitation" and social equality in a society where most working-class and minority youths are tracked into dead-end or low wage jobs, in which institutional racism and sexism systematically segment people into antagonistic social relations, and where the criminal justice system is blatantly used to undermine and repress political movements. (p. 192)

Disturbed Children, Child Guidance Clinics, and Inpatient Psychiatric Facilities

There is a legacy of the Progressive Era in relation to the present-day working of the juvenile court system and its specific institution, the state training school. But more than this, the ideology of juvenile justice reform—"individualized" treatment based on "diagnosis"; a focus on the individual rather than on the act—laid the groundwork for the discovery of the "emotionally disturbed" child. The eventual consequence of the ideology was the creation of inpatient psychiatric facilities for children, the first of which appeared in 1923 at Bellevue Hospital in New York.

Psychological and psychiatric diagnosis, if not treatment, were core ideological aspects of the juvenile court system and in the larger cities, psychiatric clinics were developed in connection with the courts. They were supposed to give the court the benefit of their knowledge of human development, to diagnose the problem. The courts would determine the appropriate remedy. In reality, however, judges decided who should have examination and, most frequently, they hardly paid any attention to the clinic reports. Rothman attributes this partly to the unwillingness of judges to give up their power, partly to the undeveloped "state of the art" of psychiatry and psychology, and partly to the limited recommendations clinics could make. Their diagnoses stated the obvious—the child's problems stemmed from a parent's drunkenness or need to work—and there were only four possible recommendations: probation, military service, a state training school, or a reformatory. Often these recommendations could not be implemented—the school was overcrowded, the parents protested military service, a voluntary agency did not want responsibility for the case.

Juvenile justice reforms eventually came together with a mental hygiene movement to create child-guidance clinics and inpatient children's psychiatric services. During the early 1900s the mental hygiene movement, spurred on by Clifford Beers and Adolf Meyer, introduced several concepts into the understanding of mental illness that would eventually affect the treatment of children. Under Beers' influence, based on his own experience as a mental patient, the movement focused on reform and upgrading of asylum conditions, specifically the elimination of physical abuse. However, these reforms were based on applying a medical model of treatment within the institution—of accepting the mental patient as "sick" and in need of "medical care." Beers argued for aftercare within the community including better employment opportunities. At the same time Adolf Meyer argued for the creation of "psychopathic institutes" as opposed to "insane asylums." The concept of the psychopathic institute rested on the distinction between the chronically ill person and the acute case who "needs a few weeks' or months' respite from a troubling environment, or because they could profit from the opportunity to begin to form new habits in a more structured setting" (Rothman, 1980, p. 309). The institute would be at the core of adult community mental-health facilities. People with problems would come to an outpatient clinic and, on the basis of diagnosis by a team (a psychiatrist, psychologist, and social worker) be referred for day care (going home at night), short-term inpatient care (psychopathic hospital), or long-term care (asylums).

But the focus, as the name mental *hygiene* movement was meant to imply was on prevention. Together, Beers and Meyers formed the National Committee for Mental Hygiene which conducted surveys on the needs of the "insane" and also conducted public education about mental health. They wanted to make clinic clients financially and personally independent by providing aftercare such as home-boarding, job placement, and stipends. Social workers were used for such work. After 1910, however, they focused primarily on providing psychological support. This shift in focus resulted from their lack of success. Few clinics were opened. They became processing mills with no treatment. There was no money for stipends or home-boarding programs. Furthermore, after World War I returning "shell-shocked" soldiers made physical causes suspect and pushed toward a more psychodynamic explanation.

Levine and Levine (1970) mark 1912 as the beginning of the end of the era of Progressive reform. In that year, the Progressive Party was beaten. It had fallen apart by 1914. Many reformers were part of the pacifist movement during World War I and their reputations suffered damage. During the post-war period, from 1920 until the Depression of the 1930s, liberals and reformers had neither power nor influence. The Bolshevik Revolution served as justification for a "red scare." In the early 1920s, the Palmer raids, the Ku Klux Klan, and patriotic societies encouraged and reflected negative attitudes toward and elimination of anything not "100% American."

Levine and Levine (1970) label the 1920s as the "businessman's decade." Despite the continued poverty of many, it was called an unprecedented period of economic growth and prosperity, created and supported with the help of the courts, regulatory agencies, and legislatures. Success, as well as failure, in this decade of the "self-made man," was viewed as an individual phenomenon. "The problem in the 1920s was to make the self better. In the pre-World War I era, the problems had been to make the world better" (Levine & Levine, 1970, p. 23). Women's participation in the wage labor force increased and in 1920, women won the right to vote. It was a period of changes in concepts of sexuality and sexual behavior. Women wore short skirts; there was public smoking and drinking. The virtures of premarital chastity were being challenged with discussions of free love. The mass media picked up these sexual themes and the ideas of scientific human relations, providing an intellectual scientific rationale for what was taking place. Freud's theories seemed particularly in tune and received a great deal of coverage in popular media as did ideas from Watson, Gesell, and habit-training theorists.

With the impetus of Beers and Meyers and, in the face of the lack of respect they received from the juvenile justice system that had created their clinics, the clinics enlarged their focus by serving schools and welfare agencies as well as an adult population. The focus on prevention, along with the popularity of Freud's ideas, led to the concept that harmful experiences of childhood led to adult problems and this led to the idea of prevention in childhood.

The child-guidance clinic was the outgrowth of this thinking. In 1909, the White House Conference on the Care of Dependent Children gave federal recognition to the importance of the home in creating or preventing problems of childhood (Rosen, 1968). In the same year, Healy's clinic opened at the Chicago Juvenile Psychopathic Institute. In 1912, the Boston Psychopathic Hospital began to study children and had a section of its outpatient clinic devoted to young female parolees (Castel et al., 1982). A federal act established a Children's Bureau which was charged with the investigation of a range of children's issues including juvenile institutions (Rosen, 1968). The bureau, in an effort to educate the public, published an infant care pamphlet discussing the lasting impact of early experience and the desirability of establishing good habits early in life. In 1915, the Allentown State Hospital in Pennsylvania founded a child-guidance clinic.

But it was the decade from 1918 to 1928 that was most significant in creating the children's institutional system we have today. 1918 was called the "Children's Year" and many conferences were held about the needs of children, including their mental health. In 1919, a Massachusetts law was passed requiring examination of any child who fell more than 3 years behind in school. Thus, the question of emotional disturbance was separated from both delinquency and retardation, at least in a conceptual sense. And in that same year, with 11 children's outpatients clinics in existence, a White House Conference on Children came to the conclusion that children in need of special care were first and foremost entitled to a "normal" home life and second, needed opportunities for education, recreation, vocational preparation for life and moral, religious, and physical development (Rosen, 1968). There was increased research on child development during this decade with a focus on documenting "normal" behavior and development.

In this context, the Commonwealth Fund in 1921 provided financial support for eight demonstration child-guidance clinics which, if they proved useful, would be taken over by the communities in which they were created. In fact, all but one reached this goal (Glasscote et al., 1972). These "habit clinics" were to help parents fulfill their role in the healthy normal development of their children. Parents, schools, and social agencies were to refer or bring children with "disturbing or otherwise puzzling behavior" (Glasscote et al., 1972, p. 13). Perhaps most significant was their focus on preschool children between the ages of two and five who employed "undesirable methods to cope with their problems" (Rosen, 1968, p. 299). At the Institute for Child Guidance in New York, 3,600 cases were treated between 1926 and 1932 (Castel et al., 1982).

According to Levine and Levine (1970) the original focus in these agencies (which were all private) was on *indirect* methods or ways of influencing aspects of the *social environment*. Within 10 years, however, the goal was lost and the focus was on the *individual* and not on the social structure. Part of this was due to the tone of individualism created in the 1920s and reflected through the growing professionalism of social work and the clinics themselves, which eventuated in a shift in goals, methods, and population.

Originally the main professionals had been social workers with their focus on social treatment methods (environmental methods) and community outreach. During this period, 74% of the cases had been referred from the juvenile courts and were mainly working- and lower-class children.

During the 1920s, however, in order for social workers to be treated as professionals, they had to be trained and they had to have a "method." In 1927, an Institute for Child Guidance was established to train professional personnel, the majority of whom were social workers. But psychiatrists and psychologists also had to be trained in "method." The grant forming the Institute was for a limited five-year period, at the end of which time fellowships were awarded only in child psychiatry and given to individual clinics to attract and train psychiatric personnel. The "method" that became primary was psychoanalysis—"talking treatment." The focus was taken away from the community and placed on the individual child, but also on the parents (usually the mother). Soon, there was a requirement that parents had to participate. Quickly, most cases became self-referred and from middle- and upper middle-class groups. By 1948, 60% of the cases came from this economic background.

The number of child-guidance clinics increased dramatically into the 1940s. By 1930 there were about 500 such clinics; by 1939 there were 776 (Castel et al., 1982). The nucleus of each was a team of psychiatrist, psychologist, and social worker, each supposedly bringing their respective skills to bear in each case. In the 1940s what is now the American Association of Psychiatric Services for Children was established as a membership organization of the child-guidance clinics. It then began to set standards for those clinics ready to be designated as training clinics.

Thus, although no real central federal policy was ever put forth, these facilities amounted to a highly developed system of mental health care services for middle- and upper middle-class children, which was already in place on a nationwide scale before the beginning of World War II. Obviously the method and the social class background of the social workers, psychiatrists, and psychologists themselves eliminated the working and lower classes from the clinics. The nature of the cases changed over time from the "hard-core" delinquent to the child who appeared "nervous." By the end of the decade of the 1920s, the cases were chosen to fit the treatment rather than devising appropriate treatment. According to Levine and Levine (1970) the changes stayed despite the fact that the methods of social treatment had been effective while the evidence suggested that the newer methods were no better and in fact less effective.

Where did the "hard-core" cases of the working and lower classes get help?

Emotional Disturbance and Residential Treatment

While the exact sequence of events is hard to trace from available sources a number of trends are clear. Despert (1970) traces the use of the term "emotional disturbance" to a 1925 paper on causitive factors in skin disease. Its first use in relation to children was in 1932 by Harry Stack Sullivan. By encouraging parents to look for "disturbing" behavior, by extending the net of clinics outside the juvenile-justice system and to children who were preschool in age, with an emphasis on documenting "normal" child development and with the focus of the clinics becoming psychoanalytic treatment with upper middle-class children, there remained a group of children who needed treatment which could not be provided on an outpatient basis. Thus the development of inpatient children's services coincides with the shifts in the focus of the clinics, the failures of state training schools to rehabilitate delinquents, the focus on prevention at an early age, and the growth and training of the professions of psychiatry, psychology, and social work in psychoanalytic methods.

As a result, since the 1920s, residential treatment has developed in two major ways. One was the "psychiatrization" of existing institutions (Castel et al., 1982). Correctional institutions adopted a psychologically oriented philosophy. Second, new services were opened at hospitals to provide inpatient psychiatric services for children who could not be called "delinquent" but who were seen as being "maladjusted" and in need of treatment away from home.

The State Training Schools, themselves, incorporated aspects of the psychopathic hospital and child-guidance clinics. According to Rothman (1980), psychiatrists, psychologists, and social workers welcomed the chance to have an impact:

> In these settings, they would diagnose the causes of deviant behavior and prescribe the antidotes. "The institution," as one N.Y. psychiatrist declared, "is looked upon as a giant laboratory where the maladjusted boy may be thoroughly studied, more or less socialized and brought to understand the mechanisms back of his behavior." (p. 267)

A delinquent arriving at the institution would be assigned to a diagnostic cottage for a month's observation. He or she would be examined by a caseworker, physician, psychiatrist, and psychologist. Then, at the monthly conference, the child would be discussed in terms of psychiatric terminology and a diagnosis, prognosis, and a plan for treatment to be developed. All of this material would be added to during the child's stay. The caseworker was assigned to insure that it received appropriate schooling and vocational programs. It would be assigned to a cottage according to its classification. The caseworker would follow the child's progress in the institution and see to its adjustment in the community upon release.

Clearly, in terms of the other aspects of the State Training Schools we described earlier, psychiatric treatment and diagnosis had little relevance. Few new job lines were created. Psychologists basically did I.Q. testing. There were no programs to fit the diagnostic results and vocational training opportunities consisted of kitchen or farm work. Assignment by classification to cottages was ludicrous given the severe overcrowding.

Despite these conditions, correctional facilities of this type have continued to the present day and retain their psychiatric emphasis, though still mainly in concept rather than in the actual provision of services. They have been aided in their development and continuation by a series of federal acts which provide money for a wide range of facilities and programs mainly focused on "children from poverty areas." In fact, the focus on "delinquent" children was expanded to include the notion of "pre-delinquent children" and the facilities extended to include pre-detention centers, detention centers, and correctional facilities. According to Ohlin (1973), "delinquents" commit an act, described in state criminal laws and local ordinances, which would also be an offense for an adult but are also described as defiant of adult authority. "Pre-delinquents" commit no criminal offense but rather evidence a "premature assertion of personal autonomy and defiance of adult authority, control and directives" (Ohlin, 1973, p. 181).

As of 1966, there were 55,000 children in residential correctional institutions. These institutions are large, with 20% having over 500 children, and 70% having at least 100 children. The children are still housed in traditionally organized, large congregate juvenile training schools. Ninety-five percent go to a school in the institution and receive mainly remedial, religious, physical education, and vocational training which is still outmoded (Ohlin, 1973).

Supposedly, the children in these institutions are not "emotionally disturbed." Yet almost all are seen as having some degree of emotional disturbance. The validity of these judgments is questionable, however, since only 35% of the children are given a psychiatric diagnosis or evaluation on admission and 94% never see a psychiatrist during their stay. Over half never even see a social worker (Ohlin, 1973).

Furthermore, the reason for their incarceration in a correctional institution as opposed to a mental health facility is unclear. As recently as 1973, a law was passed in Massachusetts allowing a child "to be *arrested* for committing the behavior of a child in need of services" (Ohlin, 1973). The type of institution into which a child is placed is a function of the availability of facilities in the geographic area, admission policies, philosophy of care, and financial ability. Whether a child goes to a public correctional institution or to a private residential treatment center (which, by the way, are heavily state funded) "is determined as much by his family's economic resources as by the nature of his deviance" (Ohlin, 1973, p. 113). Yet, it is questionable whether inpatient residential treatment centers for emotionally disturbed children, developed during this same time period, are providing a "better" alternative.

In 1923, when the first inpatient children's psychiatric service was opened at New York's Bellevue Hospital, it was followed by similar services at King's Park State Hospital in New York. Their stated purpose was treating children who could no longer live in the community (Glasscote et al., 1972). By 1930 a full-time psychiatric unit for children was established as part of the pediatric clinic at Johns Hopkins, followed shortly by similar units at Columbia, Cornell, Yale, Stanford, and Minnesota (Rosen, 1968).

The 1930 White House Conference on Child Health and Protection again named the family as the most important factor in the healthy mental development of the child. However, now the specific characteristics delineated for that development included interpersonal relationships, affection, security, and encouragement.

During the 1930s it was agreed that principles for healthy development were not inherent in family structure and therefore families, as well as professionals dealing with children in any context, needed education in mental health principles. Research was stressed as a way of obtaining basic knowledge and it focused on fears, the prevalence of delinquency and behavior problems in addition to comparative studies of well-adjusted and maladjusted children. These ideas led, in 1931, to the formation of the American Academy of Pediatrics whose original committees included one on mental health. In 1935, the Academy urged the need for cooperation between health and welfare workers in dealing with the mental health of children and in 1937 the New York City Health Department instituted a mental-health training program for physicians, nurses, and dentists. The implementation of these ideas became possible with the passage of the Social Security Act of 1935 and its child welfare provisions (Rosen, 1968). Castel et al. (1982) point out that almost all welfare policy from that point until the 1960s was built around aid to dependent children.

Indeed, beginning with the mid-1930s the idea that the mental health of children was an important issue in *any* public health or welfare situation combined with numerous federal acts financing programs for children. This meant that poor and working-class children, in more and more aspects of their lives, were likely to come into contact with what became the mental health system where they were likely to be found to be "maladjusted." This thinking largely reflected the view of psychiatrists and the medical profession, which began to focus more and more on children. In 1935, of the 281 clinics operated by state hospitals, 76% had a patient load of which 40% were children; 64% had a patient load of 60% or more children (Glasscote et al., 1972).

In the 1940s the emphasis on early experience was no longer on its relation to proper habit training but on its role in determining the infant's future emotional make-up and ways of acting and feeling. Between 1940 and 1950 there was an increased development and application of mental-health concepts to research on home, family, and institutions (including the famous Spitz [1945] studies of hospitalism), and after World War II there were and continue to be increases in the number of children sent to residential treatment. The Social Security Act was amended, in 1946, to provide funds for mental problems, and the first development of our modern federally coordinated institutional system was further spurred on by the 1946 National Mental Health Act, the first step in a program formulated by the Group for the Advancement of Psychiatry (GAP).

The "industrialization" of mental health and the power of psychiatrists and of the medical profession grew in large part out of experiences during World War II. More than 15 million recruits had to be examined and almost two million were rejected for "neuropsychiatric" reasons. Another 400,000 who were initially accepted were eventually rejected on the same grounds. About 25% of men evacuated from combat areas were suffering from mental problems. The war brought new awareness of the magnitude of mental health problems (Castel et al., 1982). The military trained psychiatrists so that they could send soldiers back into combat. Psychiatrists turned out to be useful and effective but "demanded an organizational base outside of wartime conditions" (Castel et al., 1982). The extent of the wartime problems meant that "one American in 10 was suffering from mental problems serious enough to impair his or her performance" (Castel et al., 1982). Given this projection, the system of state hospitals seemed obsolete. The alternate system, the clinics, was not centrally coordinated. There was a push to provide a public system of service capable of dealing with the full range of problems. The GAP worked hard to get these ideas put into practice.

The GAP was formed near the end of the war by psychiatrists who had served during the war and wanted to pursue their work in civilian life. They saw themselves as reformers. Karl Menninger was its first leader and among its initial members were men who subsequently became the head of the American Psychiatric Association, the editor of the American Journal of Psychiatry, the head of the Joint Commission on Mental Illness, and the director of the National Institute of Mental Health (Castel et al., 1982). They actively lobbied in Washington and with foundations to push for a strong role for psychiatry in serving the public interest.

Their first step in affecting change in the mental health system was the National Mental Health Act in 1946. The bill essentially left state mental hospitals intact, but appropriated funds for research, training, and new services. It was based on the principle that institutional care of the psychotic was a state responsibility but prevention was a national responsibility. The bill established the National Institute of Mental Health (which had an original budget of $8 million but by 1963 had a budget of $134 million).

A major thrust of the bill was the training of psychiatrists. By 1964 there were 17,000 as compared to 3,000 in 1940 while health professionals, as a whole, increased only 30% in the same time period (Castel et al., 1982). This bill also established experimental programs and research, many in private hospitals and universities. The GAP (according to Glasscote et al., 1972) had a strong interest in services for children and issued a number of reports on such services.

The second step in GAP's plan culminated in the 1955 Mental Health Act, which created the Joint Commission on Mental Illness. The Commission was to report to Congress and give an objective, thorough, nationwide analysis and evaluation of the human and economic problems of mental illness (Castel et al., 1982). In 1960, they published their report, titled "Action for Mental Health." It stressed the need to examine state hospital systems, which they saw as outmoded, and to develop new types of services and ties to the community.

It was also during the 1950s that psychopharmacological drugs were introduced on a large scale. By 1954 drugs became the treatment of choice (Magaro et al., 1978). In May 1954 Thorazine was introduced and 8 months later 2 million patients had taken it (Castel et al., 1982). The availability of these drugs and their usefulness as palliatives (rather than cures) became important in arguing for the emptying out of chronic institutions and moving patients into the community. Indeed between 1963 and 1973 the number of adult patients in the hospitals was reduced by 50% and state budgets for state institutions dropped by one half with the money going now to other places, most noticeably nursing homes.

The move of patients into the community was part of the 1950s development of community psychiatry. This third phase of the GAP plan eventuated in the formation of the Comprehensive Community Mental Health Centers Act (1963) which was to replace custodial mental institutions by therapeutic centers. This new strategy came in the wake of riots in poor Black communities and of rising political power in the Black community. These series of events became defined as problems to be researched.

> Poverty became a central social issue and elimination of the threat of it became a political imperative. Poverty now came to mean not merely lack of resources, but rather a condition of deprivation in which unemployment, poor housing, racial segregation, juvenile delinquency, physical illness and psychic imbalance took a terrible toll on a large number of cases. These conditions were not only destructive for those who had to endure them but dangerous for the government and society at large, which might have to deal with the rebellion that widespread social misery could easily produce. (Castel et al., 1982, p. 72)

Part of the attack on these problems was focused, supposedly, on economic conditions, though at the height of Johnson's war on poverty in 1966 an average of only $95 in supplemental benefits was added to each welfare monthly check (Castel et al., 1982). The largest part of the policy focused on increased government intervention in the heart of areas that were seen as having been "neglected" and were also the site of most of the severe rioting and political organizing—in the cities. A large number of bills were passed including the Juvenile Delinquency and Youth Offense Control Act (1961); the Community Mental Health Centers Act (1963); Medicare and Medicaid, Amendments to the Social Security Act of 1935; Regional Medical Program Act and Comprehensive Health Planning Act (1966); and Safe Streets and Omnibus Crime Act (1968). "The main targets were chronic poverty and despair within the ghettos" (Castel et al., 1982). Castel et al. quote Piven and Cloward (1971) as stating:

> It made little difference whether the funds were appropriated under delinquency prevention, mental health, anti-poverty or model-cities legislation; in the streets of the ghettoes, many aspects of these programs looked very much alike. (p. 261)

During this same period, with the official rhetoric and laws focusing on replacing the institution, on Community Mental Health Centers and so on, the number of inpatient children's psychiatric units and residential treatment centers grew dramatically. If we backtrack for a moment, we can see that the first impetus had come from the training of child psychiatrists under the 1946 Mental Health Act. In 1947, the first eight psychiatric trainees entered Massachusetts General and the Philadelphia Child Guidance Clinic (Glasscote et al., 1972). The 1950 White House Conference on Children stressed the importance of mental health services for children of all ages, including preschool, school age, and adolescent ages. The 1955 Mental Health Act pushed the psychiatrist more into the community and provided money for investigations of emotional disturbance among children. For instance, in 1959 the University of Indiana did a statewide survey of emotionally disturbed children and estimated that 2% of the children required professional treatment. It was in this same year that plans were approved for the children's psychiatric hospital we eventually studied, a state hospital designed for 192 inpatient emotionally disturbed children.

During the 1960s the focus on children increased, spurred on by many psychiatrists and other professionals. According to Glasscote et al. (1972), the original work of the Joint Commission hardly focused on children. In 1963, as part of the Community Mental Health Centers Act, federal funds were made available to states to plan and organize comprehensive mental health services. Each state submitted its proposals. An analysis of these in 1963 revealed that many did not include proposals for services to children.

> Alarmed by this information, the American Psychiatric Association, the American Academy of Child Psychiatry, the American Association of Psychiatric Services for Children and the American Orthopsychiatric Association called a conference for the purpose of developing principles and guidelines for planning services for children—as a result some of the states which had not included children and adolescents in their mental health plans subsequently did so. (Glasscote et al., 1972, p. 3)

By 1965 the Congress created a second commission, this time to deal specifically with the mental health problems of children and young people. "Instead of focusing mainly on the mentally ill population, it addressed itself to the emotional needs and problems of all children in America" (Glasscote et al., 1972). The 1966 Census of Children's Institutions revealed that there were 307 residential institutions for emotionally disturbed children, 283 private and 24 public, and 145 inpatient psychiatric units, 65 private and 80 public (Taylor, 1973).

In 1967, first-grade teachers in 12 Chicago schools rated their pupils and reported that 70% of them had some degree of maladjustment (Glasscote et al., 1972). In 1968, another study showed that of the new Community Mental Health Centers, few provided services for children and in 1969 persons under 19 accounted for 26% of admissions to Community Mental Health Centers—a figure Glasscote et al consider as showing the lack of services since people under 19 accounted for 40% of the general population in that year. By 1970, there were amendments to federal legislation which authorized specific sums for the development of services for children.

The increased federal intervention into mental health services in general, and specifically for children, resulted in the fact that in 1972, three times as many younger people were admitted for treatment as in 1955 (Castel et al., 1982) whether figured in numbers or percentages of admissions. And, in the 10-year period between 1966 and 1976, there was a 150% increase in the number of young children and adolescents hospitalized (Castel et al., 1982). By 1976, there were 20 state mental hospitals devoted *exclusively* to children which provided for 20% of these hospitalized under 18 years of age (Castel et al., 1982).

The notion of "community" mental health suggested by the idea of Community Mental Health Centers (CMHCs) did not do away with residential institutions any more than the progressive era reforms did. In fact, it helped to consolidate existing community services and to add new ones to fill in the gaps. In a study of community mental health centers that existed in 1970-71, the range of service provided included what were called "five essential services" (Glasscote et al., 1972)—outpatient, inpatient, emergency, partial hospitalization, and consultation and education service. Based on a questionnaire sent to all of the 206 federally assisted community mental health services then operating, 79% of the 143 responding reported that they provided inpatient service for children and 92% provided inpatient services for adolescents. Often a CMHC was not "one place" but a consortium of places under one administration. A child sent for referral could then be assigned to the type of treatment considered necessary. Often, centers had schools attached to them; other provided screening services for children in Headstart programs as a means to identify those who, when they enter school, have special educational needs. One center studied operated a school in conjunction with the school system; another introduced a program for teaching techniques in several schools in an effort to manage academic and referral problems in the schools without referral to the center. Yet referrals for service came heavily from the schools, and next from parents, with even fewer referrals from the courts. Thus, the notion of community treatment, which can conjure up the image of storefront drop-in services, does not really represent what in actuality have become large conglomerates. Most of these are university and medical school affiliated, and provide for teaching and training of psychiatrists, social workers, psychologists.

If we examine this period from the 1950s through the early 1970s, the reasons for institutionalization are varied but the descriptions of problems are no more clear than they are for children sent to correctional institutions. In their review of CMHCs, Glasscote et al. (1972) report that the majority of children obtaining services fall into categories such as "adaptation reaction of childhood," "adaptation reaction of adolescence," "overanxious reaction to childhood," and the like. In

1976, 26,000 children were admitted to hospitals: 3,000 were identified as retarded (and should have been in other institutions) and 15,000 were classified as suffering from "personality disorders," "adaptation reaction," and "behavioral problems" (Castel et al., 1982). Often children are referred not for their own good, but for the benefit of their parents or other family members. "One child's hyperactivity interfered with the routine of household and disturbed family members" (Koocher, 1976). Other times they are referred because their behavior does not match what is considered "appropriate" by a teacher or a school.

The daily treatment of children in institutions is not well documented. However, between 1966 and 1976, with children as with adults, there was heavy reliance on psychotropic drugs. Major tranquilizers are given to many "aggressive" children, especially those living in institutions. The use of drugs (especially Ritalin) for dealing with "hyperactivity" in school children has been a widely discussed issue. After research indicated that those drugs were not being used to treat a specific disease, the control implication became clear. In terms of "therapy" in institutions, the major focus in the past 10 years has been on behavior modification techniques, also "a control" technique. These sound surprisingly like the "ranking" of the Progressive era, with rewards and punishments meted out for appropriate and inappropriate behavior.

Though the range of services provided for children has expanded, the use of institutionalization continues. Still retaining the legacy of the Progressive era, each service provides a back-up for yet another service, although now the entire system is centrally coordinated through federal funding and federal regulations and begins at an early age with the psychological screening in some states, of all children in school to detect pre-delinquent or adjustment problems (Castel et al., 1982). Indeed, beginning in 1971 there began a series of legal cases against adult institutions which eventuated in a decision that those in such institutions were entitled to physically humane surroundings, adequate number of trained personnel and programs tailored to each case. Once this happened the bulk of federal money went back into chronic adult institutions with the idea of cleaning them up and "normalizing them." Thus the ideology shifted back to the days of moral treatment. The psychiatric hospital care for adults, however, is far from dead. As a result of these cases, about 80% of the state mental health budget in New York, for example, is still poured into chronic care institutions, and while the number of patients actually in the hospital at any one moment has decreased, the number of admissions on the national level has increased considerably, more than double in 1975 as compared to 1955 (Castel et al., 1982), a policy now called "the revolving door." The "normalization" ideology has helped empty institutions for the mentally retarded although many originally emptied out during the early 1970s are now serving as "transitional" care facilities and in some cases as "congregate group homes." Yet no such move has begun to empty the children's psychiatric facilities and residential treatment centers. Indeed, the children's psychiatric hospital we studied, which had difficulty "recruiting" clients in 1969, now has more inpatients than it ever did, despite the fact or perhaps because of the fact that it is now part of a comprehensive community mental health center which has connections to schools, the local emergency admitting unit in a city hospital, day programs for adolescents in need of remedial training, and so on.

Thus the institution we studied must be viewed in its historical perspective, having been planned in the late 1950s when services were being extended for children, built during the 1960s "war on poverty," and serving children largely from poor, urban areas. It opened in 1969 with a director focusing on community care running an inpatient psychiatric hospital for emotionally disturbed children. As we studied this hospital through to 1976, and as we have followed it informally up to the present day, it becomes clear that the prior history of the treatment of children, of the definitions of emotional disturbance and who fits into these categories and the history of the types of institutions built to take care of such children have all had an impact on its eventual form and functioning.

REFERENCES

Apter, S. J. (1976). The rights of children in teaching institutions. In G. P. Koocher (Ed.), *Children's rights and the mental health professions*. New York: Wiley.

Baker, H. H. (1910). Procedure of the Boston Juvenile Court, The Survey, XXIII, Feb. 5, 1910, as excerpted in R. H. Bremner (Ed.). (1971). *Children and youth in America: A documentary history: Vol. 2. 1866–1932* (pp. 520–523). Cambridge, MA: Harvard University Press.

Beyer, H. A., & Wilson J. P. (1976). The reluctant volunteer: A child's right to resist commitment. In G. P. Koocher (Ed.), *Children's rights and the mental health professions*. New York: Wiley.

Braginsky, D., & Braginsky, B. (1971). *Hansels and Gretels: Studies of children in institutions for the mentally retarded*. New York: Holt, Rinehart & Winston.

Braginsky, B., Braginsky, D., & Ring, K. (1969). *Methods of madness: The mental hospital as a last resort*. New York: Holt, Rinehart & Winston.

Bremner, R. H., (Ed.). (1970). *Children and youth in America: A documentary history: Vol. 1. 1600–1865*. Cambridge, MA: Harvard University Press.

(1971). *Children and youth in America: A documentary history: Vol. 2. 1866–1932*. Cambridge, MA: Harvard University Press.

(1974). *Children and youth in America: A documentary history: Vol. 3. 1933–1973*. Cambridge, MA: Harvard University Press.

Castel, R., Castel, F., & Lovell, A. (1982). (A. Goldhammer Trans.). *The psychiatric society*. New York: Columbia University Press.

Caudill, W. (1958). *The psychiatric hospital as a small society*. Cambridge, MA: Harvard University Press.

Despert, J. L. (1970). *The emotionally disturbed child: An inquiry into family patterns*. New York: Anchor Books.

Devoe, E. (1848). The refuge system or prison discipline applied to juvenile delinquents, New York. In R. H. Bremner (Ed.). (1970). *Children and youth in America: A documentary history: Vol. 1. 1600–1865* (pp. 689–691). Cambridge, MA: Harvard University Press.

Glasscote, R. M., Fishman, M. E., & Sonis, M. (1972). *Children and mental health centers: Programs, problems, prospects*. Washington, DC: The Joint Information Service of the American Psychiatric Association and the National Association for Mental Health.

Goffman, E. (1961). *Asylums*. Garden City, NY: Doubleday.

Koocher, G. P. (1976). *Children's rights and the mental health professions*. New York: Wiley.

Kugel, R. B., & Wolfensberger, W. (1972). *Changing patterns in residential services for the mentally retarded*. Presidential Committee on Mental Retardation. Washington, DC: U.S. Department of Health, Education and Welfare, Social and Rehabilitative Services Administration, Division of Developmental Disabilities.

Laing, R. D. (1967). *The politics of experience*. New York: Ballantine Books.

Levine, M., & Levine, A. (1970). The more things change: A case history of child guidance clinics. *Journal of Social Issues*, 26 (3), 19–34.

Magaro, P. A., Gripp, R., & McDowell, D. J. (1978). *The mental health industry: A cultural phenomenon*. New York: Wiley.

Mercer, J. R. (1973). *Labeling the mentally retarded: Clinical and social system perspectives on mental retardation*. Berkeley: University of California Press.

Ohlin, L. E. (1973). Institutions for predelinquent or delinquent children. In D. M. Pappenfort, D. M. Kilpatrick, & R. W. Roberts (Eds.), *Child caring, social policy and the institution* . Chicago: Aldine.

Piven, F. F., & Cloward, R. A. (1971). *Regulating the poor*. New York: Pantheon.

Platt, A. M. (1977). *The child savers: The invention of delinquency* (2nd ed.) Chicago: University of Chicago Press.

Plumb, J. H. (1973). Children: The victims of time. In J. H. Plumb, *In the light of history*. Boston: Houghton Mifflin.

Rosen, G. (1968). *Madness in society: Chapters in the historical sociology of mental illness*. Chicago: University of Chicago Press.

Rothman, D. J. (1971). *The discovery of the asylum: Social order and disorder in the new republic*. Boston: Little, Brown.

Rothman, D. J. (1980). *From conscience to convenience: The asylum and its alternatives in progressive America*. Boston: Little, Brown.

Scheff, T. J. (1966). *Being mentally ill: A sociological theory*. Chicago: Aldine.

Spitz, R. A. (1945). Hospitalism: An inquiry into the genesis of psychiatric conditions in early childhood. *Psychoanalytic Study of the Child.* Vol. 1, 53–74. New York: International Universities Press.

Stanton, A. H., & Schwartz, M. (1954). *The mental hospital.* New York: Basic Books.

Szasz, T. S. (1961). *The myth of mental illness.* New York: Harper & Row.

Taylor, S. H. (1973). Institutions with therapeutic residential programs for children. In D. H. Pappenfort, D. M. Kilpatrick, & R. W. Roberts (Eds.), *Child caring, social policy and the institution.* Chicago: Aldine.

Whittaker, J. K. (1979). *Caring for troubled children. Residential treatment in a community context.* San Francisco: Jossey-Bass.

Wolfensberger, W. (1972). The origin and nature of our institutional models. In R. B. Kugel & W. Wolfensberger (Eds.), *Changing patterns in residential services for the mentally retarded.* Presidential Committee on Mental Retardation. Washington, DC: U.S. Department of Health, Education and Welfare, Social and Rehabilitative Services Administration, Division of Developmental Disabilities.

CHAPTER 4

Settings for Deviant Children: A Present Day Example of the Evolution of an Institution

THE PHYSICAL SETTING: PLANS, PROMISES, AND REALITY

For over six years we spent many hours in a modern children's psychiatric hospital, working with a small group of researchers to understand what was happening on a day-to-day basis. We took advantage of the unique opportunity to enter the hospital before it had opened its doors to children, enabling us to trace the development of patterns of use and the evolution of the treatment program and therapeutic philosophy as well as the physical changes made to the building. By going there repeatedly we were able to gain an intimate view of this complex place from the early days and to look at it from many perspectives, but mainly from the children's view. Since we were not involved in the operation of the hospital, we could examine different aspects of its functioning that might not be seen by people who were focused on their daily lives and responsibilities. We have followed the evolution of the hospital from a "therapeutic community" for children into an institution, and it is this process that we will describe.

With the principles cited in Chapter One as the framework, our goal is to use all the information gathered for this case study to question whether it is possible to provide "therapy" for children placed in such a residential setting. While the time lag between the design of the hospital and the eventual occupancy created discontinuities and difficulties in implementing a non-institutional therapeutic program, one could question whether a place such as the one studied could ever provide the necessary support for children with emotional problems. In state-run facilities, where the programming is written within a bureaucratic structure out of reach of the people it serves, the ideology of containment is unquestioned. The hospital that we will describe is one such place, part of an institutional complex where the total lives of the residents are accommodated largely within the hospital walls and away from their communities.

A Picture of the Hospital

As we discussed in the last chapter, historically the form of institutions both reflected and created the prevailing concepts of deviance, their causes and solutions. The children's hospital is no exception. It is located in a marginal area on the edge of a large city. The area is marginal in the sense that it is a mix of factories, warehouses, and empty lots, crisscrossed by a network of highways moving enormous amounts of traffic. The property itself is state-owned, in our terms, an "institutional park." Much like industrial parks, it has a concentration of places of similar function, in this case state-owned and operated facilities for people defined as "deviant." Walking from the distant public transportation or driving into the site we find it bounded by a chain-link fence, a symbolic barrier between the institution within and the so-called normal world beyond. A guard in a small kiosk is the only sign of human life, and he waves in all cars and people, leaving one wondering what services he provides other than announcing that this is a place requiring a visible gatekeeper. The scene is dominated by three high-rise brick buildings making up an adult psychiatric hospital that opened in the 1950s. A series of winding walkways leads to other buildings whose designs and purposes vary—a research unit, a staff residence, an outpatient rehabilitation unit, and a controversial residential center for the retarded that is the children's hospital's nearest neighbor. In light of the many buildings we pass, the site is remarkably devoid of people and vegetation. There is little traffic and it is not unusual to see no one on the vast expanse of open land.

As we approach the children's hospital, on one of the farthermost sections of the property, we see a line cutting across the grass, a "natural path" created by the hundreds of feet aiming for a shortcut through the vast terrain. The beige brick building, designed in the late 1950s and completed in 1968, contrasts sharply with the other parts of the compound surrounding it. The low-rise design and irregular roofs create the impression that the hospital is made up of a number of structures. In fact, it is a single building designed to resemble a cluster of cottages or houses, a contrast to the other buildings in this compound.

The facade is rather anonymous-looking with a small sign announcing its identity. Entering, one finds a cathedral-ceilinged lobby containing plastic-covered couches and chairs, some public telephone booths, vending machines which dispense drinks and snacks, and a small counter which, at times, has a receptionist behind it. To the rear of the lobby, facing the entrance, are glass doors leading to a central open space that contains a clock tower (see Figure 4.1 for a floor plan). The building is organized around this central court. The main circulation route rings this court, with various wings of the building radiating from it. The wings

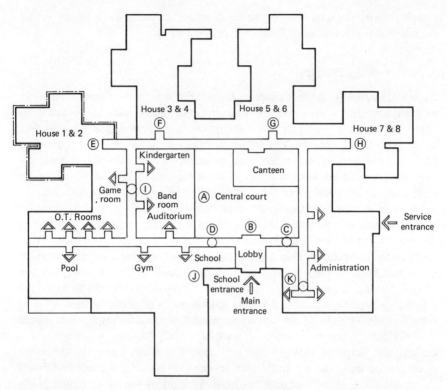

Figure 4.1.   Floorplan, building

consist of a series of "houses" or residential areas, a school, and administrative offices. The corridor system is complex, winding, and confusing to a visitor unfamiliar with the layout. Floors throughout the hospital are covered with shiny beige tiles which reflect the fluorescent lighting above.

Walking along the corridors we pass through a rather neutral if not bland environment, differentiated only by a series of doors identifying rooms of various functions. Walls are cinder block, painted beige with pastel graphic designs. This decorative feature is repeated throughout all the areas in which children can be found. Although sports figures are the graphic motif around the gym and pool, the wall mural or design is predominant. The fluorescent lighting creates a yellow pallor over everything, enhancing the homogeneous look. The winding corridors connecting the wings have a maze-like appearance with some corridors extending the length of a city block or longer (see Figure 4.2).

Eight "houses" or residential units accommodate twenty-four children each. Pairs of houses share a communal dining room located on the main floor. On entering the dining room, the first impression is the strong, often stale, odor of

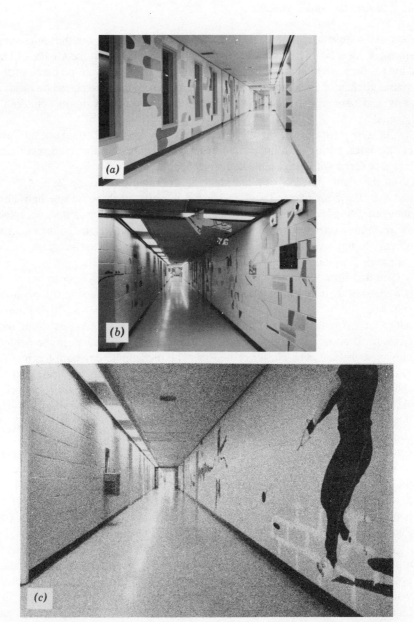

Figure 4.2. Block length hospital corridors with pastel graphic designs and sports motif near gym and pool

food, the leftovers of past meals in a windowless room. It is not the welcoming aroma of food being prepared because food is not cooked in the kitchens. The dining rooms are really small cafeterias, serving meals that are prepared in the central kitchen of the adult psychiatric hospital where they are placed on heating units and sent via a connecting underground passageway to the children's hospital.

The appearance of the dining room is that of a functional, stainless steel and cinder block setting with little resemblance to a kitchen or dinette. Small round tables covered with vinyl tablecloths provide the only color.

Of the eight "houses," six are identical in design (see houses 2, 3, 4, 5, 6, and 8 in the floor plan). They are located in pairs, each house one-half story above the main level. During our research only four of the houses were occupied; the remaining ones were used for a variety of other functions, including business offices. Some were used by state programs unrelated to the program of the children's hospital.

The first impression on opening the glass-paneled, locked door to the house is a smell of disinfectant and the sight of a glass-enclosed nursing station at the apex of the corridor. The central corridor leads to three eight-person "living units" which were originally called "apartments" (see Figure 4.3). An open, communal dayroom is on one side of the corridor, and this room looks out on the outdoor play areas behind each cluster of houses. The rectangular dayroom has a small kitchenette on one end but a metal sliding door (much like the ones used for shops as security measures) generally closes off this area. Couches and chairs are distributed around the room, enough seating space for all the residents. The furniture, made of easy-care materials, was replaced during the years of our work, but the original furniture and the replacements had the same heavy, institutional appearance. The only other furniture is a television set, sometimes on with no watchers, and frequently out of order. Overhead lighting also provides illumination here, and throughout the living unit. There is little else in the dayroom, and the appearance is distinctive for what is *not* there: small objects, lamps, toys, games—the equipment of daily life where there are children (see Figure 4.4).

The dayroom is directly across from the glass-enclosed nurses' station, a small room that looks out on all major spaces in the unit. Outside the nurses' station is a bench area opposite another seating area in the corridor. The cinder block walls of the corridor are covered with graphics, cartoon images of people-like toothbrushes, toothpaste tubes, and watches, a reminder of the activities and qualities valued by the institution.

A laundry room and a small room (used for a variety of purposes during our six years of study) complete the spaces in the communal areas of the house. The small room originally functioned as an office, used by staff to write up their patient records. It was later converted into a "quiet room," a place to isolate

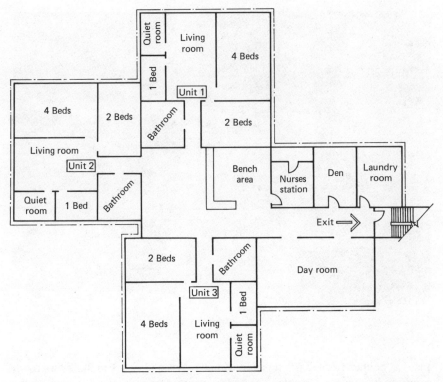

Figure 4.3.   House 1, typical

children perceived to be out of control. Its final state, in the time we were there, was its conversion into a small, den-like space, a process in which we were involved.

The appearance of the house does not change when we enter the eight-person apartments. We go through another glass-paneled door and are in a small entry foyer with a closet and communal bathroom nearby. In its original state the toilet stalls had no doors and it took over three and one-half years before they were installed. An open area in the center serves as a living room and its large picture window has a window seat below it. Four bedrooms are entered from the living room, two of them single rooms, one a double room, and one a four-bed room. Originally the bedrooms had no doors and, despite the director's efforts, they were not installed until the same time as the doors on bathroom stalls.

Furnishings in the apartments can best be described as functional with washable materials covering the floors and the heavy upholstered chairs. Indoor-outdoor carpeting initially installed in the apartments was removed and replaced with tiles soon after the hospital opened, since the covering quickly became torn

Figure 4.4.   Children's dayroom

and was neither cleaned nor repaired. Some tables and chairs in the living room complete its meager contents. The bedroom furniture is identical in each of the apartments; it consists of bed-wardrobe units with a place for displaying personal items. These rooms looked much the same before and after the building was occupied. Signs that children are living there are remarkably absent and there are few of the personal items and toys that one expects to see in bedrooms occupied by children.

The two houses that are of a different layout were designed to accommodate "autistic" children. These are houses 1 and 7 on the floor plan. Although they have the same amount of space as the other houses, only two rooms in each eight-person unit have walls. The arrangement provides a large dormitory-type room designed for six children, and one two-person room. In addition, there is a living room much like that in other apartments. The autistic units never served the purpose for which they were designed. In fact, the open design planned by the architect was considered inappropriate for its stated purposes and the units were assigned many other functions over the years.

There are 25 different rooms in the building used by the residents on a daily basis. Most are in a portion of the hospital that we designated as "community areas" along two main corridors (Figure 4.1, D and I). When the building opened, the names given to the various spaces were game room, kindergarten suite, and music room. There were four occupational therapy rooms, an Olympic-sized swimming pool, a full-sized gym, a small library, and an auditorium designed for hundreds. The canteen in the rear corridor opposite two of the houses was to serve a variety of social functions—for parties, games, and general arts and crafts. Also along the rear corridor is a hair salon where both boys and girls can be accommodated.

In addition, the original plans provided an infirmary, a school, and various offices. The school occupies its own wing with entry points both from outside the building and along the main corridor. Offices for administration and the psychiatrists, psychologists, and social workers who are part of the therapeutic team are also contained within one wing. In contrast to other spaces, these are most comfortably furnished, with carpets, plants, wood paneling, and personal belongings. Over the years there was gradual acquisition of other spaces for administrative functions.

The infirmary began as a fully equipped hospital, on the second floor of the rear section of the building. It has never been used as intended, since the director felt that minor illnesses should be treated in the houses and truly serious ones in a regular hospital. The infirmary has been turned over to a variety of programs operating out of the children's hospital and most recently has been used as an outpatient mental health clinic serving the same catchment areas as the hospital.

The inner court of the building was designed as a play area, with a series of free-form, gray concrete sculptures in the shape of fruits and animals. On one side, behind a low mural-covered wall, is a playground for young children, originally conceived as a place for the kindergarten unit, a suite of rooms accommodating the needs of a preschool group.

Other outdoor play areas are behind the house wings overlooking the highway system. Two contain playground equipment, and a basketball court and baseball field are in the others. The remaining space contains barbeque grills, benches, and water fountains, a parklike stretch of land that might be an inviting setting were it not for the absence of trees and other vegetation, and the forbidding traffic beyond. There is a door leading from each pair of houses to the outdoor recreational area, and a small "mud room" provides a bathroom and a place to hang clothing. This easy access to the outdoors and the physical supports for using the play areas suggest the permeability of the inside and outside, the closeness of the outer world. Yet, in actual practice, the outer world was far more distant than the physical reality would suggest.

This tour has taken us through a variety of internal and outdoor spaces designed to meet the total needs of the residents and the work of the staff. We have described a complete community encompassing places to live, play, learn, and receive therapy, all in and around one building.

Eventually daily life for the children in this physical setting would reflect the state program which mandated its construction, the designer's attempts to move the program in a more progressive direction, the director's community-based philosophy, the staff's view of the appropriate treatment for these children, and the children's attempts to construct their own lives within this environment.

The State Program, the Architect's Intentions, and the Director's Philosophy

The children's hospital was built out of a physical program that was formulated in the 1950s during the first post-war period of intensive building of state psychiatric facilities. The prevailing philosophy at the time the program was formulated was a medical model providing inpatient care and complete institutionalization. According to this original plan, removing children from their homes would relieve the community of the disruptive presence of the child while providing opportunities for the child to learn to deal with their "aberrant internal control systems."

The intent was to use the hospital as the therapeutic instrument with a hierarchy of children's services available, all placed in one site. The state program detailed these services and mandated the division of the 80,885 square foot building into specific amounts of space for each one. Thus we have a total life environment, one that depends little on the external setting or community.

Our interviews with the architect revealed the obstacles and limitations that he faced but also his illusions and lack of understanding of the nature of institutionalization. Working within the constraints of the state program, his intention was to design a place that would enable children to have the experience of living in a small community. Going from place to place within the building would be like moving through a town, with opportunities for chance meetings and casual encounters that would stimulate social behavior. His original design contained corridors that were 12 feet wide, much like streets, as well as places that would attract small groups. Similarly, initially he had individual cottages, rather than one large building, and included other features he saw as being non-institutional—glass-paneled hallways, carpeting in residential areas, and individual bed-storage units that he had designed himself.

Economic constraints led to the reduction of the width of the corridors from 12 feet to 8 feet, while resistance on the part of the State Department of Mental Hygiene prevented the design of cottages physically separated from the main building. These pre-construction changes led to a physical setting that was different from the architect's original conceptions. Even where the final physical setting reflected his views, his lack of understanding of the realities of psychiatric care was revealed in the actual use of the building.

The architect's conception, growing out of the state physical planning program and his own point of view, was to provide children with a wide range of living

experiences similar to those in the outside community with possibilities ranging
from individual privacy to large group gatherings. In his design of the house
areas the architect's image of the space as it would be used and the needs it
would meet might be likened to a floor in a small multifamily dwelling. There
were the apartments, the private domain of the eight-person "family," and within
them the bedroom, living room, and bathroom spaces. The bedrooms accommodated one, two, or four persons while the living room and bathroom were to be
shared by all eight residents. These individual apartments opened into common
spaces for the 24 residents of the three apartments. In the context of the hospital
and its program, the common spaces—a corridor, dayroom, and bench area—
were for intermediate size social groups, less private than the apartment but
more private than the spaces outside the house areas. Each set of two houses
shared a common dining-room space with 48 people making up the next largest
social reference group. The remaining spaces, such as the school, library, gym,
and outdoor open space, were the "community" areas to serve all residents—
192 of them according to the original plans.

The building was near completion when the director was appointed so that
his therapeutic philosophy could not be incorporated into the hospital's design.
Trained in the post-World War II era, his views, which he identified as an
"ecological model," supported the use of both the hospital environment and the
staff to create a "community" for the children, encouraging development of
personal skills and strengths. It was a philosophy based on connections to the
children's total environment, including the communities from which they had
come. It anticipated use of community-based clinics (some of which never developed) as well as services from a local medical school, both of which could
enable continuity of care for the children.

The perspective taken by the director and revealed in the early program
outlines had a strong community thrust. It did not support long periods of
hospitalization but saw value in exposing children to the community, as the
director said, "even at the height of their discontent with one another." He did
not believe that the children's total lives should be contained within this building,
however differentiated the spaces might be. His image of the way he would run
the hospital, as opposed to the way it was designed and conceived by the state,
included efforts to build channels of communication with the community, selecting staff from the community, and using all community resources in the interests
of the children. Children were to use community-based facilities whenever possible,
and the community was to be encouraged to use the hospital's facilities—the
recreational areas, the auditorium, and the meeting rooms. In addition, although
the hospital was built as an inpatient setting, as part of his community outreach
the director planned for the admission of a range of other children who would
use the hospital's services, mainly as day patients.

From Therapeutic Environment to Psychiatric Institution

After standing unoccupied for one year following its completion, the children's hospital opened during the last week of December in 1969, the official opening being something of a "political coup." The facility had been physically ready to admit clients for one year, having a core staff of administrative and therapeutic personnel as well. However, the state budget, which had provided $43 million in capital funds for construction and core personnel, provided inadequate money for operating expenses and for additional line staff required to begin admitting children. By inviting local politicians, community groups, and the press to an "official" ribbon-cutting ceremony, the first 12 day-care children were admitted to this 80,000 square foot, award-winning facility. By March 1970, the first four full-care children were admitted and the facility was funded more adequately.

The plan originally called for admitting 24 children per month, 16 of them adolescents. It was anticipated that at the end of the first six months of functioning there would be 72 inpatients (based on a discharge rate of 50%). Yet, six months after the opening there were only 13 full-care and 15 day-care children. By May 1971, 14 months after opening, there were only 23 full-care and 30 day-care children. The reality after 14 months, in terms of numbers and categories, was different from what had been originally anticipated, with far fewer children being referred in the early months, and more day-care than full-care.

Over time, it has become clear that the number and type of children who were admitted reflected more than either the "community's needs," abstractly defined, or a therapeutic philosophy specific to this particular facility. It was a product of a variety of forces, some external to the facility and others a reflection of its attempts at survival within the mental-health system. From the time the facility opened, the director had been trying in a variety of ways to have the official occupancy of 192 full-care children reduced. Finally in 1973 he did manage to get it reduced to 125. Yet, in reality, during the six years we were working at the facility, the highest census obtained was 50 full-care in addition to 30 or so day-care children. On the average, the total group rarely exceeded 60.

Given the official policy of focusing on community care, and institutionalization as a last resort, the low intake and census should not have proved problematic. In fact, it would seem to have followed directly from the community mental health emphasis and would suggest that it was working. Yet here was a 192-bed facility, newly opened, with very few inpatients and a growing operating budget.

From the perspective of the mental-health system at the time with the emphasis, at least on paper, on community care, and with budget cuts forcing several older state psychiatric facilities to close as they "deinstitutionalized" their populations, the continual operation of a new children's hospital could be viewed as an unwarranted luxury. In this context, despite a freeze on staff hiring, pressure was put on the director to admit more children. Indeed, in contrast to the slow admissions up to this point, in a two-month period during the summer of 1971, one day-care and 10 full-care children were admitted. In addition, since space was being underutilized, and a developmental center was still under construction next door, parents and community groups brought pressure on the State Department of Mental Hygiene and Mental Retardation, who brought pressure on the director to allow one living unit to become a temporary home for retarded children. These clients eventually would move into a new facility when it was completed. This occurred despite the director's stated view that it was incorrect to house mentally retarded children with emotionally disturbed children, despite the need to spend funds reconstructing part of the facility to create an appropriate play area, and despite the fact that the programming of these children had to be entirely separate from the programming for the children who were already there.

Over the 12 years of functioning, the hospital administration has demonstrated its ability and flexibility in assuring that the facility is viewed as contributing significantly to community health needs and, therefore, assuring its continued existence. When there was a low inpatient census, various other programs were developed such as a half-day tutorial program for older children who were not hospital clients. Later, an outpatient clinic for the community was located on the unused infirmary floor. An adolescent program, originally housed in the adjacent adult hospital, was moved into the children's facility and the age range extended to 18. Several attempts were made to affiliate with private agencies to provide community-based care when that was being funded and, when money was available for bilingual programs, the hospital developed one and increased the number of Hispanic children relative to the number of Black and white children. In short, a building constructed under a medical model of care became, almost in and of itself, a "community mental health center," but one located outside the community.

The hospital administration now oversees a range of children's services in its geographic area including the city hospital's children's psychiatric unit which serves as a feeder to this and other state facilities, and a program for learning-disabled children in a local public school which they hope will eventually become a complete therapeutic school. (It now has 30 children in attendance.) With 75 inpatients in their own on-site school, staff has doubled in the 12 years and the range of staff positions has expanded to include speech and hearing therapists. Affiliation with a local medical school provides interns and residents in psychiatric training, and other institutional affiliations provide interns in psychology, social work, and medical records.

On one level, these attempts can be viewed as opportunistic, that is, they reflect a desire to keep the institution going in any way possible. From another perspective, some attempts reflect sincere desire, within the context of the system, to provide for needs that are perceived as going unmet. However, having to find financial sources to ensure economic viability and the mandate to prove one's necessary role in the mental health bureaucracy in order to continue functioning, creates its own dynamic. This can undermine stated goals and may prove negative, or at least useless, in actually providing for children's needs.

At one of our early meetings with the director, just as the facility was opening, he spoke about an Hispanic child who had been brought to the hospital. He acknowledged that this boy's problem could easily be explained by his being uprooted from Puerto Rico and the horrifying conditions under which he was forced to live in a deteriorating area of the city. He felt that while the child could obtain some help at the children's hospital he would do far better if the same money could be used to give him periodic trips back to Puerto Rico. He said that one such trip financed by his family had done wonders for the child. Now the facility has a bilingual program, rather than a vacation program to Puerto Rico.

Beginning with a therapeutic philosophy supportive of community and short-term crisis treatment, 12 years after opening the facility has become a long-term residential treatment center with a hierarchy of treatment plans for different categories of children. During the early studies the head of clinical services complained of the difficulties in giving short-term community care in such a traditionally defined and designed facility. The same person 12 years later attributed the low census during the early years to the lack of outreach into the community rather than to a conscious policy of supporting community care where possible. He criticized the earlier admissions policies for taking in children whom they could not help—street kids who did not need an institution. And, he described the hospital as having finally "found its niche as a long-term residential treatment center for very disturbed children."

In the initial days of the hospital's functioning, with four full-care and 12 day-care children, staff attitudes and the philosophy of care were almost the opposite of this view. Our early years on the units found a very open child-centered program and style. Each child had an individual program formulated to meet his or her particular needs, including schooling and free time. Doors to various program areas were kept unlocked—in fact, few of them even had locks—and were used spontaneously as wanted or needed for a variety of activities. There was a fairly unlimited choice of activities using spaces in creative ways, including roller skating in the corridors when they were empty.

When children were perceived as being "disruptive" or "acting out" a crisis intervention technique was used, the child remaining where he or she was with staff gathering to give support, thus enabling the child to remain involved in the activity. The use of drugs was kept to a minimum. The general atmosphere was informal, high-spirited, and optimistic despite the emptiness of the building, the small number of staff, and the small number of children. As one walked through the public areas during the early days people were around and the building, enormous as it was, seemed more populated than the census would support.

Not that the staff thought that everything was perfect. Interviews revealed that there were some aspects of this building that were viewed with some concern. They feared that the low hanging lights could be broken easily by children. The tremendous amount of glass and carpet needed high maintenance and could easily fall into disrepair. The lack of a physical place for day-care children made it difficult to integrate them into the program. The system of food preparation and delivery made a very impersonal activity out of what could have been an important aspect of group living. The absence of doors on the bathroom stalls and showers did not support privacy in these types of personal activities. The fully equipped pool, gymnasium, library, and school were seen as going counter to the philosophy of using community resources.

On the positive side, staff thought that it was significant that there were no isolation rooms as was usual in state facilities. They appreciated the specially designed rooms for occupational therapy, including a woodworking room. The availability of outdoor spaces, the variety of bedroom sizes, the kitchenettes, and the provision of wardrobe/bed units were all seen as contributing to a non-institutional atmosphere.

Yet two months after opening, many changes had already occurred. The number of full-care children had increased to 12, one of them a female. One house, which had been opened but only sparsely occupied, now had one full apartment, and some children living in a second apartment. But, even with only 23 children in all, the specially designed occupational therapy rooms were having problems, the staff complaining they were too small and suited only to groups of four or five. For general crafts, the rooms in the school building were preferred. Even though most spaces were still not furnished there was considerable wear and tear visible on carpets and several windows had been broken and were boarded up. Suddenly, during our formal observations, we found ourselves recording the locking and unlocking of doors and the addition of locks to doors that had not had them before.

Changes had taken place programmatically and administratively, as well. Children had been divided into groups for activities, with one or two child-development workers assigned to each group. There was an increased structuring of the child's day. Some degree of choice still existed in that rooms could be unlocked upon request. But there were several indications that attempts were being made to impose more control on the children. Sheets of paper were placed over the glass panels of many activity room doors, to prevent the children inside from being "distracted" and the children outside from being "disruptive."

Explanations for the changes focused on the need to keep track of the children as they roamed around the large underoccupied building. Staff cited instances of children climbing onto the roof, wandering into administrative areas, hiding in the unused infirmary.

Six months after the hospital's opening the census had reached 15 day-care and 13 full-care children, two of them female. Children were assigned to specific groups with whom they went to all activities. Every child was obliged to carry a program card specifying where they were to be at each time period. If a child did not want to go to the defined activity he or she was confined to the house. If children were disruptive during activities they were returned to their house. Practically all freedom of choice and movement had disappeared. Doors were uniformly locked, whether or not a room was occupied. The game room, formerly a popular area, now rarely was used. Despite the addition of candy machines to the canteen, the room was sparsely furnished and used for organized crafts activities rather than as a free time, social space.

Within the next eight months, the census doubled in each category of care. At about the same time a decision was made to divide children into two groups according to age—one an adolescent group, the other made up of younger children. Not only were activities age-segregated but the living areas were as well. This decision necessitated moving all children to two new houses and coincided with the conversion of the office space in each house into an isolation or "quiet" room.

Other changes were happening outside the living space. The occupational therapy program was moved into an unused house, requiring major physical modifications. In the same house, the lower floor was used for autistic children, also necessitating extensive renovations of the indoor space and access to the outdoors. The room that had been custom-made for these children, with easy access to the outdoor play area, was now converted to a staff library and the outdoor area ceased to be used and maintained. Some of the furnishings and equipment from the game room were moved into the canteen and the game room, as such, ceased to exist.

The major physical changes over the next 11 years reflect the growing institutionalization and controlling aspects of this setting. Carpeting was removed from all areas and much of the glass was replaced by plexiglass. "Quiet" rooms were eventually placed in almost all community spaces as well as adding one in each of the three units or apartments that made up each house. Built-in benches which had been a popular sitting area close to the nurses' station in each house were removed despite the fact that more children used these areas than used the dayrooms. Television sets were enclosed in massive wooden structures and anchored to the floor. Administrative offices took over almost all unused house areas.

The increasing institutionalization becomes apparent when reflecting on changes in the quality and diversity of activities as well as the locations of these activities. Over time, the so-called public spaces such as the gym, the outdoor play areas, and canteen showed a general decline in spontaneous, vigorous activities and an increase in sedentary organized activities—generally group arts and crafts or table games. The central court for which we had a few hundred thousand separate observations, had a total of 36 occasions in which it was used, and these were all during the first few months of occupancy. The outdoor recreation spaces were rarely used. The houses, which early on were used only rarely during the day, became places to send children when the staff felt they were too difficult to manage during school hours or activity times. The house became defined as a place for withdrawal and detention of children. This characterization was enhanced by the fact that the public and private life spaces were separated but close enough to enable the living area to become part of the disciplining of children even during their school hours. Since most of the children eventually were disciplined in this way, the house became associated with passive, alone, withdrawing behaviors which included a heavy dose of watching TV to pass the time.

The institution became focused on "disobedience" and there was a general tension underlying the day-to-day living, a tension produced by the view that the children were basically volatile and that only specific procedures would keep them from erupting. These included the use of drugs, detention in the house, called "restriction," and even the requirement that children detained in the house wear their pajamas during the entire day aptly called "control precaution" to discourage children from running away (termed "eloping" in hospital jargon). Sometimes the precautions were extended to activities outside the house as well. The atmosphere of the hospital developed a lethargic quality—the combination of drugs, pajamas, watching television, and an emphasis on submissive, regimented behaviors in areas that could be readily surveilled.

Thus the days of roller-skating in the corridor gave way, within one year, to a pattern of totally structuring the children's daily lives, programmatically as well as spatially, a pattern which continued over the next 11 years.

The State Concept of Psychiatric Care Prevails

It is clear that neither the architect's nor the director's conceptions were realized or realistic. The architect's plan embodied an image of space and of living based on the illusion that children here would have the same freedom as children in the outside community. The designer did not understand the extent to which the institution and its goals would constrain the spontaneity and freedom of children to a degree far beyond that of children outside the institution. The director's image denied or underestimated the reality of a site that was geographically, socially, and symbolically isolated from the community. His image also implied a flexibility on the part of the therapeutic program and staff that would lead to the use of resources within the community. This flexibility was not evident nor possible given the difficulties of access to the community, the lack of community resources, and the limits resulting from the size of the staff and the work required. He underestimated the resistance to change from the mental-health system with its carefully delineated job categories and salaries, its bureaucratic and political requirements, and its interest in the capital investment in this physical facility.

The designer's image of a bustling community was not realized in this site either, partly because the planned size of the population never materialized. However, this explanation is a limited one. Even when the hospital accommodated a series of different programs with a potentially large population from which to draw, including a day-care program for autistic children, a half-time remedial education program for adolescents, and a program for developmentally disabled children, their schedules and programs were purposefully separated in space and time. This programming only allowed a small, defined number of residents to be in any space at one time. There would be eight children using the Olympic-sized swimming pool or the regulation-sized gym; three or four children in the library; the auditorium and canteen were empty except on special occasions; and the outdoors spaces were virtually deserted. Walking through the corridors, the "main community streets," it was hard to imagine that there were as many people in the building as we knew there were.

It was difficult for the director to get community people to use the resources in the building. This was due, at least in part, to the location of the hospital and its inaccessibility by public transportation. It also was due to the conceptions held by community people that this building housed "deviants," people with whom they would rather not mingle. When the facilities were offered to the adult psychiatric hospital, located on the same site, for a while their residents used the pool and gym. However, the staff became concerned about "strangers" in the building, people they did not know and could not control. In any event, these users were not what the director had in mind as "community people." Finally, the use of space fell to decisions made by on-line staff and unit chiefs rather than to the director, who became occupied with obtaining funding, lobbying, and other political and administrative matters. The staff did not necessarily share the director's philosophy since many were trained in traditional institutions.

The semi-public areas leading to the houses and within them did not live up to their planned use as places for casual social encounters. A sitting area outside the doors leading to the house areas was rarely occupied by anyone other than one or two staff members taking a break. The internal house corridor, the semi-public space shared by the inhabitants of the three apartments, did work well in the early stages as a hangout for the teenagers in the adolescent unit. It would appear that either its success was not recognized, or that it was considered unimportant, or that the use of the area was seen as inappropriate or annoying. The part of it that was most popular, the bench area, was eventually removed, supposedly to accommodate a larger nurses' station. These corridors functioned mainly as places to administer medications and to line up residents in preparation for leaving the house.

The planned use of the dayroom, the unit's other semi-public space, was predicated on the notion that residents would freely choose it as the space to meet members of their "apartment house" community. However, due to the institution's perceived need for surveillance and efficient use of staff time, residents were ordinarily herded into the dayroom without choice. There, under the watchful eye of the nurse behind the glass window of the adjacent nurses' station, social activities were minimal. This was partly due to the absence of materials and equipment that would be supportive and interesting. There were no table games, no magazines, nothing that would attract the residents and keep them busy. The most common item available was the TV set and for a short while the adolescent unit had a phonograph. But more than that, the schedule of the hospital did not provide much time for social activities within the house. Rather, these activities were programmed for "community" spaces as part of the therapy rather than as part of living.

The eight-person apartments did not live up to their image either. The living rooms were never used for small group gatherings; in fact, they were rarely used at all. Although the furnishings there were minimal, the more compelling reason for their lack of use was the unwillingness of the staff to allow residents to be there since it was difficult to surveil them. The dayroom was more expedient. The bathrooms were almost as public as the living rooms, especially when the stalls and showers lacked doors. When these were added, the staff kept the doors to the bathrooms propped open for easy surveillance. This approach reflects the inconsistency and incongruity of the goal of developing appropriate or socialized behavior. While verbally espousing the emotional immaturity of the residents and their problems especially in regard to their bodily functioning and sexuality, the enforced publicness of the bathroom would hardly be a supportive way to cope with these issues. Yet in this instance, surveillance predominated over a therapeutic goal, questionable as both were.

Since aloneness was considered suspect and was defined as withdrawal rather than as privacy, children's voluntary attempts to be alone in their bedrooms were often thwarted. In reality, during the day bedrooms rarely had more than one person in them. Most often, these were children being punished during the program times when other children were off the unit. Therefore, the predominant activities in all bedrooms, regardless of the number of assigned occupants, were sleeping, lying awake, and sitting (with no other observable behavior). The total surveillance of bedroom spaces when they were occupied severely limited their use for more personal or social activities. When doors were installed this did not measurably change the use of these rooms because doors were closed only when rooms were unoccupied. The exercise of rules that doors be left open when rooms were occupied contradicted their stated purpose.

There was no possibility for the children to choose when to use their bedrooms or what they could do once inside them. It might, however, have been possible for the residents to create some sense of their own identities in their spaces by putting things in the rooms that had personal meanings, and thus making the rooms reflect those who lived there. This did not and could not happen. Each child had a bed-unit, bed cover, sheets, pillow, and pillowcases exactly like all the others. The beige cinder block walls would not hold anything tacked to them for more than a few hours or at most a few days. There was no place for a small lamp, a small table, a comfortable chair. Yet the impersonal quality that this homogeneous, unresponsive environment created (impervious to individual imprint) was the "home" for children for, in some cases, as long as six years.

The pervasive public quality of life was enmeshed in the public quality of the physical environment. Other than sheer size, there was little to distinguish the living room of the apartment, intended as an intimate space for no more than eight people, from the dayroom of the unit, intended for 24 people, or from the canteen intended for use by all the residents. The walls did not vary, the lighting did not vary, the materials available were virtually all similar. The intended range of life experiences, from the most private to the most public, envisioned by the designer, was an illusion in a system in which all aspects of residents' lives are assumed to be public and in which publicness is rationalized as vital to the therapeutic goal. The casual social relationships that might have developed in more public areas were also not possible because being in these spaces was still a matter of program rather than choice. Once in the space, the types of acceptable behaviors were also predetermined.

In the end, the state's concept of psychiatric care prevailed, even though it was assumed to be anachronistic. The guiding principles underlying this setting involved a definition of who these children were, a conceptualization of their problems and the role of hospitalization in providing a cure.

SOME IMPLICATIONS OF THE INSTITUTIONALIZATION OF CHILDREN

Placing young children in custody, whether for protection, education, or therapy, involves a series of definitions. These include definitions of the children, their families, definition of the care they are to receive and the places in which they will receive this care. In the case of the children in the hospital that we have studied, their admission as "patients" implied that their problems required such special attention that they could not be addressed in the course of their schooling or home life. Neither parental attention nor therapy from specialists would be sufficient to deal with what had been identified by specialists as their problems—problems which were defined as something more than the expected developmental difficulties. What made the distinction between the expected and the uncommon, at least in the population we studied, was a matter of poverty, an easily available labeling system, and inadequate services in the community.

The Children

Although designed for children who would be full-time residents, from its opening the hospital continued a mix of day-care and full-care children. The term "day-care" refers to children who live with their natural or foster families and come to the hospital on weekdays for a combination of therapy and school. Full-care status children live at the hospital although occasionally they spend weekends and holidays at home. Both categories of care involve the same kinds of children, those diagnosed as seriously disturbed and in need of help, presumably beyond what could be provided through schools and community services. Over the years of our work we saw many children shift in status, moving from day-care to full-care, and also in the reverse direction, sometimes shifting more than once. In general, the day-care group was about half the size of the full-time residents.

During the six-year course of our research, 193 different children were admitted to the hospital, 131 of them males and 62 females. They ranged in age from 6 to 18. After reaching 18 the residents were either sent to an adult hospital, turned over to the community programs, or discharged to their natural or foster families.

If we examine the ages of this cumulative group, we see that the majority of the children fell between the ages of 9 and 14, although there were differences between the percentage of boys and girls in some age categories. Above 14, the percentage of boys and girls was fairly even. In the younger age groups, however, boys were underrepresented in the 9 to 11 age group and girls were overrepresented in the 12 to 14 age group. This suggests that there were different criteria applied to the behavior of each, bringing them into contact with the mental-health system at different times in their lives.

The number of years the children remained hospitalized captures another important quality of hospital life. Despite the intention to provide "short-term" care, we found that the average stay for males was 14.1 months and for females it was 16.5 months. The range extended from a few days to six years.

The hospital used the classification system developed by the Group for the Advancement of Psychiatry. Although there was turnover of children in the years we worked in the hospital the diagnostic patterns remained essentially the same, with the possible exception of a gradual increase in the numbers of severely "acting-out" girls, that is, girls identified as unable to fit the prevailing social stereotype of passivity. Most of the patients came from poor families and state-provided residential care was really the only option available to them.

A profile of 30 children during our first two studies in the early years of the hospital's functioning provides a picture of the kinds of problems that were listed in the charts. Twenty of the 30 youngsters fell under the "personality disorder" grouping, two of these with "borderline psychotic" features. Within this broad category, the most common label was "impulse ridden," with eight children so described. The remaining 10 patients were considered to have psychotic features, two of them "borderline," three with "psychosis of early childhood," three "schizo-phrenic-form psychotics," and two with "psychotic disorders of adolescence." During most of the research period there was an autistic unit for a small group of young children (under age 10) with a day program designed for their needs.

Beyond the psychiatric labels applied to the children and their designation as mainly poor and mainly Black and Hispanic,* they were urban children from poor and working-class areas of a large city. Some had records documenting years of contacts with clinics and hospitals. Many had been identified by school authorities who defined their problems as too serious for management within the usual system. Others had been in another hospital either as residents or clinic patients, prior to their admission to the children's hospital. In a few cases the children had been removed from their families and characterized by the courts as children in need of special services, an assumption made that their home environment did not provide adequate care or supervision.

The clinical labels and demographic information provide an impoverished sense of the children and what they were like. Over the course of our six years in the hospital we got to know them quite well, and the children also became familiar with our research team. Many of them asked us to explain our work which we did, and most understood quite well what we were doing. They called us the "space people" and occasionally would help us with observations or tease us by calling out a code number to describe an activity they were involved in.

They were as varied a group as one might expect in any setting where children can be found. Some were lively; others were subdued and shy. Most were friendly and happy to see us or indifferent when we appeared, full of enthusiasm, good humor, energy, and pride, in many ways *not* an unusual group in their overall behavior. In fact, their behavior became more unusual when they were placed on a prescribed regime of psychotropic medication. They would become lethargic and unresponsive, sometimes so drowsy that they spent the days sleeping or staring off into space.

Labeling and Hospitalization

In all of our contacts, casual and formal, we saw few instances of extreme pathological behavior. There is no reason to doubt that these did appear in *some* of the children some of the time; or that many of the children clearly needed

* During our data collection the hospital had a total of 193 different patients on whom we had ethnic data: 44% of them Black, 39% Hispanic, and 17% white.

help with the problems confronting them in their daily lives. Yet, when it is easy to view children as having problems that cannot be managed through ordinary means and when there is an available system for care, there is always the temptation to use the system as the easiest course. Middle-class and upper-class children might receive counseling or tutoring. The reasons for their truancy might be questioned. But for the children in the hospital we studied, few options existed. Once the term "maladjusted" or "abnormal" had been applied, they were drawn into a system that had been set up for children with their labels, a system with a defined set of goals based on a specific conception of normalcy. The result was, first, to make the child fit a standard of normal that may be alien to his or her background and functionally inappropriate for the child's future life in the community. Second, it was easy to use the children's deviant labels as a means of explaining all of their behavior and minimizing their competence. Activities that might seem normal outside the hospital and its population were interpreted within the "overall rational plan" (Goffman, 1961) of the setting. Some examples from our work come easily to mind.

For instance our own observations found children rarely to be aggressive. Yet aggression was extremely upsetting to staff when it did occur, however infrequently. We would hear such behavior described vividly after the fact as we watched measures set up in anticipation of future outbreaks. There was a question for us as to what fell under the category of "aggression." Times when we felt that the children were high-spirited or engaged in playful roughhousing would often be viewed by the staff as instances of aggression. Similarly, questions or challenges to the staff's authority were seen as deliberate aggressive acts. The staff seemed to expect absolute obedience to authority and a passive, compliant mode of behavior.

A second example was staff's perceptions of children's privacy needs. In talking to the staff about whether privacy was an issue for the children, the chief psychiatrist of the children's unit replied:

> Yes, kids are always in a group. They can't be private. It's good in relation to breaking down defensive structure. The private room hasn't been good. I'm opposed to individual rooms, because when kids aren't closed off, you know more about their problems.

Without any motivation to question these labels, the entire experience within the setting's walls was organized to meet its so-called therapeutic goals. This covered not only the labels worn by children on entering and on their behavior while in the hospital but extended to the places open and closed to them and the physical qualities of these places, as well. In response to the question, "Is privacy an issue for the kids?" a child-development worker said:

I never hear them speak about anyone invading their privacy. I never heard kids talking about requiring it. This is a hospital and in a hospital there is none and none expected. There's nothing that they do that requires privacy. All share bathrooms and showers.

Thus the ascriptions continued to follow the children since alternative views rarely had an opportunity to exercise their power, in the site.

A final example (but one that we were able to test) was related to the children's ability to understand the spatial layout of the hospital building. Concerns were expressed by various staff members about "spatial orientation" within the building. The director of nursing thought that the vastness and "complexity" of the building made independent movement through it difficult for the children. Independent movement appeared to be a programmatic goal thwarted by the physical design of the building. The director of nursing questioned the value of existing signage and wanted to find ways of improving them for "these" children who suffered from "disorientation in time and space," a classic textbook description based on paper-and-pencil psychological tests. The psychologist supported this view of the children and thought that there might be value in developing a research project documenting the relationship between "hemispheral dominance and orientation problems," identifying ways the physical environment of the institution could be used to compensate for such difficulties. We agreed to conduct a study of the children's ability to find their way around the building.

We developed a series of orientation tasks which involved having children draw a map of the hospital, then trace a series of paths to various places in the hospital and finally having children take us on walks to and from specific places. We found that while the children could not always draw an accurate map of the building, they easily marked off paths after locating themselves spatially in relation to the entry. Their actual walks were even more revealing of their knowledge of the building as a social as well as a physical setting. As children took us on these walks they provided rich detail on the various parts of the building, including staff spaces and changes in staffing and physical location that had occurred over time. Here is a description of our tour with Richard, age 14, who had been in the children's hospital for one and a half years:

We visited the second floor offices. After viewing each office, Richard turned to retrace direction and stated it would be easier to go down the same way we entered. I asked where the other way would lead and he said, "to the green door, but further from the downstairs offices. . . ." Not only did Richard tell me who was occupying each office presently, he frequently described all the moves that had taken place over time. The rest of the hospital was toured with similar thoroughness.

Mike, age 15, had only been in the hospital *one month*:

> Mike originally claimed he couldn't show me around since he didn't know the hospital well enough. With reassurance that I'd be pleased to be shown the parts of the hospital he knew, he was an eager guide . . . In fact, he knew the hospital well and gained increased confidence as he went around. . . . He was able to locate all the places I named, with the exception of the school area which he seemed not to have heard of previously. (In fact, he had not attended school since he was admitted during the summer.) Mike knew the rest of the hospital well. In the office area he informed me that there were 17 offices and then proceeded to count them.

Maria, age 14, had been in the hospital exactly *one year*. She could not draw a map, nor could she accurately trace her path on one. Nevertheless she knew her way around:

> Maria was quite thorough, explaining every room we passed covering the entire length of each corridor. When we reached the school area, she described the equipment within each of the closed doors, specifying ovens, sewing machines, and so forth.

Our experiences clearly indicated that the children, including new arrivals, were neither confused nor disoriented by the building. They had clear images of the spaces, and in many cases a historical view of them. Their lack of independent movement, then, was not a function of their incapacity. Even when informed of these findings the constraints on their movements were not removed.

We found repeated evidence of the confusion between labels and reality and of the contradiction between stated goals and actual program. There was a reification of categories that led the staff to fail to recognize the needs and competencies of these children, eliminating a whole range of experiences from their lives. The result was a daily routine that was rigid and stultifying—a routine which helped generate exactly the behavior that was considered inappropriate.

The Daily Lives of the Children

A typical day for both the young children and the adolescents started at 7 A.M. when they were awakened. After about an hour for washing and dressing they lined up in the house corridor to be led to the dining room. Once in the dining room the children lined up again to obtain their food which was served from a counter. Food trays were taken to one of the small round tables and breakfast was quickly eaten. After everyone had completed the meal the children lined up again, returning to the house and then going off to school. Moving as a group through the corridors they were ushered into the wing of the building housing the school.

By 9 A.M. the children were in their classes with day-care children joining them after arriving in the hospital's minibus. A one-hour break for lunch began with the children lining up and marching to the dining room assigned to their house. The meal itself usually lasted only 15 or 20 minutes, and the rest of the time was spent in the house. At the end of the hour the children went back to school, again moving in a group. They stayed in school until the traditional 3 P.M. By 5 P.M. all of the day-care children had been returned to their homes in the community.

The full-care children touched base in their house, then from about 3 P.M. to 4:30 P.M. were involved in a formal recreational program—either in the gym, the pool, the occupational therapy suite, the game room, or the music room, supervised by staff members who led them from area to area.

Between 4:30 P.M. and 5 P.M. there was a free period, a break before dinner. At this time the children were allowed to use their bedrooms, although most could be found in the dayroom. At 5 P.M. children lined up to receive medications. Dinner was preceded and followed by the usual lining-up ritual and the meal itself took a scant 15 minutes. After dinner, another formal recreational program involved everyone. Preparation for bedtime began at 9 P.M. for the adolescent units, about an hour earlier for the younger children. Snacks, which came from a central supply in the adult hospital, were served as the children showered and went to bed.

Formal therapy sessions took place during the afternoon, consisting of a weekly or twice-weekly meeting with the social worker or psychologist assigned to each case. It has been estimated that the unprogrammed time available to the children and adolescents in this hospital covers a maximum of two hours (Golan, 1978), with limited opportunities to exercise some choice of what to do, although residents were still spatially restricted to the house during this time.

Weekends followed a somewhat looser schedule since school was not part of the program. On Friday afternoons some inpatients left to visit their families. Most of the day children remained at home when the school was closed. Whenever possible, the staff planned some community activities for the remaining children. However, apart from these the groups followed a program of recreation and crafts within the building with a much reduced staff supervising the activities. Despite their small numbers, food still was prepared in the adult hospital and carted to their dining rooms and all other hospital routines continued.

It is essential to contrast this schedule with the lives of young people outside an institutional setting, especially in terms of the degree and forms of structuring of their time, in thinking of the balance between public and private life available to individual children and in terms of the institutional mechanisms used to enforce the schedule.

The Imposition of Order

On the surface, the school hours of the children might be perceived to resemble the lives of children living outside an institution though there was an enormous qualitative difference when the surface was scratched, even slightly. When after-school hours were examined, any resemblance disappeared. A look at the guide-lines for the evening nursing staff provides a picture of rhetoric versus reality. According to this document, the objectives of this time period from 3 P.M. through bedtime at 9 P.M. were:

> To attempt to provide a homelike structured environment to children by understanding, teaching, and giving guidance needed to develop basic social, behavioral patterns and maintain individual character development.

This was to be attained by the following methods:

1. small group interactions,
2. utilizing facilities of the hospital, and
3. gradually reduce tension and activity stimulus and prepare for sleep and rest.

The detailed program that was to reflect these objectives and methods appears in Table 4.1.

Behind this schedule is an order and rigidity that raises questions as to how "homelike" life in the hospital could be. The daily repetition of exactly the same activities in exactly the same sequence leaves little latitude for the reality that daily life varies somewhat for most people. Regardless of schedules fixed by working, chores, and other obligations, there are days when one is not hungry at 5 P.M. and not ready for sleep at 9 P.M.; showering is not an absolute necessity (nor is a set time) every day, nor are we always hungry for a snack before bed. The absence of any opportunity for spontaneous feeling and activities also elimi-nates the pleasure of unexpected events which is and should be a part of daily life.

The belief that such order is necessary for therapeutic purposes requires the development of strategies for imposing this kind of structure on the lives of children. One predominant institutional ritual used in this hospital to ensure adherence to this schedule was *lining up*.

Within an hour of awakening, children lined up inside the house to be led to breakfast in the dining room. Food was obtained by lining up and moving through the cafeteria line. Breakfast time ended, and the children again were lined up to return to the house, and almost immediately upon return, lined up once more to go to the school. During school hours, lining up was a recurrent activity as

TABLE 4.1   Guidelines for the Evening Nursing Staff–Children's Unit—Unit III

Routine	
3 PM	All children to be returned to unit, accompanied by group leader or coordinator
3–3:30 PM	Evening staff receive day report—assignments
3:20–3:30 PM	Evening group leaders take children to their areas for activities
4:45–5 PM	All children and staff return to unit
	1. Children as ordered, receive 5 PM meds
	2. Prepare for supper (encourage hand washing)
5–5:30 PM	Supper, cafeteria style
	1. Group leaders eat with own children
	2. Head nurse discuss activities plans for the evening and make announcements
5:30 PM	All children and staff leave dining area and report to designated area of first scheduled activity
5:30–8 PM	Activity involvement
	1. Staff takes assigned supper break
	Wednesdays: 5:30–6:00 group meeting
	6:00–7:00 post-meeting
	6:00–8:00 activities
8–8:30 PM	Snack time and free hour group leaders involved with own patients as much as possible
	1. Table games
	2. T.V.
	3. Canteen
	4. Game room
8:30– 9 PM	Prepare children for bath/shower and bed
	(a) Laying out clean clothes for next day
	(b) Staff assist in developing personal hygiene habits
9 PM	Children to be in room and in bed
	Group leaders stay in room or area of group to read stories or to just sit in area
9–10 PM	Alternate bed check, at one-half-hour intervals by group leader and nurse
10–10:30 PM	Head nurse and staff discuss and evaluate evening happenings
	Head nurse writes evening report
11–11:30 PM	Head nurse gives oral report and makes rounds with night staff

children moved from room to room and also as they went to and from their house at lunch. The end of the school day meant lining up to return to the house, staying for a few minutes, and once again lining up to go to some formal programmed activity, lining up to leave the activity, and returning again to the house. There was one-half hour of free time before dinner, but lining up for medication took part of this time. The lining up before, during, and after dinner was followed by another lining up to go to evening program and to return to the house.

In following the course of one particular child's day, an observer recorded the following, as a group of 10-year-olds walked from their living area to the gym during their evening "homelike structured" time. This walk could easily be done within two minutes, but took ten minutes instead:

(6:15 P.M.) The kids are lined up waiting to go to the gym. Marie sits on the floor, tying her shoelace and playfully hits Joel's foot. After about a minute she gets up and leans on the wall, pulling on the doorknob of the room behind her. She's watching all of the activity going on around her, laughing at something one staff member says to other kids who are in front of her on the line. Most of the children are now laughing hysterically and Marie joins in, listening and laughing. A staff member says, "Marie, if you can't get quiet you are going to the back of the line." Marie says, "I can't help it. He's making me laugh," pointing to another staff member. And that staff member warns, "I'll really make you laugh," but keeps cracking little jokes with the boys which continues to amuse Marie. . . . The first staff member says, "Is everybody ready?" . . . They're still lined up at 6:19 and finally a staff member opens the door and the kids file out. They start walking past the canteen, past the kindergarten area. Marie begins to prance and begins a mild verbal argument with Joel. She shoves him slightly and scowls. At 6:20 everyone is directed to sit down against the wall and Marie sits down quickly. One staff member says, "We can sit here through the whole day." (None of this is directed at Marie. The staff is talking to several other kids while everyone else waits.) While sitting, Marie hits another child and says, "Stop doing that," and begins to tap her fingers very impatiently. The kids are still sitting and at 6:23 the staff person says, "Are we ready to try again?" The kids all respond with a loud, "Yes." Marie is one of the first to stand up, and the staff member says, "O.K. We're going to try it again." They all walk single file against the wall. Marie is not saying anything but some of the other children are talking. At 6:25 they enter the gym.

The same child waits on the cafeteria line to get her lunch tray and soon finds herself threatened with the punishment of the "quiet room":

Marie waits in the dayroom of her house listening for her name to be called to line up for lunch. Nine children have already gotten in line and at 12:03 the group is finally on its way, with Marie as tenth and last in line. By 12:04 Marie is on line in the dining room waiting to be served cafeteria style. She waits for a tray and talks in a friendly manner to the kids around her. She leans against the door and suddenly it opens as a staff member enters. Marie almost loses her balance and gets very angry, says a few angry words to the staff member, who apologizes. At 12:05 she's still waiting, looking at the children on line, unresponsive to their comments. At 12:07 she picks up her tray, wipes it with a napkin, and takes her silverware. She watches the food being distributed. At 12:08 she whispers to the boy in front of her and he tries to give her his dessert. She puts it back on his tray. At 12:09 Marie takes a dessert and milk and is finally given her plate of food. She says, "I'm not going to eat that!" A staff member assures her that she doesn't have to. An angry exchange follows, anyway, and Marie says, "I'm tired of supervisors." The staff member replies, "If you don't stop that you're going to be in the quiet room all by yourself." Marie takes her seat in the dining room without taking her main course.

In another example, on one of the rare instances in which the children were using outdoor play areas, the children are subjected to an arbitrary time limit:

The kids have been outside for 40 minutes and have been involved in a variety of high energy outdoor activities including using the slides and swings. Joe, the staff member shouts, "O.K. Everybody line up!" The kids continue to play. Two minutes later, Joe says again, "I said to line up, please." Most of the kids are involved on the slide and no one listens. Marie is organizing them into a game in which they slide down under her body which is arched over the slide as a bridge. Marie looks up and says, "You'd better hurry." She goes down the slide. Joe threatens that he's not going to bring people outside anymore. Marie takes her jump rope and is the first to line up by Joe who continues to threaten as she says pleadingly, "Please, Joe." It's three minutes after his first call and they're all lined up by the exit door. Joe is checking off, on a list, all of the kids who did not get in line immediately. As he checks off Marie, Marie says, "Joe, I got on line!" and she argues with him. Finally, he agrees. By four minutes after the initial line-up call, they were back in the building.

In these examples, Marie is reprimanded when others are not and others are reprimanded when she is not with no clear indication of the behavior that is acceptable or non-acceptable. In the outdoor example, children have no access to a clock and they have no way to judge when an activity is going to end, yet the staff person becomes upset when it takes all of four minutes for 10 children to respond to his order. If one reflects on experiences outside of such an institution, it is clear that assembling children to leave a playground when they are deeply involved in activities is a difficult and lengthy chore even when one or two children are involved. Yet, here, three minutes is seen as being a long enough time to require the punishment of so-called tardy children. When Marie finally gets angry in the dining room she has been waiting on line first in the house and then in the food distribution area, and her impatience increases as time passes. The restlessness and irritability of people waiting on bus lines or movie lines, or, indeed, waiting to be served in a restaurant, would be considered a "normal" part of life, yet Marie's restlessness becomes the basis for the threat of isolation.

Lining up is more than simply a functional mechanism for getting children from one place to another. It occurs within a context of a total structuring of the children's days, where ordinary activities lose their sense of flow, becoming bounded and compartmentalized as discrete activities that are not freely chosen. Lining up then becomes the glue that connects what can be essentially unrelated activities to one another at the same time that it becomes the boundary that separates them. The sheer tedium of sitting or standing in one spot repeatedly over the day denies the spontaneity and need for activity that children have. And, in an overly structured and programmed day, it uses up precious time that could belong to the children and be used by them for their own purposes.

Lining up is common to most children in school and even small amounts leads to impatient and disruptive behavior. In the context of the hospital, given its frequency and pervasiveness, it creates a quality of regimentation in life which underscores the children's lack of personhood. Lining up becomes reified as an activity, for example, making it the major part of "eating," instead of the way to get to the dining room. Requiring such regimentation in this context and with such intensity, guarantees the self-fulfilling prophecy of children's disruptive behavior.

The philosophy of care stresses that "these" children need structure but in its translation into practice it requires that children demonstrate their submission to arbitrary and unpredictable demands. In the guise of having a therapeutic goal, lining up imposes a rule system that is impossible for the children to comply with, making demands on them that inevitably cannot be met. This leads to the use of all kinds of power mechanisms by the staff in order to achieve compliance.

This same philosophy of care stresses that "these" children need social experience. Reflected in the daily routine, in addition to order, is the constant participation of children in group activities and the absence of opportunities for privacy. The pervasiveness of public life demonstrates the contradictions between this aspect of the so-called therapeutic goal and the strategies for achieving it.

The Elimination of Privacy

The chief psychiatrist of the adolescent unit had this to say about privacy as an issue for adolescent residents:

> Sure, we try to force the kids to mix with others; forcing out of defensive structure and forces change; at unit meetings kids can't be private. Those are the rules of the group throughout the day and night.

When the same person was asked how the residents manage to get privacy, he said:

> by rocking, sleeping . . . defensive maneuvers, using bizarre behavior. . .

Other staff members mentioned other extreme forms of achieving privacy such as "hiding in the closet," "running away," "blowing up (acting out) in order to get it." These behaviors were considered inappropriate and were some of the reasons children and adolescents were (and continue to be) institutionalized. Yet the environment—physically and socially—reinforced their occurrence.

In this institution, as in others, childen spent almost all of their time in the presence of other people, engaged in various personal and group activities. The experience was one of co-participating with others in the activities as well as being under the surveillance of staff. In addition to the structured daily program which left limited time for private endeavors of any sort, the physical design of the hospital seemed aimed at preventing privacy for the children. Not only that, the staff discouraged children from wanting to be alone. Going off to one's own room, whether a single bedroom or not, even to read, was interpreted as a negative kind of withdrawal even when it was obvious that the group had nothing to offer the child.

In effect, a child who wanted privacy was considered to be wanting a "bad" thing—and had to break rules to achieve it through being confined in the "quiet room."

As described earlier, the apartment units never functioned for small groups. Instead, children were herded into the larger dayroom which was located opposite the glass enclosed nursing station, thus providing easy group surveillance. Doors on bedrooms and bathrooms, once installed, did not provide physical privacy since staff could and did enter at will in the name of "therapeutic goals" and "security."

The impact of the "labels" given to the children was reflected clearly in the administration's views about the children's needs for privacy. The chief of service, in describing his expectations regarding the addition of bedroom doors, anticipated problems which he defined as "homosexual activities," especially among the adolescents. He felt that since these were "not normal" youngsters, they would not be able to "handle" opportunities for privacy.

Nurses, child-development workers, and teachers were asked whether privacy was an issue for the children and whether kids having privacy would create problems. Most of these staff members were conflicted, being more sensitive than their administrators about the issue of privacy for children and adolescents, yet fearful about residents' "behavior problems." Therefore their view of the children and of their jobs undermined the very basis of privacy:

(Issue for kids?) Yes, they need it, but they don't have it. It's human nature to be alone. Kids are always in a group in the living area and there's no place to go to think things over when staff and (other) kids bug you. (Create problems?) In the living areas I can see difficulties, because if the kids are private, *the staff wonders what the kid is doing* and doesn't know when to *intervene—the kid may be cutting his wrist.* (Teacher)

(Issue for kids?) Yes, a minor problem. They're taught to do things in groups, with little time for themselves. (Create problems?) "It's a problem at times, because

you must know what the kids are doing at all times in order to protect them.
(Nurse, children's unit)

(Issue for kids?) Yes, a person learns most when he examines himself. It's hard
to learn when others are around. (Creates problems?) It's no problem when they
get it, because *I judge* when a kid should be alone. (Child-development worker,
adolescent male unit.)

The ability to have privacy when parents came to visit was subordinated to
the staff wish to observe the interaction between parents and children. As a
result, the policy was that parents were not permitted in the apartment areas and
visiting took place in large public spaces.

Yet another way in which institutional needs and so-called therapeutic needs
overrode the children's individual needs for privacy was in terms of information
privacy. The "team" structure, while it supported a holistic therapeutic approach
to the child, raised issues of confidentiality. The therapists mentioned residents'
requests for them to keep information that came out during therapy sessions from
other staff members. Staff had to explain to residents that this couldn't be done.
The policy made the staff uncomfortable but they did not feel that they could
change it because it was an integral part of the therapeutic milieu:

kids worry—who knows about them. What do people know about them. . . . Have
to be careful in terms of information shared about the kids. A therapeutic community
makes it difficult because everything's supposed to be shared. I would rather ask
kids: what would you like to share? (Nurse, children's unit)

Records were kept for each shift and shared with staff from the next shift. The
context of therapy sessions was not confidential. Children were expected to
communicate feelings to each other and with the staff:

privacy is an issue kids bring up—when something happens in their life that only
the coordinator should know—but it can't be so. The team has to know. The kids
don't always accept it. (Psychiatrist, children's unit)

There were two acceptable types of reasons for children having "privacy"—
the need to deal with emotional upset and what was called "sexual/hygienic
needs." When asked in which situations children needed privacy most, more
than half the staff said it was to deal with emotional upset. Yet, in talking about
this situation, the staff interpreted "privacy" to mean "isolation":

Any extreme emotion, for example, depression. A child who is feeling unwanted
or persecuted. They have moments when they want to be alone. Or a kid who's
physically blowing up—that is, assaultive. (Child-development worker, children's
unit)

When they're uncontrollable, they need it. (Child-development worker, children's unit)

If they have things bugging them and have to work it out in their head. They were talking about a room where kids could beat the shit out of things—I'm all for it instead of the kids beating up on people. (Teacher)

When they're upset . . . should be isolated . . . (Nurse, adolescent unit)

If a kid acts out, he has an audience, maybe he should be alone . . . (Child-development worker, children's unit)

When asked why the children would need doors to their bedrooms, sexual needs and modesty were the prevalent answers from the staff:

For changing clothes. They need to learn you should do this in privacy. (Director of nursing)

Adolescent boys need it for masturbation. Maybe if the stalls were closed, it might be more helpful. (Chief psychiatrist, children's unit)

Getting up in the morning and their own hygienic tasks. (Nurse, girls' adolescent unit)

Trouble with masturbation. There's always somebody walking into the room or bathroom. (Child-development worker, boys' adolescent unit)

Girls who start to menstruate early. There are those who started and those who haven't. They need that sense of privacy. Personal hygiene is in the bathroom, but they still need privacy in their rooms. There's been a problem with male visitors who come to the unit. This has created a sense of loss of privacy. (Child-development worker, girls' adolescent unit)

It was very rare for the staff to talk about the sexual needs of girls or privacy as a need unconnected to either pathological or sexual and modesty needs. Yet one or two staff members did realize the significance of privacy for self-reflection and recognized that the absence of physical privacy led to forms of psychological withdrawal:

I do think kids need privacy and it's hard for them to be alone here. There's no place—the way the unit is built, there's no place that's isolated, private. Sometimes a kid may want to go to a place without having to ask. The only place he could be alone is outside, and he'd have to ask. (When kids get privacy does it create problems for you?) I can't say, because I haven't had the opportunity to be with kids who've had privacy. The only privacy I see is psychological, but in the physical presence of others. (Nurse)

The importance of the so-called quiet room to privacy came out in our in-depth interviews with residents. When asked where they went to be alone, or when they wanted to do something without interruption, more than half named the "quiet room." Only two mentioned their bedroom while other places mentioned included the bathroom and unoccupied spaces. Yet, while the "quiet room" was perceived as one of the only places where residents could be alone and, in fact, was the only private place, there was a clear conflict created by its use for this purpose:

The quiet room is good 'cause it's quiet and nobody'll disturb you. . . . (If you could change the hospital what would you do?) First of all, I'd have no quiet room. (Adolescent boy)

(Where would you go in order to be alone and uninterrupted?) The seclusion room. (Why?) It helps keep you calm. (Is there a place you don't like to be alone in?) The seclusion room. (Adolescent girl)

Although initially associated with punishment and with the need to calm down when overly aggressive or acting out, children and adolescents soon learned that the seclusion room was the only place in which they could be physically alone. While a number of residents named the quiet room as the most uncomfortable area of the hospital, some of the same residents said they actually feigned emotional upset to have the luxury of aloneness. Even though we question the quality of this aloneness, the feigning of emotional upset demonstrates the residents' attempts to exert some control over their environment and their lives. However, within the context of the institution and its power structure the consequences were great. Children could continue to be institutionalized for these behaviors, because actual control was out of their hands. In fact, the goal of institutionalization was control and throughout the years of our work this goal surfaced despite philosophical statements to the contrary.

The Use of Space as a Mechanism for Control: From Detention to Isolation

Although many aspects of the hospitalization reified the control maintained over the children, the use of space and space policies were among the most powerful forces. In the first year, there was the increasing tendency, described earlier, to lock doors both in unused spaces and in areas in which children could be found. A second mode, also described earlier, was confining children to their houses, the unit living areas, which eventually was accompanied by the wearing of pajamas. A few years after the opening of the facility, a yellow line was painted on the floor of the corridor area that connected children's spaces to the front lobby and the administrative areas. This was a message to the children that they were not to pass into those sections of the building. Although this rule was supposed to be self-enforced—a type of behavior modification technique—during breaks in program time the line was patrolled by staff who directed children to their proper locations.

When the behavior of a significant number of adolescents was perceived to be "disruptive" or "out of control," *all* of the adolescents were kept in their house area for 24 hours, behind a locked door. Meals were brought in to them and, at times, the program staff itself would organize activities there. It was anticipated that this extreme action would motivate the adolescents to "pull themselves together," mainly through group action and pressure; they did not like having the unit closed and it was expected that the "leaders" of the group would exert pressure on others to shape up. After a while this procedure was banned from the adolescent unit (it was unclear why but we suspect that it only created more difficulties), but resurfaced in the children's unit. There it was used as punishment for actions such as boys going into the girls' unit, or someone throwing a chair (an extremely rare event), and in situations where a child was defined as "not being able to remain in program"—a vaguely defined term.

A system of rewards and punishments was developed based on restricting or expanding children's free range of movement. If one behaved "well" one could have the privilege of walking to program unaccompanied by staff. The next level extended the privilege to walking to the lobby unaccompanied. Freedom of movement gradually expanded, depending on the staff's perception of the child's self-control, and included trips outside of the building but remaining on the grounds, going to the local shopping area (which required a bus ride), or going home on the weekend. Infractions of rules resulted in lowering the child's level of privilege to the steps below.

The one conventional psychiatric hospital mechanism for control that was consciously *excluded* from the original physical design and therapeutic philosophy of this facility was the existence of a "seclusion room." In early discussions with the director the absence of such a space was described as extremely progressive and an indication of a newer philosophy. Yet, within one and one-half years of operation, an office in each of the house units, directly adjacent to the nurses' stations, had been turned into what was now called a "quiet room." This 10 by 6 foot room was totally empty except for a mattress on the floor. It had a door which was locked (see Figure 4.5).

The supposed policy of the hospital was to follow state regulations which required that a staff person accompany a child during time spent in this room in order to provide support for working through the difficulties. However, this did not usually occur. Generally children were in there alone. A peephole was drilled into the solid door to enable staff surveillance.

The use of on-the-spot crisis intervention was replaced by a policy of detention in the house, then became detention in the "quiet room." Isolation became viewed as valuable for quieting down a child who was "out of control." It was to be used for individual children when:

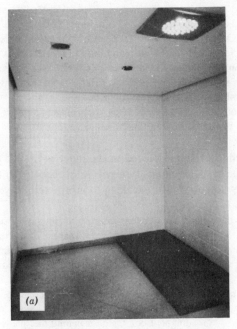

Figure 4.5. Office converted to "quiet room"

His behavior has gotten out of his control to a degree such that *all other means of attempting to promote internal control has failed*. The theory of seclusion is that a temporary reduction in interpersonal contacts which have become ungratifying and unmanageable for *whatever reason* will help a youngster to regain control of his unacceptable behavior. (Hospital Policy Memorandum #7407. Emphasis ours.)

Earlier we described how the threat of isolation in the quiet room was a way of dealing with Marie when she argued about the quality of the food. Another incident, from observations of the same child, shows the latitude the staff had in defining what is "unmanageable" and "ungratifying," the supposed use of isolation as a last resort, and its arbitrary use with one child as opposed to another:

(Again, during mealtime in the dining room). Sarah and Marie have been consistently picking on each other during the meal, both being provocative: Sarah laughed and said something and Marie says something about beating "the shit" out of Sarah and reprimanding her. . . . Sarah laughs at Marie and says, "Someone's going to beat the hell out of you." Marie laughs. Sarah was teasing Marie. Finally a staff member tells them both to sit down and Sarah sits down. Sarah and Marie start arguing verbally again. Staff says, "Keep on talking" angrily or half angrily, walks over to Marie and places her hands around the base of Marie's neck, resting on her shoulders, and shakes her a bit. Finally she says, "Marie, you want to go into the quiet room?" Marie ignores her. Staff says, "Come on, kids." (Apparently referring to both Sarah and Marie but really only to Marie.) "Let's go upstairs," touching Marie on the shoulder. Marie doesn't listen. She is really annoyed at Sarah. Staff again says, "Let's go, let's go, Marie." Apparently Marie was now talking about Sarah's mother who had died because staff says, "We don't talk about anyone's mother that way." Staff takes Marie out and Marie is still muttering. Staff leads Marie into the house and into the quiet room.

Following the child as she is placed in the quiet room and the responses of both herself and the staff member leads one to question who is out of control and what value the isolation has other than to affirm authority:

The staff unlocks the quiet room door and Marie goes in, saying something about sleeping in there. She goes willingly and says, "Thanks for the mat. I can go to sleep on that." The staff says, "No. I'll take them out." She closes and locks the door. Marie drags some of the mats around and when the staff member returns she finds it difficult to open the door. The staff pulls the mats out and Marie says, "Thanks. You're moving the mats. It's cooler for me. Want me to help you?" She actually helps the staff to move the mats out. When the second mat is removed Marie cheerily says, "Goodnight. Lock the door behind me, please. Goodnight."

Marie stays inside. She talks to herself, counts to herself, sings, bangs against the door as other kids go by on their way back from dinner. Finally, after only six minutes, the staff member peeks in to see what Marie is doing but Marie ignores her. Then, just as arbitrarily as she was put in, she gets taken out, although her "attitude" has not changed:

The staff member walks over to the quiet room and unlocks the door. Marie is just sitting inside. Staff member says, "Up!" and Marie says, "Thank you for letting me in the quiet room," and walks through the corridor toward her apartment. The staff member says, "Marie! Did you hear what I said? You're not going to sleep now." And Marie walks back into the corridor.

This example, in which Marie shows as much strength as the staff person though she definitely has less power, does not reflect the trauma associated with this experience for most children, or perhaps even for Marie on a less than obvious level. Often children were dragged kicking and screaming into this room, crying loudly and with great personal pain during large parts of their confinement. They could be heard kicking the walls and door—all of this with little, if any, response from the staff other than threatening continued isolation until the child calmed down.

Beginning with one room in each house unit, within six months a room in each public area was converted into a place for isolation. At this point, one of the top administrators, who one and one-half years earlier talked about the *lack* of a seclusion room as being "progressive" was heard describing to a group of visitors the "foresight" of the programmers and designers in providing a seclusion room for every house.

The proliferation of seclusion rooms did not stop, even here. Eventually, one bedroom in each apartment was made into a seclusion room, that is, three per house area. Although the amount of aggressive behavior we observed in the hospital did not change at all, over all of the years of our study, the number of seclusion rooms increased tenfold. By the end of our research, given the average census, there was one seclusion room for every six children.

The seclusion room now became part of the treatment plan, moved from its *ad hoc* placement in an empty office to a new space now specially designed, from the point of view of the administration, to take care of children's needs in that situation (see Figure 4.6). That is, as opposed to bare walls against which the children could injure themselves, and a tile floor that was cold and hard, a room was created that had carpeted walls and floor, a built-in mattress, and windows (albeit screened) so that they could see out during their containment. The ceiling was lowered so that electrical wiring and ventilation units were beyond the reach of the children. All metal plates on the wall were covered. The door had a peephole and no door handle, only a lock. A small alcove in the wall was sealed off so there would be no unseen corners. The high level of "safety" precautions that had to be built into the rooms delayed their use for over a year. The delays and problems in achieving this level of safety focused on being able to devise a system such that the entire room could be seen through the window in the door. When this was accomplished a second problem arose when they found that the children were able to rip off, and indeed did rip off, the metal edging of the carpet.

A great deal of time, effort and planning went into the creation of these spaces. The administration saw this focus on *"safe" seclusion* as the progressive move—as opposed to their earlier view that it was the *absence of any seclusion room* that reflected their progressive institution. We could not help but view the new "quiet" rooms as yet another, albeit modern, version of the "padded cell." Yet being in this padded cell, as painful as the experience was, represented one of the few instances in this institution when a child could be alone.

The experience of being spatially confined as a form of coercion and punishment is not a phenomenon unique to psychiatric institutions. Many parents "ground" their children, restricting them to their home and within that to their rooms as a form of punishment. Yet if parents outside of an institution locked their child into a room we would consider them to be abusive. And there would

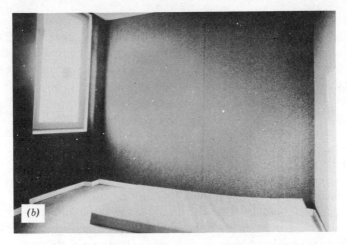

Figure 4.6.   Bedroom converted to "safe" seclusion room

be no doubt about this designation if they had constructed a room specifically designed for this purpose.

The powerlessness of being a child in relation to adults which often limits children's abilities to leave this type of home situation, or even to share with others the event itself, is magnified when one considers children within an institution. They have already been defined as less than "normal" in their judgment and therefore their ability to challenge such arbitrary actions is lessened by the probability that they will not be believed. If they do challenge such action the system that defines them and orchestrates their daily life has the power to define such challenges as an indication of the problems that led to their incarceration in the first place. It is also possible that after enough years in such an institution they themselves would stop questioning these actions because they would have internalized the system that defines them and gives others power over them. The process of "re-socialization" in such a setting needs to be carefully examined.

The Institutional Environment as a Mechanism of Socialization

Underlying the placement of children in a setting outside the community was the assumption, as well as the expectation, that they would be returned to the community from which they came *after* they had learned to behave "appropriately." Thus the children were assumed to have been inadequately socialized and their experiences within the institutional environment were to be part of a resocialization process.

While the average length of stay in this setting was approximately 15 months, one-third of the children remained for over two and one-half years and some as long as six years. Some children entering as young as nine years of age did not leave until they were 13 or 14, having spent more than one-third to one-half of their lives in this setting. Young people admitted at 13 or older usually stayed until they reached the age limit (16 or 18, depending on what the institution defined as the age limit at a specific time).

Since many children remained here for several years, we would argue that this hospital (and others like it) was a primary agent of socialization. What then were children taught about who they were and what was expected of them from the society in which they lived? What was the role of the physical environment as part of this process?

What we have described up to this point can be seen as part of a socialization process. Children were taught that proper behavior was being with others. The notion of others and the notion of aloneness were two absolute extremes, the one involving the presence of many persons, the other total isolation. In fact, children were taught that the primary function of physical aloneness was to deal with emotional upset, with someone else determining when that was occurring, that being locked in a room devoid of stimulation, both physical and social, was the way to control the upset, and judgment of recovery also had to be made by others.

Healthy young people, the children were taught, are low-keyed, well-controlled, and self-disciplined. The spontaneous expression of emotion had to be controlled because it would inevitably lead to aggression. What the children were not taught was how to predict what would be perceived by those in authority as an acceptable level of emotional expression and what would be seen as uncontrollable emotional upset. Furthermore, the children learned that they could not be trusted to monitor their own behavior. Surveillance was necessary "for their own good." Adults could intrude on them at any time, under any circumstance, even in the privacy of the toilet or shower.

Age and sex segregation of housing gave the message that same-sex agemates were the most appropriate companions except in sexual behavior (and such activity was taboo and pathological). One should be sexually and physically modest yet not question the group-programmed nature of showering and toileting activities as well as the unlimited access by professional staff to bathrooms and bedrooms. Boys and girls were to behave differently: if you were a girl you were to be passive and accommodating, without withdrawing; if you were a boy you were to be active and confident without being "out of control." What the children did not learn was how to do this or why behavior that did not fit sex stereotypes was unacceptable.

The model for daily life was based on following a strict routine with every activity given a definite time slot and a definite place for its performance. Life was planned by others, and the children's role was to follow that plan by being at the appropriate place at the appropriate time. Their role did not include the planning of activities or any deviation from the schedule such as sleeping late, staying up late, or choosing not to participate. Children were being taught that there had to be a reason for everything that a person does. All activities had to be either therapeutic or functional. One did not play; one had recreational therapy. One did not draw; one had occupational therapy. Eating was not a social activity but purely a matter of obtaining nourishment as swiftly as possible in a place designated for that purpose.

These children were being taught a way of life totally isolated from their communities and community values and, in many instances, in contradiction with them. Despite some variation in ethnicity, race, and class within the staff, the overwhelming way of life that was being taught was white, middle class, and with a mainstream ethic. This ranged from the food to the value of rigid time schedules to the notion that well-controlled emotion was healthy. The appropriateness of this newly learned way of life for the children's sense of self-identity and their reintegration into their communities was not questioned.

Often when we raise these issues with people who work within the psychiatric system they protest that we are unrealistic in our views. Apparently, we do not recognize the severity of the problems these children have or the volatile nature of their behavior. We should understand the importance of "re-socialization" as being in the best interests of the children. In our research we have, in fact, seen some behavior that could be considered "extreme" and which required skillful support. However, after many years in both adult's and children's psychiatric facilities, it is clear that to a large extent these behaviors are more of a response to the nature of the psychiatric environment than an indication of internal pathology. In the children's hospital the opportunity to work with a group of adolescents put into question the assumptions and rationalizations that are used to continue the existence of these types of settings.

The Red Room: An Attempt to Challenge the System

While documenting the development of the therapeutic, administrative, and physical use of the facility for the first few years of its existence we actively sought ways of providing feedback to the staff and of creating interventions that could potentially improve the quality of life for children there. Initially, information was given to the director and other upper-echelon staff who had been our first contacts. For example, when we had identified the pattern of increased locking of doors we met with the director to discuss the implications of this change. We also described the placing of children into seclusion rooms with no adult present. Subsequently, we attempted to intervene when a team of designers from a university-based program came up with a plan to place statues in the halls and graphics on the walls. We tried to persuade the team to involve the children and adolescents in the planning and execution of the project so that it would reflect their aesthetic and personal choices and make them active participants in changes to their own living environment. That attempt was thwarted, nor was there any interest in our offer to evaluate the changes.

During this time the building itself was undergoing a great deal of change. These changes were being dealt with on a piecemeal basis, and reflected the impact of momentary crises, the "political" allocation of space, and the lack of any systematic planning process which could reflect on the impact of specific changes as well as processes of change. We felt that the implementation of systematic "space and space-use planning" would be a vehicle for raising consciousness about a broad range of institutional issues. We attempted to organize a permanent "space-planning" committee. Clearly, this did not rate as a high-priority issue. Staff insisted that the existing "room-assignment" group played this role although the arbitrary nature of many of their decisions raised serious questions about their procedures. It was clear that people did not want to risk upsetting the prevailing power structure.

We had always viewed the nature of our work as having the goal of implementation yet it was clear that despite the fact that we were well-known by most staff and that we were available to cooperate in space planning we were denied any role in decision-making that involved the issues on which we had information. Our project was used more to legitimate the commitment of the facility to research and its role as a teaching institution than as a means to reflect on and change policies within the hospital. It was apparent that the only way that we might influence changes was to enter the system more fully. We arranged for one of our staff members* to work full-time, going to the hospital on a daily basis. She attended unit meetings in each of the house areas and meetings for all levels and types of staff. She maintained daily contacts with unit heads, psychologists, on-line direct-care staff, teachers, recreational and occupational therapists. In short, she focused on understanding the staff and the staff dynamics, gathering information about institutional changes that could serve as a basis for interventions on our part. She became a visible, non-threatening presence that represented our project, continually suggesting ways that we could be helpful.

The first results of this were a series of workshops with staff of all levels, in which we presented the findings from our work. We raised issues that we thought they might want to consider as part of policy decision-making and day-to-day functioning. The small amount of time given to the workshops (they were a minor part of a long series of in-service training sessions) limited their impact and provided no vehicle for following through on ideas that were generated.

Finally, during our fourth year we found out that the proliferation of seclusion rooms was soon to encompass the children's apartments. Plans called for the conversion of one single bedroom in each of the apartments (three per house) into a custom-designed isolation unit. This meant that the existing seclusion

---

* Dr. Arza Churchman served in this capacity.

room, which had been created through the conversion of an office, would now be vacated.

With the daily participation of our staff person we had gained knowledge of these plans prior to decision-making about the disposition of the vacated space. We previously had conducted two studies in which we interviewed both staff (at all levels) and children about issues connected to privacy and the expectations and need for doors on bedrooms. The studies served to raise consciousness about these issues and bring to the surface contradictions and conflicts staff had about the lack of space and opportunity for children's privacy. The lead time in knowing about the plans allowed us to generate a proposal for the use of the vacated spaces which built upon the findings of the research and the newly raised consciousness about the setting.

We proposed to obtain funding to renovate these rooms to provide some type of private and/or intimate spaces that children could use. The need for this type of space and experience had been clearly articulated by the children.

This renovation could have been done in a number of ways. We could have had one of the architects on our research team or an architect from the State Department of Mental Hygiene design rooms following our specifications. We could have suggested workshops with the staff alone, so that the final products would represent their view of the children's needs. As in past changes, the hospital maintenance department could have undertaken this work with the research team simply providing funds. However, we had a particular point of view regarding change. We wanted to undertake a planning and design process with the children and involve them in all phases of redesign including the actual construction work. The process we eventually utilized was a compromise between what we believed should be done and the reality of the limits placed by the administration.

We proposed the total process of planning and construction be done by the children with our team acting as facilitators. We believed that the children were capable of participating in the decision making and actual work. It was through interviews with them that the need for such a space had been articulated. We felt confident that this collaborative work project would demonstrate to the staff that their view of the children as being limited in competence would have to be revised.

We were not anxious for staff participation in the process since we felt that their presence in the planning groups would inhibit the free expression of the children's ideas. We also were concerned that staff might use their power to force their ideas on the children. We felt that the participation of the children would give them a sense of their own competence in an environment that did not offer this support. We did not want to limit the physical changes to the addition of traditional furniture nor did we want to prevent that. Our goal was to open up the range of alternatives and help the children make their own decisions. We hoped that the physical presence of space designed by children for themselves would, in an environment created by and symbolizing the values of others, continue to be a reminder of another possibility.

The final process did not totally match our ideal vision. We were limited to working with the adolescent group. The staff and administration would not permit them to be involved in any of the construction citing union and safety issues. They required that some staff participate citing their institutional responsibility for the children which they could not abdicate to us. We were not allowed new construction and in the use of furniture were limited to a state-approved supplier, even though fire and safety specifications could have been met elsewhere.

The final project involved the renovation of two of the vacated rooms, one on each of the adolescent units (girls' and boys'). We formed a planning group for each unit composed of four adolescents, one staff person, and one of our staff people. The adolescents involved were selected by the staff, although we considered them to be representative of the range of adolescents on the units. We met several times with each group in the living room of one of their apartment units.

During the first session we explained what the project involved, making it clear that this was to be their room and they would be able to design it as they chose within certain spatial, financial, and institutional constraints. We suggested the range of things that might be altered or newly acquired without specifying what had to be done. For instance, we told them they could paint walls, paper walls, panel walls, or leave them as they were; they could carpet the floor or leave it alone; they could put in various types of furniture and decorations. We emphasized the need to plan with spatial issues in mind, such as the size and amount of furniture selected in relation to the size of the space. We also made it clear that they were limited to selecting furniture from a state-approved supplier and that we could not do any construction but were limited to interior decoration changes.

With this as the context, the first part of the discussion focused on what images they had of the room, what they would like it to be, and what functions they saw it serving. What emerged from these discussions was the desire for a "comfortable" room where they could go whenever they wanted and either be by themselves or with another person. During these discussions, in which the adolescents participated quite reasonably and with ease, they raised the whole issue of how they were going to decide who used the room, how long they could use it, and what they would use it for. These concerns were raised by the adolescents and were not precipitated by staff pressure. They realized that they needed a set of rules and we agreed that they could be the ones to set those rules. While the rules were somewhat different for each unit, each group developed a set of rules that attempted to strike a balance between individual and group needs, reflecting reasonable criteria for making decisions and a desire to make the room a special place. Concretely what this meant was the decision that when the room was empty anyone could use it and they could continue using it for as long as they liked (or as was possible given hospital programming). If someone else wanted to be there, and the person who was inside had been there for thirty minutes, the second person would be entitled to access. In both units the adolescents decided that in order to keep maintenance to a minimum food would not be allowed in the room.

During the subsequent workshops the participants looked through different furniture and floor-covering catalogues, talked about what to do with the walls and used a floor plan of the room with templates representing furniture of different sizes and shapes to get some idea of what would fit into the room. They selected the covering for the furniture as well as its color.

The discussion during planning and the decisions that were made revealed the adolescents' awareness of the deprivations of the institutional environment and ways they could make up for some of its inadequacies. It also displayed the discrepancy between staff and adolescents' sense of aesthetics and definitions of space, the administration's efforts to control the process, and the fears that remained among the staff about the potential difficulty such a space would create.

Both planning groups, working independently, selected soft, lounge-like furniture that was completely upholstered with no visible metal or wood. It was in direct contrast with hard, framed furniture elsewhere in the hospital. The color was also contrasted with what existed in the space. Each group chose a bright red fabric; the furniture in the hospital was generally pale tones of blue and green, whether fabric or plastic. One discussion focused on the care of the fabric with staff suggesting that furniture be covered with plastic. The adolescents were opposed to this and the solution was to make removable covers of treated fabric that was stain resistant, and to immediately purchase a second set. While each group selected seating of slightly different design they each included a low, occasional table, originally intended to hold a lamp. The lamp was the next issue. The administration refused to allow any small-scale, movable lighting. When we suggested that lamps could be permanently attached to the tables, they still refused for fear that light bulbs could be used as weapons. We suggested replacing the florescent overhead lighting with incandescent lighting and that was also vetoed. In order to create somewhat of the atmosphere the adolescents desired we eventually suggested that the use of a filter covering the overhead lighting would soften its effect, an idea that appealed to the adolescents.

In both groups, the carpet selected was also red. In going through the samples the adolescents commented on the desire for "thickness" and chose a deep pile as opposed to a flat tweed. The staff tried to convince the children that a red carpet would quickly get soiled and that a tweed would be "more practical." In this instance, as in others, we found ourselves advocating for the adolescents and being able to help them get their ideas adopted. This was not because they were unable to clearly articulate their ideas but because their ideas were not always taken seriously by the staff. The position of another adult had to be taken seriously.

The issue of what to do with the walls served as a catalyst for the intervention of the administration into the design process. In the course of discussion with the administration about who would do the painting, if required, we were "offered" both paint and wall paneling. The wall paneling did not present a problem since the adolescents could decide whether or not they wanted it, and which of the three colors available they preferred. The paint was another matter. We had intended to allow the adolescents to select their paint from a wide range of colors available on the general market. The safety codes presented no problem. However, the hospital insisted that they had paint available and that it should be used. Unfortunately, the colors were the usual institutional pastels. From among the available colors, each group selected "cherry pink" whose intensity was in name only. One group argued very strongly for red walls but the administration would not yield. The group liked the idea of wall paneling and both decided to put it on one wall opposite the door (see Figure 4.7).

The door could have become the major stumbling block in creating a place that children wanted to serve their need for privacy. Despite staff acknowledgement that this was the main purpose of the room, their fear of children's behavior led them to insist that the door have a glass panel so that they could check out what was happening inside. The apparent contradiction between purpose and design did not seem to register. Again, here we became advocates for the adolescents' point of view and when they failed we attempted to find a solution that would address the staff's concerns without negating the purpose of the space. The eventual solution was an extremely narrow glass window, about 2 inches wide and 18 inches long. The glass panel was so narrow that staff could not use it as an ordinary surveillance device. In order to really see what was happening they would have had to obviously peer through the window as they stood right next to it. We relied on social conformity as an inhibitor to behavior that had the quality of "snooping." The staff, as in other instances we have confronted, accepted this solution which provided them with at least the symbol of surveillance.

It was apparent, to us, from what the children selected that this new room was to be a dramatic contrast to the surrounding space. Indeed, later on when we interviewed the adolescents, they described the room in exactly this way. But during the planning process one discussion made it profoundly clear that the quality of an institutional environment as represented in its physical characteristics carries symbolic meaning that is consciously understood. At one point during the discussion of what could go on the walls, a staff person suggested the possibility of "painting a mural on the wall." There was a loud shout of

Figure 4.7.   "Quiet room" converted to Red Room

disapproval—No!—as one young man proclaimed, "No *hospital art* " (see Figure 4.8 and Figure 4.2). Another added, "You wouldn't put that on your walls at home."

In the end, the rooms they created would not qualify for interior design awards and were modest by virtue of limits on the budget, the new construction, and range of furniture (see Figure 4.7). Yet both the staff and the residents of the units liked the rooms very much. During the physical process of change the children were continually checking on the progress. They talked to the workers and when the furniture arrived several of the children helped carry it in and put it in place. Once the room was completed the adolescents insisted that we take a picture of them in the "new room."

After waiting several months after the time the room was completed we conducted a series of observations of its use as well as interviews with children, adolescents, and staff about their attitudes toward it and their use of it. By the time we returned to interview people, the room had acquired its own identity and was referred to as "the red room," a name that has persisted over the years. When we spoke to staff and adolescents, some of whom had not been in the hospital during the planning or design phase, both groups liked the room very much. When two people needed a space for visiting, talking, or even occasionally for a therapeutic meeting, they chose the red room, and both staff and adolescents felt it served this purpose very well.

The staff made a clear distinction between the users of the red room and the adolescents placed into the seclusion room. They felt that the red room was a place for children "in-control," a place where a child could choose to talk over problems and issues. In contrast, they said that the seclusion room was a place for children "out-of-control," to be used as a calming device without the adolescent's choice. Their view of the room was still within the therapeutic mode. The adolescents saw the room as a good place to get away from the staff and used it in that way, often being in there alone. While some used it more often than others, we did not find any way of distinguishing the frequent, infrequent, and non-users in a way that was comparable to staff views. Both the staff and the adolescents liked the decor and felt it to be the only "homelike" space in the hospital. Even those who did not use it often liked it and liked the fact that it was on the unit. Earlier staff fears that the room would be physically damaged, if not destroyed, did not materialize. In fact, the staff acknowledged that there was excellent maintenance of the rooms by the adolescents with no signs of damage—in marked contrast with the remainder of the hospital. The rules that

Figure 4.8.   Hospital art

the adolescents had set up for use of the room were respected and there was no evidence of conflict over use of the space. A sign-in sheet system was developed which gave the adolescents the control of room use and we saw no instances in which the staff interfered with that system.

Our experience with the adolescents throughout the planning and design process, as well as our observations and discussions with them and the staff subsequently, reinforced our original views. The adolescents were perfectly capable, despite their labeled pathology and staff misgivings, of being part of this process, with no apparent difficulties. They appreciated and were aware of the barrenness of the existing institutional space and were capable of articulating an alternative. They also showed that when they were part of the decision-making processes they would take responsibility organizing its maintenance and use.

The red rooms remained in use for several years after they were created. We did not follow this process closely, although on our occasional visits they continued to be well-maintained and used and we often heard comments from the staff that they were such special places. We can't say what effect they had on the staff's view of the adolescents or in changing the staff attitudes toward the competencies of newer residents.

Despite our success in implementing this process and in helping to create these spaces, the eventual disposition of these spaces underscores the priorities of an institutional system and reminds us that the physical environment is only one aspect of that system. An evaluation, as part of the accreditation process, criticized the hospital for failure to have adequate record space on each unit as opposed to the centralized system that was in use. In order to comply with these regulations, the red rooms on each unit were totally dismantled and the space became an extension of the nursing station, to be used for record-keeping purposes. On a recent visit the Director of Nursing assured us that it was the administration's intention to re-create these rooms because they had been so successful. They had not been restored during the two years since compliance with the regulation. We believe they are unlikely to be restored given the administration's attitude that current residents are so much more "disturbed" than the adolescents with whom we had worked.

IN THE BEST INTERESTS OF CHILDREN

This children's psychiatric facility is the outgrowth of a long history of attempts within this country to provide places and ways of dealing with children perceived to be deviant. After many years of working in this and other children's psychiatric institutions it is questionable to us whether this is a solution to the problem.

Since World War II, there are more and more children entering institutions despite the rhetoric of deinstitutionalization. These children are overwhelmingly poor and United States minority children who are reached through a net that extends broader and broader and has more and more minimal requirements for inclusion. The modern veneer of the building and the good intentions of the staff as compared to the image of a snake pit and its attendants provides a superficial message that we have progressed. Yet the dominant values that are inherent in the system and, indeed, the very fact that it is a system, emphasize and provoke deviance as opposed to eliminating it. The institution itself, through the imposition of order, its mechanisms of social control, drugs, punishment, and isolation, is more akin to its predecessors than most would admit. The concept that the goal of the institution is to socialize children to return to their communities is contradicted in several ways. First, children remain institutionalized for many years before their final release, occurring mainly when they reach maximum age. What they are being socialized to is also questionable. Second, as our work has shown, the institution and its sociophysical environment support the very behavior for which children were supposedly hospitalized in the first place. The whole concept of what is "appropriate" behavior is problematic but clearly it is not fostered by this institutionalization experience. Finally, the whole question of "appropriate to the community" seems to be defined by mainstream American values and would not serve to reintegrate children into their actual diverse communities.

This system, and the adults who implement its principles, has an incredible amount of control over the daily and yearly lives of these children. That power is virtually absolute and unquestioned. The definition of the children as "deviant" invalidates their views as legitimate, realistic perceptions of what is happening in their daily lives. Yet in the face of such power the children attempt to exert some influence over their lives, to find some way to get what they need, and to be who they are or want to be. Often these attempts expose them to even greater difficulties and more labeling and invalidation. Few of their experiences provide concrete proof of their competence, more often they emphasize the children's incompetence.

The physical environment, as part of that system, supports its values materially and symbolically and is used to enforce its powers. The use of space as a mechanism of control and, in particular, using it to isolate children, is one example. Historically, this type of space has had many different names—padded cell, isolation room, seclusion room, quiet room, and now—time-out room. However, despite these changes of name their functions and their message is the same. They are places of punishment for children who are told that they are so out of control that contact with other human beings is neither possible nor desirable.

It is conventional to review such a study and to suggest the implications such work has for improving the system. It is our conviction that any piecemeal attempts at improvements to a system that is basically questionable at its roots is like putting a band-aid on a gaping wound. The definition of these children as "deviant," the view that such deviance is internally sustained and of psycho-dynamic origin, has created a system dependent on the continuation of the deviance. Whether consciously intended or not, these attitudes make it literally impossible for anything else to happen. Since children spend such a large portion of their childhood here, few were able to see beyond the labels attached to themselves and to maintain a sense of themselves as valuable human beings. But our hope lies with children like Marie, who, when asked how this place should be changed said:

> There would be no certain times you had to come in, no certain time you had to go to bed, no strict rules. It would be run with some strictness to it but not that much because I don't think it's right for them to say what time you've got to be in, what time you've got to be out, like your trainers or something, where you have to do what they say. People have their own minds, one person may think one way and another person thinks another way. You have to have your own mind and do what you want to.

REFERENCES

Goffman, E. (1961). *Asylums*. Garden City, NY: Doubleday.

Golan, M.B. (1978). *Children in institutional settings: Privacy, social interaction, and self-esteem*. Doctoral dissertation, City University of New York.

CHAPTER 5

Settings for Childhood Learning:
A Historical Perspective

The institution we have just described is what some have called a total institution (Goffman, 1961). However, the distinction between partial and total institutions is not entirely clear. Most often it is based on the amount of time children spend in them and the degree of control the institution has over the children's lives. Children confined in total institutions for any part of their lives, whether in residential psychiatric facilities, centers for the developmentally disabled, or community group homes, are almost totally cut off from their homes and communities. Every aspect of their daily lives is controlled by others and influenced by the assumptions underlying the facilities' existence, what Goffman (1961) has called the "overall, rational plan." Children in these settings have little possibility of seeing alternative ways of living and have little power to make changes of any kind.

However, most children spend large portions of their days for many years in settings that share certain common features with those we have described. These places are partial institutions, and schools are usually placed in this category. Yet children do not freely choose to spend their time in such places and their parents have little choice either. Schooling is compulsory and in most school systems parents have minimal influence, if any, on the policy or daily program. If children do not follow the rules for acceptable behavior, they can be suspended or expelled, referred for testing or psychological treatment, or moved to special schools and even total institutions. If school authorities consider parents to be neglectful they will be subject to various forms of institutional control such as fines, imprisonment, or even having their children taken from them. While there are cases where parents are not providing a positive environment for a child and even situations in which children are physically, mentally, or sexually abused by their parents, very often the removal of the child from the home is not based on these kinds of incidents (Massachusetts Childbearing Rights Alliance, 1982).

As we have suggested, the institutions described in the previous chapters provide back-up sanctions for the ones we will be describing in this chapter and the next—the schools. We will see that schools—their policies, programs, and physical forms—have been shaped by the political, social, and economic contexts in which they developed. Labeling the school as a partial institution obscures the less obvious power that it has had over the lives of children and their families. We will see that schools, both historically and today, share the qualities that are associated with total institutions. Why this is so and how it has happened can be best understood by looking at the history of schools in the United States.

Schools existed in the United States prior to the nineteenth century, but they played a minor role in childrearing and socialization. Children were taught in homes and communities but only the things considered appropriate to their race, class status, sex, and family work lives. Education beyond the family for white children of the "common classes" consisted mainly of apprenticeships. In some instances, instead of private tutors, children of the upper classes attended Dame Schools—a group of children taught basic reading, writing, and computational skills by a literate woman in the informal atmosphere of her kitchen. There were some charity schools for poor children stressing military discipline and drill. The accepted view was that white children of different classes and sexes would attend different types of institutions (Bowles and Gintes, 1976). Yet, at a maximum, only 10% of white children attended a school and usually for only limited parts of the day and during certain times of the year. The majority of Black children were slaves and, as such, legally were not allowed to gain any literacy skills, although it is clear that they managed to do so even under the threat of death (Davis, 1971). Children of household slaves were sometimes part of play schools arranged for the young white children of their owners. Others, mostly freed Blacks, received education in schools for Blacks, an outgrowth of the missionary activity of various churches, including the Quakers, schools which developed from 1765 to 1785 (Bullock, 1967). However, most often any literacy training Blacks received was done secretly and illegally.

Following the American Revolution and the War of 1812 there was a surge of nationalism and reform. The creation of a new country meant the emergence of diverse social and religious groups. The beginning of rapid industrialization also brought urbanization. "In 1790 there was not one American city with more than 50,000 people. By 1830, almost half a million lived in cities of that size" (Nasaw, 1979, p. 12). People no longer able to earn their livelihoods on farms relocated to urban areas, becoming poorly paid wage laborers. During this time different movements for schooling began with a view toward educating the poor white child. Merchant and financial elites, with the assistance of church authorities, moved to expand charity schools in the large Northeastern cities which were absorbing most of the rural migrants. Three different types of schools developed, all modeled after their English counterparts.

The most popular and widespread educational method supported during the early part of the nineteenth century were the Lancasterian schools (Spring, 1972). These schools were seen as beneficial because they maintained order and compelled the poor children, for whom they were designed, to internalize respect for authority

(Nasaw, 1979) and to accept subordination (Spring, 1972). The system used older students as unpaid monitors and a scientific arrangement of the classroom to make schooling efficient and inexpensive. Engravings of an early Lancasterian school showed a large room, divided into 12 sections, holding a total of 450 students (Spring, 1972). In fact, it was claimed that one teacher could be used for as many as 1,000 pupils. Schoolrooms were arranged in hierarchical fashion, the teacher seated on a raised platform above the students and monitors. Monitors marched along the rows of students carrying the teacher's instructions and maintaining order. Students were punished for all types of offenses including talking, playing, inattention, moving after the bell rang, having dirty faces and hands, coming to school late, not coming to school, and even for making noise in the streets when leaving schools. Every day, in every lesson, students advanced or moved back depending on how well they performed (Nasaw, 1979).

Sunday schools were a second attempt to socialize the children of the poor to respect authority. Volunteers taught whatever they could in one day, with a heavy emphasis on manners, morals, and Protestant religion, although they were not affiliated with a specific church or denomination.

The third type of school, the Infant school, taken from the British model, had as its goal reaching poor children at an early age, removing them from their parents for as much time as possible so they would not learn from bad examples. These schools were our first day-care centers, with children ranging in age from 18 months to six years. Through activities performed in unison, including marching in procession, they were taught that being obedient and well-mannered were signs of good moral character.

By 1830 these three types of schools were established throughout the Northeast. Yet they did not achieve their goals. The urban poor avoided them whenever possible. Most did not want charity and recognized that their lack of money was not their fault. They also knew that there was no guarantee of better jobs for their children, even after such schooling. Charity school organizers attempted to increase attendance by altering their image. They changed their names to "Public Schools" and invited lower middle-class families to send their children there for a nominal fee. These attempts failed, for the most part; families kept their children in private or church schools. Some of these schools had public money for support yet public, non-sectarian, tax-supported schooling was not the clear direction in the early years of the nineteenth century (Katz, 1971).

COMMON SCHOOLS

The first major turning point in the U.S. educational system is considered to be the Common School reform, lasting from 1830 until the end of the nineteenth century. Wishy (1968) believes that the spread of common school education after 1830 started a full-scale American debate about educational theory that has continued with enormous vigor down to today. (p. 67)

Central themes in this debate have been and still are: the role of religious versus secular values; the role of heredity versus environment; the need for global versus specialized education and its relationship to social class, race, and sex; the child as a passive recipient or an active learner; obedience to authority versus self-actualization; and the school's role in maintaining the status quo or supporting social change. Underneath these debates have been the issues of who will control the education of children and toward what end. Wishy's characterization of the Common School era has been true of other eras as well. Whether by force of ideology or due to the political and social conflicts among diverse groups, "too much seemed at stake in American society for anyone to ignore the power of education" (Wishy, 1968, p. 68).

During the latter part of the development of the charity schools, and as settlement moved westward, many local communities, towns, and small cities were creating their own small schools, the one-room schoolhouses. Some were religious, some private, and some public, although they charged tuition for attendance. A group of reformers based in the Northeast argued for free, universal education. They, too, claimed to be interested in educating the poor and adhered to Protestant morality and the Puritan work ethic, believing that the poor were themselves to blame for their inability to deal with the changing economy and, therefore, for their poverty. Yet, they differed from the charity school supporters in their stated belief in upward mobility. Indeed, in some ways they began the "Great School Legend" which Greer (1976) describes, the idea that schooling was the road to economic prosperity. Horace Mann, one of the main proponents of the Common School movement, claimed that wage laborers could become independent entrepreneurs through hard work, just as he had done.

In addition, the extension of the vote to all white men, regardless of property or social standing, meant, to reformers, that those who had the vote had to be educated to use it properly. Thus, while proclaiming that the Common Schools they sought would be free of political teaching and church affiliation, the content of their curriculum was highly political and religious. It supported the values of republican citizenship, patriotism, and Protestantism. Their models were the New England Common Schools open to all within the community, albeit a community which, while differing in class, was otherwise homogeneous. Reformers felt that children from the poorer classes with "weak minds and morals" could learn through contact with the wealthy, while the children of the rich would learn to appreciate their advantages and responsibilities. All would learn their positions within the society and how to work together for the common good.

Forming a net of reformers across the country they supported school taxation, the training of appropriate teachers (preferably "gentlemen"), and the creation of new school facilities, maintaining that existing ones lacked comfort and were unhealthy. In fact, Barnard, another major common-school reformer, conducted a survey of school buildings in order to substantiate his case. Barnard found that school buildings were often little more than shacks, reflecting the least possible expense in design, construction, location, and upkeep. The buildings frequently were located next to dirt roads and dust filled the air inside the building. The few windows were small, without shading, and in winter and hot summer days this lack of ventilation was oppressive to those crowded inside. Heat was usually provided by a stove that had to compete with cold air rushing in through cracks in the siding and under the doors. Teaching equipment, such as it was, slates and maps, and even clocks, chairs, and desks were rarely provided. Many buildings lacked a water supply and toilet facilities. Barnard observed, in summarizing the state of schoolhouses:

> . . . after an extensive and careful examination of the state of a great number of school-houses in this and other states, we are constrained to believe that in regard to accommodation, the convicts in the State Prisons, except those condemned to solitary and perpetual confinement, and we are not certain that in all cases these should be excepted, are better provided for than the dear children of New England. (McClintock and McClintock, 1970, p. 53).

Reformers had some limited impact during the early decades of the nineteenth century. For instance, Illinois passed the first law for publicly supported schools open to all white students ages 5 to 21 (Daniel, 1980). In trying to increase their impact, reformers allied themselves with manufacturers and received their support by maintaining that common schooling would produce a docile workforce trained to the needs of mass production including punctuality, personal cleanliness, good social habits, and loyalty to their jobs. With the election of Jackson in 1829 and his expressed support for the "common" man, others joined the movement. In addition, the influx of Irish immigrants into Massachusetts, particularly to Boston, added some support because of arguments that the city was being taken over by immigrants, in this case especially suspect because they were Catholic (Butts & Cremin, 1953). Yet, even after Jackson's election, the main issue remained school taxation. Local communities were opposed largely because it would shift control of their schools to the state. Taxation laws went through periods of passage and repeal and in the end those passed were not enforced. Instead, most communities retained control of their own schools though state-levied property taxes provided some of the financing. The addition of state-levied property taxes sharply reduced the number of private schools since moderate-income families could not afford both the new taxes and local tuition (Butts & Cremin, 1953; Nasaw, 1976).

There was a period of a few years during which workers supported the Common School movement (1828–1831), but with reservations. They made their own demands for less discipline, better teachers, and less rote learning (Nasaw, 1976). Yet, eventually they abandoned it while continuing their own community education projects including libraries and reading rooms (Butts & Cremin, 1953). The Irish, especially, refused to send their children to these schools on religious grounds (Bowles & Gintes, 1977; Butts & Cremin, 1953; Nasaw, 1979). Reformers' response to their unwillingness was first to use their political connections to gain the passage of laws removing public funding from religious schools. While this affected Catholic schools, it also adversely affected other privately run Protestant schools and added to their decline. Finally, in the face of continued resistance of the Irish who demanded that, at a minimum, the Protestant content be eliminated, Massachusetts became the first state in 1852, to pass compulsory schooling legislation. Its intention was to use state authority to force Catholics to send their children to the Common Schools. The bill was passed on the basis that:

> The parent is not the absolute owner of the child. The child is a member of the community, has certain rights, and is bound to perform certain duties, and so far as these relate to the public, Government has the same right of control over the child that it has over the parents. . . . Those children should be brought within the jurisdiction of the Public Schools, from whom, through their vagrant habits, our property is most in danger, and who, of all other, most need the protecting of the State. (Boston School Committee, 1853, as cited in Nasaw, 1979, p. 77, emphasis ours)

The Houses of Refuge, being developed during this time, provided a backup sanction for compliance with the compulsory education law. The largest proportion of inmates at this time were "foreign born." Most were Irish and entered as truants (Nasaw, 1979; Rothman, 1971; Shultz, 1973).

The Common School movement laid the groundwork for future public school education in several ways. It articulated the ideology of the school and state as guardians of children, rather than the family and community. In the smaller school districts the one room schoolhouse remained the norm:

> Because of the great diversity within each group, the teacher would have to deal with each student separately. Therefore, the early district schoolroom was most often a picture of a teacher seated at a central desk, with one child after another approaching, reciting from text or memory, being rewarded with a smile or a blow depending on the effectiveness of the recitation and returning to his seat. (Butts & Cremin, 1953, p. 275)

But in the cities the Lancasterian model gained wider acceptance since it could handle the rapidly increasing school population with efficiency and low cost (Butts & Cremin, 1953). School attendance by white children increased dramatically during this period, from 38% in 1840 to 69% in 1860 (Katz, 1971). In the urban areas graded classrooms began to appear. They were proposed by Horace Mann on the basis of his observations of Prussian schools. Apparently, his idea could be implemented since different school buildings were being constructed to house older and younger children. This led to the use of one larger school building to house different age groups of children being taught in separate classrooms. It was also during this period that women teachers became the norm (Butts & Cremin, 1953). While ideologically the arguments could be made on the basis of Jackson's philosophy, that any qualified person should be able to fill a job, it was, without doubt, economically best for local districts. The teacher's salary was the highest item in the budget and women earned far less money than men for the same job. By the beginning of the Civil War, the American elementary school teacher was a woman.

By 1860 the Common School had a near monopoly on elementary education (Butts & Cremin, 1953; Katz, 1971). Yet its reality did not match its ideology of free, universal education. Attendance was limited by race and religion and Common Schools were not accepted in all parts of the country, particularly in the South. With slavery as the basis for the economic and social structure, wealthy white Southerners used private tutors, military academies, and their own colleges. The teaching of Blacks was prohibited by law in most states and some schools, which had been allowed to exist earlier, were closed by force. This move has been considered an attempt on the part of Southern leaders to prevent the spread of anti-slavery literature which they felt was responsible for a number of slave rebellions (Bullock, 1967).

But the South was not alone in its attitudes toward Blacks. In the West and North, most states also opposed allowing Blacks into their Common Schools. In 1847, for example, the Illinois legislature agreed that Black parents should get their tax money returned because their children could not use the public schools (Daniel, 1980). In the same year in Massachusetts, the state in which the major battle for Common Schools had been fought, the Massachusetts Supreme Court ruled that separate schools for Black and white children were acceptable provided that they were equal, thus denying the appeal of a Black man whose five-year-old daughter had been refused admission to a white public school in Boston (Butts & Cremin, 1953). Though Massachusetts abolished separate schools only six years later, this case was used as precedent for the U.S. Supreme Court decision in 1896 making "separate but equal" a nationally accepted policy, one that lasted until the mid-twentieth century.

Native American children also were excluded from Common Schools. They were placed in boarding schools, a form of total institutionalization, because it was deemed necessary to isolate them from their unChristian surroundings in order that they be trained appropriately.

PROGRESSIVE ERA

The period after the Civil War up to 1930 is considered by most educational historians to be the second major turning point in U.S. educational history. While identified as the "Progressive Era" by many, there remain critical questions as to whom the benefits accrued.

The urban population swelled as the United States was industrialized. The use of machinery in agriculture meant that many small farmers could not survive economically against large-scale competition. With their families they moved to cities and became wage laborers (Nasaw, 1979). In the South, there were 4 million freed Blacks, many of whom moved in and around cities looking for work (Butts & Cremin, 1953). In 1900, 50% of them still lived in the South but with the establishment of "Jim Crow" laws in the South the move to Northern cities began as well. Toward the latter part of the century, there was massive immigration of Southern and Eastern European immigrants, some lured to the United States by advertisements of well-paying jobs, others leaving Europe to escape political repression. They went to work in the factories as low paid, unskilled laborers and by 1910 had become an essential component of the American workforce. Included in this group were large numbers of women working in the mills of New England and the garment industry of New York. The urban population rose from 9.9 million in 1870 to 20 million in 1900, while the total population of the country went from 30 million in 1860 to 100 million in 1920, with 50% of the people living in urban areas (Butts & Cremin, 1953; Dropkin & Tobier, 1976).

Large corporations blossomed from the 1880s onward supported by congressional aid which included protective tariffs, credit laws, and laws allowing the importation of indentured labor from Europe (Butts & Cremin, 1953). This so-called industrial boom, however, did not mean that all Americans profited. During this time several severe economic depressions hit the country. Without changing the conditions of work or the low wages, many large corporations developed company towns in an attempt to keep workers quiet and to prevent the development of independent labor unions (Callahan, 1962; Spring, 1972). Yet unions gained strength. There were frequent and extensive strikes through the early decades of the twentieth century.

With the tacit agreement of two presidents, the government sought to maintain the status of Blacks in the South. Legislatures of Southern states enacted Black Codes, including laws which specified the types of jobs Blacks were allowed to have, forced them to work or be subject to arrest for vagrancy, limited their rights to own land, prohibited interracial marriages, made the rape of a white female by a Black male punishable by death, prohibited the free assembly of Blacks, and required permits for travel from one state to another (Bullock, 1967;

Butts, & Cremin, 1953). Black children without "apparent support" could be apprenticed out, with preference given to their former master, remaining until they reached the age of maturity (Bullock, 1967). The Congressional response included the Civil Rights Act of 1866, the 14th Amendment, the Reconstruction Act of 1867, and the 15th Amendment. For a time there were some reforms of the tax system, political democracy, relief, and education. But much of this was eventually sabotaged by business interest in an area where developing industry needed to utilize low-paid wage labor (Butts & Cremin, 1953). The federal government had no support from former Southern ruling groups. The Ku Klux Klan and the Knights of the White Camelia developed. Lynching became widespread and the anti-lynching movement developed in response (Apteker, 1982). Yet the Supreme Court rulings of "states' rights" beginning in 1873 and the withdrawal of the federal government from the South in 1877 restored the power of white supremacists (Butts & Cremin, 1953). With the "Jim Crow" laws found to be constitutional the "New South" was firmly rooted in racial segregation (Thompson, 1966). Conditions of Blacks and their treatment by government was not much better in other parts of the country. From the end of the nineteenth century through the early decades of the twentieth century, Blacks were attacked by whites in race riots in many cities (Marx, 1970).

The women's suffrage movement had also developed during this time, as well as the movement for contraception and abortion. Over these decades many women were arrested for their activities. In 1919, women finally won the right to vote, but contraception and abortion remained illegal and voting was still a middle-class and upper middle-class activity (Zinn, 1980). Socialist parties had also begun to appear after the Civil War and by the 1920 election they polled over 1 million votes (Butts & Cremin, 1953). But the entry of the United States into World War I in 1917 served to consolidate the hold of conservative political elements.

Zinn (1984) contends that there was some truth to the idea of the prosperity of the 1920s. Wages went up and consumerism flourished as new gadgets were introduced. Yet many unskilled jobs were being eliminated in the factories with the introduction of the new technology, and membership in unions dropped through the decade. While $2,000 was considered a sufficient basic necessity income in 1929 over 60% of American families were earning below this level (Zinn, 1984; Allen, 1952).

There was a resurgence of patriotism and nativism (Levine & Levine, 1970). In 1917 the passing of a literacy test in some language was required of all newcomers and a few years later virtually all immigration from Southern and Eastern Europe was stopped (Butts & Cremin, 1953; Zinn, 1984). The Ku Klux Klan was revived in the 1920s and had 4.5 million members by 1924. The Scopes trial was a victory for Fundamentalists, and it succeeded in keeping the theories of evolution out of the classroom (Butts & Cremin, 1953).

During the period from 1865 to 1900 the public school system consolidated, and Michael Katz (1971) asserts that by 1880 the modern school system, much as we know it now, was the norm in the urban Northeast:

> American education had acquired its fundamental structural characteristics, they have not altered since. Public education was universal, tax supported, free, compulsory, bureaucratically arranged, class-based and racist. (p. 106)

It was sexist as well. Women were not counted in statistics nor were they educated (Hein, 1975).

Compulsory attendance was one of the major issues of this period. Initially, it was advocated as a way of making immigrants fit for their role in society. Gradually education became a child's right and was linked to child labor reform. Compulsory education was called the "best child labor law" (Takanishi, 1978). It would keep children out of factories and off the streets and prepare them for their future occupations. By 1900, 32 states had compulsory schooling and in 1918 Mississippi became the last state to enact this type of law. Yet in 1920, 1 million children of school age were still working and an enforceable child labor law was not passed until 1938. The juvenile justice system was used to back up compulsory attendance. Thus the right to an education was actualized through the reform of compulsory school attendance (Takanishi, 1978). Parents were held responsible for their children's failure to attend school while employers were under no legal obligation to refrain from hiring children.

In the South, the question of compulsory attendance was also central after the Civil War and was combined with the issues of taxation and integrated schools. Without a prior history of publicly supported schooling for whites, the possibility of a system that would include Blacks had even less support among the white population. A series of Freedman's Schools had started in 1861, after the Emancipation Proclamation, funded and organized mainly through Northern-based churches, although Blacks themselves had contributed financially as well. By 1865 there were 875 schools, and about 60% of Black children aged 5 through 12 were enrolled, although most were concentrated in the cities of a few states. This system had a New England style, was graded, and stressed acculturation as well as literacy. With the creation of the Bureau of Refugees, Freedmen, and Abandoned Lands in 1865, Congress focused on education as the freedman's hope for success (Bullock, 1967). Yet under the Black Codes many of these schools were closed and those remaining open were controlled by whites. Blacks would be threatened with losing their jobs or housing if their children attended school (Bullock, 1967). During Radical Reconstruction, Black representatives to constitutional conventions introduced provisions for publicly supported schools, open to all. Most states created a publicly supported system but remained silent on the question of compulsory attendance and racial policy. The systems often were built on the structure of the Freedman's Schools and attendance of both Black and white children began to increase. However, the opposition of white Southerners was expressed in unpaid taxes and by keeping white children out of the schools. With the withdrawal of the North, the return to "States' Rights," and the replacement of slavery by racial segregation, Black citizens had no control over educational policies. They could not vote for school boards nor could they serve on them. With the *Plessy* v. *Ferguson* ruling of 1896, there was national legal justification for "separate but equal" schools. Two years later, the Conference on Southern Education accepted racial segregation as the basic fact of the Southern system. Without legal power but with incredible influence, this group of Northern and Southern educators, acceptable to the white leaders of the South, shaped the Southern public school system. By sacrificing the principle of racial equality they hoped to convince white Southerners to accept the notion of "Negro education" (Bullock, 1967). With the energy and political and economic connections of their earlier Northern common-school counterparts, they pushed for public acceptance of segregated, compulsory, publicly supported schooling on the grounds that it would preserve Southern tradition and benefit whites by insuring that Blacks would learn their place in the "New South" (Bullock, 1967; Butts & Cremin, 1953; Thompson, 1966).

The inability of Southern Blacks to control the school system that was to educate their children had a parallel in the other sections of the country—the centralization of the public school system. Based on the view that immigrants were ignorant, reformers argued that "schooling had become far too important a social institution to be left in the hands of parents and neighborhood residents, rural or urban" (Nasaw, 1979, p. 111). Arguing that local school boards were not handling issues of overcrowding and sanitation responsibly, between 1897 and 1905 reformers managed to influence 20 states to authorize consolidation. Local school boards, representative of their constituencies, had previously made all decisions about curriculum, maintenance, building, and hiring. They were replaced by boards voted on a city-wide basis through laws passed in state legislatures which had already been gerrymandered to bypass immigrant representation. By the second decade of the twentieth century almost every city had been centralized, and by 1916 most school committee members in cities were from the business and professional classes (Bowles & Gintes, 1976; Callahan, 1962; Greer, 1976; Nasaw, 1979; Spring, 1972).

Issues of overcrowding and unhealthy conditions were used, not only to gain control over school administration but also to build new schools and introduce new structures for school organization. It was between 1865 and 1920 that many of today's schools were constructed, and by 1918 education had become "big business, with a plant valued at two billion dollars" (Butts & Cremin, 1953, p. 405). Specifications were developed for both urban and rural schools. The majority were "large boxes enclosed by red brick walls and covered by a steep slanted roof. The large boxes were subdivided into smaller, uniform cubicles called classrooms" (Castaldi, 1968, p. 120).

The main focus was on sanitation, safety, comfort, light, heating, and ventilation. Indeed, with the large number of children who were now attending schools and the limited money previously invested in the system, the basic physical conditions of many schools were horrible. In hearings in 1917 before the Committee on General Welfare of the New York City Board of Aldermen (1974) it was revealed, for example, that there were 200 kindergarten classes with 50 pupils and nearly 300 with over 50. In the elementary grades there were over 1,000 classes with more than 50 pupils and many thousands with 40 or more. A large number of schools were on double shifts with children attending only part-time. One school, not unlike many others, had 3,786 pupils and only 1,699 seats. Many children had to carry their coats around for lack of storage space and toilet facilities were incredibly inadequate and antiquated. In some schools there was what amounted to 4 square feet of space per child. Parents complained that schools were built next to railroads and elevated subway lines with resulting noise that made it impossible for children to hear teachers or each other. Yet it was also clear that the physical conditions and siting of school buildings, the equipment that was available as well as the overcrowding were not uniform across all schools. Those in wealthier districts did not have the same problems as those in poorer ones (New York Board of Aldermen, 1974; Greer, 1976).

In the South, the public school system expanded more slowly, with even more of an imbalance between facilities and programs for Black and white children. By 1892 the concept of "special education" was a definite ideology. Blacks would be trained for their "appropriate" places in agricultural, mechanical, and household industries and such education would be "character building" (Bullock, 1967). There were arguments for and against such a view within the Black and white communities but by the early 1900s the ideal of "special education" was in place (Bullock, 1967). The Conference on Southern Education continued this philosophy.

The Conference surveyed the state of the Southern public school system. They found that buildings were small, classes were held in churches, lodge halls, and abandoned huts. There were leaking roofs, huge holes in the walls, few seats, little furniture, and no closets. If rural children went to school at all, they had to walk miles to reach one. And as late as 1910, there was not one single eighth grade rural public school for Black children (Bullock, 1967). Funneled through the Conference, a large amount of money for school improvement came from Northern industrialists such as Rockefeller, Peabody, and Slater (Bullock, 1967; Butts & Cremin, 1953). The Rosenwald Fund, in particular, heavily supported the building of schools for rural Black children, through a system in which their partial funding was contingent on Black parents donating money as well as labor, and showing a commitment to the education of their children. With the help of the fund, which lasted from 1913 to 1932, 5,367 public schools, shops, and teachers' homes as well as industrial high schools resulted (Bullock, 1967).

However, the dispersion of money was left in the hands of the Conference and, through them, in the hands of Southern whites. The money was distributed unevenly with more going to the white schools with the explanation that it cost less to maintain a school for Blacks. Only 9.6% of the building budget, in 1915, was spent on Black schools (Bullock, 1967). It was not only in building that the disparity was clear. The school term for Black children was 27 days shorter than for whites. Since many Blacks were farm tenants, owners pressured them to have their children work and arranged for them to be excused from school.

By 1930 over 80 percent of Black children were enrolled in school. Although the literacy rate of the Blacks had increased 93.8 percent during the period from 1890 to 1930, many in elementary schools were students in the 15 to 20 age group and considered to be "overaged" for their class level. The Rosenwald Fund in 1933 explicitly stated its philosophy of education for Black children:

> . . . the kind of preparation children needed for rural living included the ability to read and write clearly; some skill in the use of figures; a knowledge of farming, including some general understanding of biological processes and appreciation of nature; manual dexterity, especially in the handling of wood, fabrics and other utensils as related to simple mechanics, and a grasp of the fundamentals of sanitation and health. (Bullock, 1967, p. 142)

The training of urban children was in industrial arts. According to Bullock (1967),

> By the third decade of the 20th century, a complete financial structure for educating Negroes along special lines had been laid . . . and the South's fears that these changes would lead to social equality between the races had been reduced by placing supervision of the work ultimately in the hands of white school officials. (p. 127)

The influence of industrialists and industrial needs was felt in the rest of the country as well. In both the building and operation of schools there was a focus on management and efficiency, similar to that in the factory. In 1907 Bagley's *Classroom Management* was published. It was reprinted 30 times between 1907 and 1927 (Spring, 1972). In it he claimed, for example, that "the expert observer could immediately gauge the efficiency of the teacher by the manner in which lines pass to and from the room" (Spring, 1972, p. 46). An argument was made for more efficient school plant utilization and one proposal was a 12-month school year. According to Callahan (1962) this idea was not accepted due to opposition by parents and groups such as the National Child Labor Committee. They felt that efficiency was not a sound basis for an educational system. From their view children needed leisure time and, if utilizing the school building more fully was the goal, it could be used for after-school and summer recreational programs. However, efficiency did become the focus and affected elementary schools in many ways. Various accounting and record-keeping systems were developed, including estimates of efficiency based on the cost per pupil of teaching different subjects. Eventually, this led to cost efficiency measured in terms of dropout rates, with teacher and schools judged more efficient if they had fewer students leaving school (Callahan, 1962). But it was in the "Gary Plan" that efficiency was uppermost, and it was initially tied to the concept of enriched or "progressive education."

"Progressive education" emerged especially through the ideas of John Dewey (1966), who was active in the reform movement. For "progressive educators," the child was a individual whose enthusiasm for knowledge should be excited rather than deadened with the "old system of lockstep procedure and memorization" (Dropkin & Tobier, 1976, p. 175). Learning was to be child-centered rather than subject-centered with children viewed as active learners who needed access to materials so that they could direct their own learning. The school was seen as a community and a microcosm of the larger society. It would reflect the diversity of the larger society, its art, history, and science and would foster cooperation between children of different backgrounds. In 1919, progressive educators formed an association, lecturing and becoming involved in public schooling. However, although several private elementary progressive schools opened, they mainly served the upper middle-class white community. Progressive education was never applied in its original form to the public elementary school. Instead, certain aspects of Deweyan philosophy, such as the need for hands-on learning, the usefulness of manual training, and the idea of social cooperation were applied as they served other interests. The cooptation of these ideas can be attributed to progressive educators' lack of control over the dissemination of their ideas. However, others argue that they carry much of the responsibility because of their pragmatism (Spring, 1972) and their desire to see their ideas implemented in any form. By the 1930s the Progressive Education Association had become academic and took few stands on the issues of inequality, segregation, testing, or tracking (Perrone, 1976).

The connection of progressive education to efficiency and economy produced the Gary Plan. It was introduced by Wirt, a student of Dewey's who had become the administrator of the schools of Gary, Indiana, a company-town (Callahan, 1972). The Gary Plan called for enriching the regular academic program by adding nature study, art, music, and industrial education. It also provided an organizational plan which was economical and efficient.

This would be done through a departmentalized system in which the students moved from room to room. The plan was arranged so that all of the rooms, either home rooms or special rooms were in constant use. For example, while one group was in home room receiving instruction in reading, writing and arithmetic, another group was in the music room, another in the shop, another on the playground, etc. When the bell rang, the students would shift to the next class. (Callahan, 1962, p. 129)

School administrators adopted this idea, especially after 1915 with the national focus on efficiency and productivity. It advocated both economy and enriched education and provided an answer to the overcrowding and the shortage of classrooms.

There were many arguments for and against the plan and it became a major issue in the mayoral election in New York City in 1917. Public hearings were held to discuss its implementation (New York City Board of Aldermen, 1974). Arguments in favor generally focused on the alleviation of overcrowding. One principal who was against the plan emphasized that the classroom was not a factory and should not be considered as such. He felt that when rooms were used successively by many teachers individualization would be impossible. He also opposed forcing children to carry their books with them throughout the day.

Callahan (1972) credits an article by Bobbit in 1912, titled "The Elimination of Waste in Education" with being central to the eventual acceptance of the Gary Plan. He, and others after him, made the economic aspects primary, including the need for fewer teachers. Bobbit also highlighted the ability of the plan to enable each child's program to be fitted to individual abilities. He pointed to the availability of manual training, or industrial education, as especially positive for students with the "motor type of mind" (Spring, 1972), who could concentrate on industrial subjects and do a minimum of academic work. Through the Gary Plan economy and efficiency became tied to differentiated schooling and, especially to industrial education. At the 1917 hearings on the Gary Plan in New York City (New York City Board of Aldermen, 1974) the representative of the Gary League put it this way:

I have heard a lot about vocational training, but gentlemen, in the Gary system it is pre-prevocational. It is taking a child . . . and giving it different tools to work with, so that the little soul finds itself, and we don't find a boy that God intended to be a first-class plumber being a mighty poor lawyer. (p. 28)

The idea of industrial education and differentiated schooling had been around since the turn of the century. In the mid to late nineteenth century, businessmen had established some trade and manual training high schools, convinced that classical education was not appropriate for the new era. They believed in teaching practical skills: sewing and cooking for girls, and carpentry, metal, and machine work for boys. Initially, this had little impact. Educators opposed them, some fearing loss of jobs; others because they believed in classical education, and some who only supported these subjects as an addition to the curriculum of classical education. Organized labor was against it; their apprenticeship system would be circumvented and a supply of cheap labor would be created. As white-collar work grew at the turn of the century, the high school grew with it (Nasaw, 1979).

With the backing of such groups as the National Association of Manufacturers, arguments were made for three different types of schooling. Immigrants and Blacks would leave after elementary school. Middle-class whites would receive traditional training, boys for college and girls to make appropriate mates. The industrial high school was earmarked for working-class white American boys and girls. These girls, who had to work, would train for the "respectable" jobs such as dressmaking, which also would make it unnecessary for them to deal with immigrant men in the factories. Domestic science would prepare them for their roles in the home. White working-class males would be educated for the supervisory and skilled jobs in the factory. In 1903, although teachers were still opposed, the National Education Association started to call for differentiated schooling, arguing that schooling should match the jobs available, and that students should be prepared for their different futures. In 1914 and 1917 the first major federal aid to education other than land grants, passed Congress as the Smith-Lever and Smith-Hughes Acts provided funding for vocational education.

Vocational high schools never were accepted totally. Comprehensive high schools became the compromise—academic and vocational training under one roof. Students were tracked into their appropriate race, sex, and class roles anyway (Nasaw, 1979; Spring, 1972). But the concept of industrial education and differentiated schooling were implanted, via shops, and through the Gary Plan into the elementary schools, as well as through the development of junior high schools (Spring, 1972).

In spite of protests, the Gary Plan spread rapidly after 1918. Research was done supporting its ideology. For example, Cox (1921) documented that 33 student hours of time were "wasted" each day in a school of 500 pupils due to the inefficiency in movement patterns during transition times. He suggested that design should decrease transition time to a minimum. Separate boys' and girls' entrances were also created to "preserve order" (Nasaw, 1979). By 1929 over 3,000 schools operated under the plan in 202 cities and 41 states (Callahan, 1962), having been adopted by centralized school boards which by that time, as described earlier, were composed of people representing business interests.

This plan and others were rationalized and supported by the development of intelligence testing. As early as 1912, a study conducted for the U.S. immigration service by Professor Harry Goddard, found that 83% of Jews, 80% of Hungarians, 79% of Italians, and 87% of Russians were feebleminded, based on "culture-free" tests (Bowles & Gintes, 1976). Initially, these results were used in the movement to restrict immigration. But professionals, like the psychologist Terman, advocated their use in the school system to determine the best education suited to a particular child (Bowles & Gintes, 1976) and to determine the careers that were most suitable for each child. Thorndike and Judd developed diverse techniques to measure every subject including spelling, handwriting, arithmetic, and composition. This work had such influence that by 1918 "the scientific movement permeated every aspect of education" (Butts & Cremin, 1953, p. 439). The Rockefeller and Carnegie foundations supported research on the possible educational uses of these tests. The idea was implemented by school administrators and high-level policy makers. Over 4,000 articles on testing were published between 1921 and 1936. In 1936 a survey of 150 school systems found three-quarters tracking students through the use of intelligence tests (Bowles & Gintes, 1976).

The supposed objectivity and scientific rigor of these tests, based on genetics, Darwinian theory, and the sophisticated statistical work of Pearson, Terman, and Thorndike hid the relationship between social background and a child's position in school (Bowles & Gintes, 1976; Greer, 1976). While I.Q. tests had been standardized to produce equal results for boys and girls, researchers such as Thorndike provided equally "scientific" justification for their separate tracking. He concluded that because boys were naturally competitive and aggressive and girls were naturally nurturing, they should not share the same curriculum but should be encouraged in different directions (Bowles & Gintes, 1976; Nasaw, 1979). By 1930 testing had become an institutionalized part of the public-school system. The Rockefeller Foundation funded the formation of the Cooperative Testing service, the forerunner of the numerous testing services still in use today. Testing began in elementary school so that children could be assigned to their appropriate tracks later on in high school, if they continued their education.

Spring (1972) contends that differentiated schooling and industrial education served to deal with only one aspect of corporate need: teaching specific people to move into their proper societal position. Phrases such as "individualized instruction" were used to describe it as a positive goal. The second aspect of corporate need was a person who cooperated well and could work in groups. Following Croley's (1909) ideas that heterogeneity was a fact of American life and, therefore, required a form of education that would unify people by stressing overriding national goals, the individualism of the nineteenth century was redefined to stress cooperation and self-sacrifice to society. This was to be achieved, through two types of social activities—an emphasis on group work in the classroom and the introduction of extracurricular school activities. Children had to be taught how to get along with others and to be shown the social value of what they learned through group activity. Methods were developed to replace overt control with social control (Ross, 1922).

Again, John Dewey's ideas were used. He had stressed the development of a sense of community as a goal of education, as a way to give meaning to life in a society that was becoming more and more alienating. However, his idea of how to achieve this goal was very different from its eventual implementation. It was Scott's redefinition of Dewey's ideas that prevailed (Spring, 1972). Dewey saw social cooperation as the end result of a specific process of education. Scott saw it as a means to an end. The end was training the child for the world of work after school. He stressed the idea that children who only were interested in learning were peculiar "bookworms." He devised methods which demanded that the child be cooperative and get along with others. Spring describes one of them in which every six weeks each child's contribution to the group was evaluated by his peers in their presence (Spring, 1972). It was this concept of social cooperation that was used in the public schools.

Another method of ensuring social cooperation was to extend the role of the school in the life of the child and the community. As discussed earlier (see Chapter 2), the perceived need to Americanize immigrants as a way of preserving the social order gave rise to the movement to save the immigrant child from the evils of the urban environment. One solution was creating parks and playgrounds. By demonstrating the relationship between juvenile delinquency and the lack of playgrounds, laws were passed in New York City that required school buildings to be built with an adjacent open-air playground or a nearby existing one to be part of the school program (Spring, 1972). These were used for after-school and summer programs. Eventually clubs and recreation centers were established in the buildings as well. Thus "the schools rapidly extended their control over the social life of students" (Spring, 1972, p. 23).

It followed quite logically that schools could serve as a social center that would reach parents and youth no longer in school. Again, John Dewey was the source of this idea, describing the social center as a "social clearing house of ideas that would interpret to the urban industrial worker the meaning of his place in the modern world" (Spring, 1972, p. 78). By 1920, 667 school districts throughout the country had social centers in their schools, providing recreational activities as well as classes in the evening (Spring, 1972). The idea of the school as a social center had an impact on school design and, therefore, on children's experience during the school day as well. One early suggestion incorporated into school design during this period was placing assembly rooms on the ground floor with easy access from the street. This was seen as a way to reduce accidents, provide for fire safety, and also to make it easier for adults who might have difficulty climbing stairs. Since the school was to have multiple uses for adults as well as children demands were made to redesign the desks, replacing those bolted to the floor with "flat-top desks that could be rearranged and utilized for club and recreational activities" (Spring, 1972). Some schools were specifically designed to function as social centers with the expectation that adult classes, community meetings, and various other services would be provided there.

The idea of the school as social center serving the needs and reflecting the desires of the neighborhood could not be implemented according to Dewey's original conception. Control of the schools was no longer in the hands of local communities since the school boards had become centralized. Program planning was also out of community control because of the professionalization of staffs.

> Since the school community lacked direct channels of influence on the schools, the social centers never became an expression of neighborhood life but functioned rather to impose a concept of organization on the community. (Spring, 1972, p. 90)

Social centers supported the concept of the school as an agent of social control.

This particular period in the history of education had great significance in creating much of the present-day school system—structurally, physically, administratively, programmatically, and conceptually. One of its major impacts is what Greer (1976) has called "the great school legend." The legend has it that through this system immigrants rapidly and efficiently assimilated into American society, achieved social mobility, and climbed up the economic ladder. Since it is believed to have done this so well, the legend has become the basis for criticizing contemporary schools, claiming that if present-day poor urban children cannot do well in school, it must be their fault.

Yet, using a wide range of statistical information about the actual functioning of urban schools during that time period as well as the present, Greer demonstrates that, in fact, the economic mobility of immigrant groups varied depending on the countries from which they came and their economic role within that country. Those groups ranking high in economic security or whose European experiences suited them for urban life showed the greatest amount of economic mobility, and it was their children who ranked highest among immigrants on school achievement tests. These included farm-holding Scandinavians, Greeks, shop-keeping Eastern European Jews, and later, in San Francisco, the Japanese. Contrary to the legend, their economic mobility preceded their educational school success. And even though some segment of these immigrant groups had children who succeeded in school, many did not.

The second part of the school legend deals with success in teaching. Perrone (1976) cites evidence disputing this belief. Based on studies of urban school systems all over the United States, Greer (1976) found that:

> In virtually every study undertaken since that made of the Chicago schools in 1898, more children have failed in school than have succeeded, both in absolute and relative numbers. (p. 108)

It is true that children stayed in school longer, and more students entered school, but these statistics owe more to compulsory education legislation, the back-up of the juvenile justice system, and the lack of jobs than to school success.

High failure rates were found in the majority of the school systems (Spring, 1972). Compulsory attendance and the desire to avoid dropouts only pushed failure into the upper grades. A study of Chicago schools between 1924 and 1931 showed that 61.4% in elementary school were performing below grade level, as were 41% of those entering ninth grade and 32% in the tenth grade. Explanations for the problem included "feeblemindedness," overcrowding, poor sanitary conditions, and financial problems. Efficiency was judged by attendance instead of academic success and school failure, especially after World War I, was consistently tied to racial and ethnic differences rather than the goals or programs of the schools.

By 1900, de facto segregation, tied to housing, was already in place. As more Blacks migrated to cities after World War I, the unskilled job market had all but disappeared. While poverty was the rule for most ethnic immigrants as well as for Blacks, the racism existing in employment and in housing meant, for example, that Blacks were replaced by immigrants in many jobs and used as a relief labor force to be called in during strikes.

According to Greer, the period from 1900 to 1914 was crucial in defining the future of the urban Blacks and the role of the schools. They were treated separately from immigrants and their problems were not seen as emanating from city life. School policy made it clear that Blacks would not gain economic mobility through education. Black children were, as in the South, categorized as needing special education and their inability to rise up the economic ladder was seen as their own fault. Although there were "studies" showing them to be mentally deficient, they were not even placed in any of the special schools set up for this purpose. By 1911 it was the deprivation of the Black family that was to blame for the situation. Despite the low number of Black children in the city, special studies were done about their school achievement. While all immigrants were shown to be doing poorly, Blacks were singled out.

> . . . poor children generally performed badly, both black and white . . . but when a Negro child performed badly, his being Negro was explanation enough. (Greer, 1976, p. 140)

In truth, however, the major difference between Blacks and whites who dropped out of school was that there were more jobs for whites, and this helped sustain the legend.

> The schools failed the white poor but no one noticed. The white poor found jobs, which did for them what the schools claimed they would do, move them upward, slowly, as a result of their own efforts. (Greer, 1976, p. 141)

By 1921, the problems of the Black children were researched and discussed within the context of "special groups" which included "the lame, the blind, the orphan and the illegitimate." No matter how similar the resulting description of the problems of Black children and poor immigrant children, Black children continued to be singled out.

In Greer's view it is the special categorization of Black children's failure which showed the limited role of the school in shaping the social upward mobility of any group. Literacy tests led to restricted immigration rather than public school improvement programs.

> While concern for the failure of public education for millions of the foreign born had culminated in immigration restriction legislation, little was done to modify the partnership which persisted between lower-class status, school failure, crime and delinquency. (1976, p. 145)

THE DEPRESSION

The 1920s were years of extravagant and conspicuous consumption for those who could afford it—now a sign of social status in a society which was beginning to cast off an earlier Puritanism. Then, in 1929, the Depression hit. Personal financial security, seemingly gained through hard work, was revealed to be based on conditions beyond individual control; it could be eliminated almost instantly.

Initially, the severity and potential longevity of the Depression were not acknowledged at the national level. Yet, as 5,000 banks failed and many businesses and factories closed, massive unemployment accelerated. Official unemployment figures showed 8.7% unemployed in 1930, 15.9% in 1931, and 23.6% in 1932 (Nasaw, 1979). In the South, one-quarter of Black families were on public assistance (Bullock, 1967). Black migration to the cities accelerated. By 1930, one-half the population of the United States was living in urban areas (Nasaw, 1979).

As the Depression took hold, 26 states had laws prohibiting the employment of married women. The majority of the nation's public schools, 43% of public utilities, and 13% of department stores enforced a restriction on the hiring of wives. Nevertheless, the Depression brought an increase in such employment. Most of these working wives were from immigrant and Black families; usually their income, however small, was desperately needed. In many cases, because women were offered low-status jobs and paid even less than men, the wives of unemployed men were able to find work, and so became the family's sole bread winners (Ryan, 1975).

In 1932, Roosevelt was elected president. His "New Deal," a mixture of concessions to business and to the populace, was intended to stabilize the economy and quell the brewing rebellion. While it did not achieve these goals, it did solidify the government's role in running the economy.

Unfortunately government economic policies had limited impact; in 1933, from one-quarter to one-third of the labor force remained unemployed (Zinn, 1984). The years from 1932 to 1935 were marked by rising worker unrest and attempts to develop labor and farm parties; in 1934 alone over 1.5 million workers struck.

A variety of militant poor people's movements now developed. Some staged sit-ins at welfare offices to demand housing, food, and jobs (Piven & Cloward, 1979), and Unemployed Councils fought off evictions. In 1935, with 83% of the population earning less than $2,000 per year, rioting erupted. In Washington, D.C. more than 20,000 World War I veterans and their families came from all over the country, demonstrated, and then camped across from the Capitol, demanding payment of their bonus certificates (Zinn, 1984; Manchester, 1973).

The Social Security Act of 1935 attempted to deal with some of the issues sparking this militancy. It provided retirement benefits, unemployment insurance, and aid to mothers and dependent children, although no health insurance. In 1938, a minimum-wage law established the 40-hour week and outlawed child labor, but the minimum wage set was low. Most poor people, especially Blacks and Mexican-Americans discriminated against because of racism in other jobs, were not helped by this legislation because it excluded tenant farmers, farm laborers, migrant workers, and domestic workers.

During the Depression years there was a brief shift in stated government policy with respect to Native American Indians. The outcome was the Indian Reorganization Act of 1934, which claimed as its goals a change in land-use management and tribal relations, giving Native Americans more control over their own affairs, and civil and cultural freedom (New, 1969, excerpted in Bremner, 1974).

The Depression and the Schools

Schools were already overcrowded, underfunded, and in poor physical condition, and thus teachers and students were among the first victims of the Depression (Bremner, 1974). Yet in a crisis of massive unemployment and the shrinkage of jobs for unskilled labor, it was even *more* important for children to remain in school (Bremner, 1974; Greer, 1976). Few had other alternatives. Indeed, it was in the context of the Depression, rather than that of the Progressive Era's "child-saving" movement, that a child labor law was finally passed in 1938. As a result of these factors, schools became even more overcrowded and the school population generally poorer, than was the case when children had dropped out to take jobs.

A report in *Literary Digest* (Parrish, 1933, reprinted in Bremner, 1974) revealed that 80,000 school teachers were unemployed across the country and hundreds of thousands were receiving no money. The states in the South and Midwest were hardest hit. School terms had been cut in half; construction and repair were at a standstill; 2,269 schools in 11 states had closed and more were ready to do so. Parts of school programs had been eliminated including night schools, Americanization programs, schools for the disabled, health activities, music, art, home economics, manual training, and physical education. With enrollment going up, 250,000 children were going part-time and thousands were being taught in portable shacks. The lack of school building also affected the building industry.

It was clear that something had to be done, yet the issue of federal aid to education was hotly debated in Congress. Two issues were paramount: first, whether aid should be given to parochial as well as to public schools, and second, whether the federal or the local government would control the money and its allocation. The first question was ignored in the education bills. The second was answered in a way which left the racially segregated school system of the Southern states essentially intact. In these states, the amount spent for schools attended by Blacks remained far below what the proportion of Black children in the population would have indicated. And the curriculum in such schools continued to focus on literacy programs, vocational education, and homemaking—"special education" (Bremner, 1974).

The aid to education took several forms. Work Progress Administration projects focused on literacy and vocational training largely for older youths. There was federal aid to rural schools through grants for salaries, but no money for supervisory or administrative work. Other funds for school building were given through non-federal WPA grants dispersed through state and local governments. This building program soon produced new schools which were strikingly similar nationwide, since their physical appearance was dictated by common requirements for heating, lighting, toilet facilities, eating facilities, and square footage per student. The classical styles that had been common as a building form gradually disappeared, replaced by a plain two-to-three story cube with rectangles cut out for windows (American School Buildings, 1949).

In contrast to the situation with Blacks, policy toward Native American Indian children during this period seemed very progressive in intent. The Indian Reorganization Act of 1937 led to the training and recruitment of Native American teachers and the introduction of bilingual programs. Between 1933 and 1943, 16 boarding schools closed and 84 day schools opened. In 1933, 75% of Indian children were in boarding schools but by 1943, 66% were in day schools (New, 1969, reprinted in Bremner, 1974).

In the North, however, the influx of Black children into the schools made underlying racism more apparent. As Black children entered the schools, the inability of the school to make a difference in the academic performance of these overwhelmingly poor children became a "social problem." Since the problem could be localized in particular neighborhoods, it was attributed to the population, rather than to educational practice, teachers, or administration. The schools were now supposed to make up for the problems of "family life." And these problems became more and more defined in racial terms (Greer, 1976).

In 1935, Harlem, the main Black area of New York City, erupted with massive rioting. The mayor's office appointed a commission, headed by Franklin Frazier, to study its causes and make recommendations. Frazier made desegregation the major issue and the school the focus of change. He felt that the exclusion of Blacks "from opportunity in society at large was now well established in the schools" (Greer, 1976, p. 147) and believed that something had to be done there quickly, including the inclusion of Black professionals in the system to prevent recurrent rioting. Frazier's study, which remained "on a shelf" for a year (Stern, 1937, reprinted in Bremner, 1974), also found that only two new schools had been built in Harlem from May 1925 to May 1935 and only nine since 1900. The borough of Queens, largely middle-class and white, had 78 new buildings in the same time period. "The official excuse for what suspiciously looks like discrimination is the declining population of Manhattan" (Stern, 1937, reprinted in Bremner, 1974, p. 1684). In 1937, two new schools were finally approved. But a new housing project would also add 500 pupils to be served by a school which had been described as overcrowded in 1930.

Stern describes a typical Harlem school:

> . . . like a prison. . . . Even the most diligent scrubbing cannot really clean a building built in the '70's and '80's . . . benches too small . . . in rooms unadorned, bleak and dingy. Teachers trying to cope with classes whose numbers average slightly more than even those in other overcrowded sections. (Stern, 1937, reprinted in Bremner, 1974, p. 1684)

Stern also describes zoning restrictions that would not allow students into schools in white districts and the overt racist remarks of teachers.

While Frazier argued for desegregation, W. E. B. DuBois presented another view. In a paper titled "Does the Negro Need Separate Schools?" (1935, reprinted in Bremner, 1974), he stated that under the present state of affairs in public education, acknowledging the racism, anti-Semitism, and the disparity in conditions for the rich and poor, he believed Blacks should have separate schools over which they could have control. He made a distinction between forced segregation and chosen separation, arguing that "becoming white" should not be the goal. He wanted schools where Black children could be treated like human beings, trained by teachers of their own race, and informed about their own history so they could develop under supportive conditions their own sense of what they wanted to become.

But it was the campaign for desegregation that was taken up. The NAACP, beginning in 1936, pressed lawsuits based on the disparity between the salaries of Black and white teachers and also on the lack of professional education for Blacks (Bullock, 1967; Bremner, 1974; Butts & Cremin, 1953). Several of these cases were won; especially in the case of salaries, however, the states found ways to evade compliance, for example, through recertification.

Throughout this period academics, especially in "progressive" education circles, debated the content and structure of education (Bremner, 1974; Butts & Cremin, 1953). In the Depression context the social role of education and the teacher was increasingly questioned: should controversial social issues, such as the economic situation and racism, be raised in the classroom and, if so, how? Yet these debates remained largely academic. The day-to-day realities—overcrowded schools, poor conditions, minimal programs, and educational inequality for children of different races and backgrounds—continued.

WORLD WAR II AND ITS AFTERMATH: 1940 TO 1950

There is wide agreement that the defense preparations eventually begun in 1940 and the United States' entry into World War II finally ended the Depression and brought the prosperity that the New Deal policies had failed to achieve. The war took 12 million people out of the job market and created millions of jobs at higher wages for those who remained at home. Business boomed as the planned economy subsidized industry and controlled wages more than prices. As the demand for labor surged, women were encouraged to enter the paid workforce. The overall participation of women jumped from 25 to 36% of the adult female population (Ryan, 1975).

The availability of industrial jobs spurred Black migration to the northern cities, although the jobs available were still at the lowest pay. The armed forces remained segregated. Unions grew, continuing the Depression years' pattern. Citing national security, the government succeeded in outlawing various forms of labor protest and union leaders agreed to no-strike pledges and wage control. However, large numbers of strikes continued.

National security was the basis for passing the Smith Act (1940), giving the government the right to intern and prosecute anyone advocating the overthrow of the government or joining organizations taking this position or publishing literature espousing this view. National security was also justification for the forcible removal from their homes of 110,000 Japanese-Americans who were placed in internment camps for the duration of the war (Zinn, 1984).

The war's end brought more than the return of the soldiers. The use of the atom bomb at Hiroshima and Nagasaki ushered in the nuclear era and raised the specter of all-out nuclear war. There also was fear that returning soldiers seeking the jobs guaranteed under the Selective Service Act of 1940, together with the end of wartime production, could plunge the country into another depression. Several governmental strategies were designed to avert these possibilities. One was the G.I. Bill, which provided funds to support college and technical education for veterans and thus keep them out of the job market for several years (Nasaw, 1979). And, to deal with the continuing wave of strikes, the 1946 Employment

Act placed a 4% lid on unemployment. Jobs within the federal government itself were maintained at a high level.

However, as Blacks tried entering the post-war industrial job market in large numbers they found that unskilled jobs had all but disappeared and the focus was on skilled and technical work supposedly requiring an education they did not possess. This contributed to a Black unemployment rate 60% higher than that for whites (Piven & Cloward, 1979). Decent housing was unavailable. The density of ghettoized neighborhoods was suffocating, but racism did not enable people of color to move elsewhere. And these neighborhoods had to absorb the new waves of Spanish-speaking people, many from Puerto Rico, who came to the U.S. mainland in increasing numbers after the war. For example, the Spanish-speaking population of East Harlem in New York City grew to well over half a million people (Steward, 1972).

During this post-war period, women workers were urged to return home. Instead, due to economic necessity, their participation in the workforce increased. But they, too, were forced out of their jobs in wartime industries. Meanwhile, the few day-care centers provided to support women's war work were almost all closed by 1946. At the same time, the birth rate was increasing dramatically, reaching its 1920 level during 1946 and 1947, after almost 20 years of decline. And, while marriages were increasing, the divorce rate was also on the rise (Allen, 1952), creating more households maintained by women.

A new high-technology consumerism began taking hold as wartime industrial plants were retooled to produce electrical appliances and other consumer products. In 1946, the FCC authorized 400 television stations, and the first antennas went up on 8,000 rooftops (Wright, 1983). And the cold war, which began in 1946, played an even greater role in maintaining industrial production and profit. With a focus on Communism and the Soviet Union as the enemy, official policy shifted from isolationist to interventionist. New military pressures and financial-aid plans opened additional markets for goods and allowed access to sources of cheap raw materials (Nasaw, 1979). Defense spending and government contracts for new military weapons continued, rationalized by the growth of Communism.

In 1947, President Truman required the Justice Department to make lists of subversive organizations. Subsequently, the Soviet Union's blockade of Berlin, the 1949 Communist victory in China, and the 1949 explosion of an atom bomb by the Soviet Union were all used to urge national unity against the "world-communist conspiracy." By the beginning of the 1950s, the foundation had been laid for the "witch-hunts" which were to come (Zinn, 1984).

The Schools: 1940 to 1950

As in the broader political arena, during the war and accelerating afterward, there were the beginning signs in education of the issues that would predominate in the 1950s. The question of whether federal aid to education should be given to parochial as well as public schools had surfaced earlier, but never had been resolved. By 1946, the direction was clear: there would be state policy control combined with federal financing. In general, money was given to parochial schools for what were defined as non-religious functions — school lunches and transportation (Butts & Cremin, 1953).

Federal aid to education was also held back by legal arguments focusing on state control, which were actually intended to continue school segregation in the South. In 1948 the Southern bloc of the Democratic party resisted the Civil Rights part of their platform citing opposition to school desegregation. Then in 1949, a case was filed in Georgia against the "separate but equal" system in elementary schools. Slowly, pressure against segregation was beginning to mount.

Frazier's account of Black children's views of their schools in the border states (Frazier, 1940, excerpted in Bremner, 1974) had shown that Black youth knew that white children had better school conditions and better equipment, and often based their view of the inferiority of their education on these grounds:

(Are black schools as good as white schools?) Definitely no! And I can prove it. In most of the schools you can't get your mind on your work for watching out for falling ceilings. . . . We always get the buildings after the whites have torn them up or when they're about to fall to pieces. We get all the out-dated equipment and used stuff. We know the program is different. (Frazier, 1940, excerpted in Bremner, 1974, p. 1666)

Brameld's study (excerpted in Bremner, 1974), eventually to be cited in the 1954 school desegregation court case, *Brown* v. *Board of Education*, showed that in the South Black children had shorter school terms, less teachers per pupil, teachers who were paid less, and an educational program preparing them for jobs that were nonexistent. In the same year the President's Commission on Higher Education reflected on the inadequacies in elementary and secondary education that resulted in inequities, especially for Blacks, on the advanced level.

The problem was not only in the South. While academic educators urged the teaching of intergroup relations (Butts & Cremin, 1953), Brameld described the *de facto* segregation in the North where approximately one-fourth of Black children were attending segregated schools:

I visited an elementary school consisting of two buildings about 500 feet apart: in one building, all Negro children, Negro faculty, Negro principal. In the other building, white children, white faculty, white assistant principal. The children did not even play together on the same playground. (Brameld, 1949, excerpted in Bremner, 1974, p. 1698)

In the large Northern and Eastern cities a pattern had developed in which, while the majority of poor children continued to fail in school, these poor children were now mainly Blacks. In 1943, 90% of the children entering high school in New York scored below the norm on reading ability although all had been awarded an elementary school diploma. Yet as Blacks became the majority of the poor, the inability of the school to fulfill its post-World War II goal as the pathway to employment and upward mobility became evident. This was explained in terms of the students' race rather than their poverty. As desegregation was pushed, "equal educational opportunity" implied that since a school had worked for poor whites, it now should work for poor Blacks—if not, they, not the schools, were somehow to blame. By 1948 the first multifaceted remedial program was developed to cope with preventing and correcting problems such as delinquency.

The situation for Native American children also worsened through the 1940s. A 1942 study of the failure of vocational education for Native American children attributed this to the lack of available jobs, but by 1944 a U.S. Congressional Committee attributed school failure to poor attendance. The committee recommended assimilation as the main goal and compulsory attendance to support it (U.S. Congress, House of Representatives, 1944, excerpted in Bremner, 1974, p. 1718). In a complete reversal of policy, they reasserted that boarding schools off the reservation were better because the surroundings were "healthful and cultural."

The continuing discussion of the social role of the school began to intensify, especially toward the end of the 1940s, but a case early in the decade foreshadowed issues to come. In 1940 two school children refused to salute the flag because they were Jehovah's Witnesses. The Supreme Court upheld the school's right to require such behavior, affirming the right of the school to train children for their place in society even by means contrary to the parents' perspective. Teaching children to be loyal citizens was a legitimate goal and the school could decide the best way to do this (*Minersville School District* v. *Gobitis*, 1940, reprinted in Bremner, 1974). In 1944, however, this decision was overturned. A school had required children to participate in a stiff arm salute to the flag or face expulsion. Children who were expelled could not return until they complied. When they were absent it was considered unlawful and they could be treated legally as delinquents. Their parents or guardians could be subject to prosecution resulting in a fine and a 30-day jail sentence. The court ruled that such compulsion was not constitutional but reaffirmed and supported the good of the procedure (*West Virginia State Board of Education* v. *Barnette*, 1943, excerpted in Bremner, 1974). During the latter part of the decade, as children were trained with "take-cover" drills to prepare them for nuclear attacks, efforts to censor textbooks had begun.

1950–1960

In 1950, the Korean War began. That same year the Internal Security Act required the registration of organizations found to be Communist or associated with Communists and created detention centers for suspected subversives. As the defense spending and anti-Communism of the late 1940s continued into the 1950s, Senator Joseph McCarthy, chairman of the House Un-American Activities Committee, told more than 11 million television viewers that Communists were infiltrating everywhere. In this atmosphere of distrust and fear, many people lost jobs based on guilt by association and it became unsafe to voice a dissident political opinion or even to suggest reforms (Bremner, 1974). In 1954, McCarthy was censured by his fellow senators, not for his anti-Communism, but for his tactics (Manchester, 1972; Zinn, 1984). The Soviet launching of Sputnik in 1957 and the successful revolution in Cuba in 1959 were presented to the public as reminders that anti-Communism was a necessity for the "free world." Religious fundamentalism was starting to be revived and the John Birch Society was forming (Manchester, 1973).

During the 1950s the participation of women in the labor force continued to increase. Between 1940 and 1960 the number of married women and women with children who were working had quadrupled (Ryan, 1975). Yet jobs remained sexually and racially segregated.

In 1950, 8 million automobiles were sold (Allen, 1952) and a network of highways was created which would help to expand the suburbs of America, all supported by federal funding. But the suburbs did nothing to ease the housing situation for Black families. Despite their illegality, restrictive covenants and discriminatory practices prevented these families from moving into suburban areas. The FHA supported these policies (Wright, 1983; Kaplan, 1977).

By 1960, 73% of all American Blacks lived in cities (Ryan, 1975). The "slum clearance" programs of the 1950s had destroyed their communities, tearing down "slums" but failing to replace them with an equivalent number of housing units. Instead, these programs created projects, many with worse living conditions than those they were supposed to replace. Blacks were still disproportionately poor and the gap between Black and white income remained (Allen, 1952). Legal battles against segregation continued.

In 1954, the Supreme Court found segregation of the schools unconstitutional (*Brown* v. *Board of Education of Topeka*, 1954). In 1955, Rosa Parks was jailed in Montgomery, Alabama for refusing to sit in the back of the bus, the section set aside for Blacks. The Black community immediately mobilized. Blacks boycotted city buses, ushering in what was to be a decade of civil rights activism, leading to the outlawing of local bus segregation and the first Civil Rights Act in 1957. Segregationist resistance, while including economic sanctions such as evictions, denial of loans, and mortgage foreclosures, generally involved a high level of violence such as the bombings of churches and homes. Much of this resistance in the late 1950s was aimed at preventing school desegregation.

1950-1960: The School Desegregation Issue

From 1950 to 1954, several cases challenging the segregation of public schools were brought to the courts, including those in California against the segregation of Mexican-American children. In a case in South Carolina, the court ruled that segregated schools were acceptable but they had to be equal. In Topeka, Kansas the court refused to outlaw segregation in the public schools. At first, court cases brought legislative counterattacks. In 1952, South Carolina voters approved a constitutional amendment which would have abolished the public school system (Butts & Cremin, 1953). In Georgia, an amendment was introduced to keep schools segregated. If necessary, the state was to turn the schools and school property over to private individuals and to give grants to citizens who could then "choose" where to attend school. Laws were also passed to take funds away from mixed schools. And the resistance was not only in the South. In Cairo, Illinois there was mob violence when Black children tried to enter a white school (Butts & Cremin, 1953).

When in 1954, in a case which focused on several of the previous rulings, the Supreme Court unanimously overturned the 1896 "separate but equal" decision, it stated that separate schools were inherently unequal (*Brown* v. *Board of Education of Topeka*, 1954 as reprinted in Bremner, 1974). The court justified its position by using social science research showing the detrimental effect of segregation on Black and white children, but especially focused on the retarding of the mental and educational development of Blacks. In a second decision, the court issued procedures for compliance calling for integration as soon as practicable, "with all deliberate speed."

The resistance, especially in the South, was immediate and massive. In 1956, 101 of the 128 national legislators from the states in the Confederacy issued the "Southern Manifesto" in which they called the decision "a clear abuse of judicial powers," and pledged to use lawful means to repeal it (Bremner, 1974; Piven & Cloward, 1979). Almost every state of the former Confederacy enacted legislation to prevent or hamper the enforcement of *Brown*, including the closing of all public schools and the creation of private academies supported by state funds, repealing compulsory education, and ending the collection of taxes. Black children in Virginia had no public education from 1959 to 1963 (Bullock, 1967).

Not all attempts to prevent integration were legislative. As Black students attempted to register at schools, the violence of whites against them escalated. The 1957 case, in Little Rock, Arkansas is perhaps most well known. It was only one of many places in which violence was used (Manchester, 1973). During this period, however, the Supreme Court started backtracking from its earlier decisions. For example, they upheld the concept of discretionary pupil placement, one of the sidestepping attempts to continue segregation. In the 10 years following the desegregation decision, the number of integrated schools in the South increased by only 1% (U.S. Commission on Civil Rights, 1967, excerpted in Bremner, 1974).

In the North, the impact of the decision was felt as well, although the issue was *de facto* segregation resulting from residential segregation and the drop in the number of white students in the schools, as a consequence of suburbanization and the use of private and parochial schools by white families. By 1957, there was a drop of 20,000 in the number of white pupils in New York City public schools. With Blacks 20.1% of the school population, 455 out of 704 schools were racially homogeneous. This meant that less than 10% of Black children were in white schools and vice versa. To change this situation, in 1958 the New York City Board of Education began to allow voluntary transfers to underutilized white schools, moving Black and Puerto Rican students to white areas.

Greer (1976) contends that urban school desegregation and the launching of Sputnik by the Soviet Union in 1957 were linked. The widespread school failure that had existed historically for the urban poor was now no longer functional. School became important both for opportunity and for economic and national security. Segregation became the explanation of the inadequacy of urban schools. Studies found that schools with high percentages of Blacks and "other" (non-white) children scored below others on achievement tests. Their school buildings were older and more crowded and the proportion of substitute teachers was high. Integration became the answer to better schooling and to better achievement.

Whether or not a firm case can be made linking the rationalization of urban school desegregation with the perception that the United States was being surpassed by Soviet technology, Soviet existence and actions had a decided impact on public school policy and programs during the decade. Bremner (1974) contends that although "American education had always placed a high premium on inculcating patriotism" (p. 1576) during the cold war, loyalty was "defined as conformity" and this made "suspect the very act of seeking improvements and reforms" (p. 1576). In 1949, the National Education Association had reported that teachers were avoiding controversial issues having to do with sex, criticism of prominent persons, separation of church and state, race relations, and communism. In the 1950s, textbooks were being screened by groups of self-appointed "patriotic" censors. By 1952, 30 states had passed laws requiring loyalty oaths and disclosure of organizational affiliation from public school teachers, and many lost their jobs (Butts & Cremin, 1953). In one of the many cases involving a teacher who was fired, the Supreme Court stated:

A teacher works in a sensitive area in a classroom. There he shapes the attitude of young minds towards the society in which they live. In this the state has a vital concern. . . . One's associates, past and present, as well as one's conduct may properly be considered in determining fitness and loyalty. (*Adler* v. *Board of Education*, 1953, as reprinted in Bremner, 1974, p. 1737)

Within this conservative context the Progressive Education Association ceased to exist in 1955. Criticism of their approach escalated and the focus became "back to basics," despite research that had shown that progressive school children tended to outdistance their non-progressive school peers on almost all of the academic and social dimensions studied (Dropkin & Tobier, 1976, p. 185).

In 1953, the mid-century report on education was published. Its goal was to describe for "educators, test-makers and interested citizens, the measurable goals of instruction in our American elementary schools" (Kearney, 1953, p. 7). In their view, technological advances, the atomic and air age, as well as reports from business that students were incompetent, required careful delineation of goals and objective assessment of outcomes. Their description of goals was broad and overwhelmingly inclusive. The authors gave goals for specific ages qualifying that they represented the average child under optimal conditions. The goals have a clear class, sex, and cultural bias. Skills and attitudes to be acquired by the end of the sixth grade included "knowing how to handle safely the machines, appliances, and gadgets encountered in the home . . . ," playing games and engaging in social activities appropriate to his age, sex, and social group, developing a desire to be clean, which for girls develops earlier; knowing what laws he is expected to obey, knowing the value of leisure time. Descriptions of measures were especially sex typed: "increasing muscular dexterity is shown by girls in their skill in sewing and handling cooking utensils" and by boys in using "hammer, saw, screw driver, plane, square, chisel, brace and bit" (Kearney, 1953, p. 53).

The issue of federal aid to education also did not advance initially during the 1950s. Elementary school enrollment was at an all-time high of 26 million in 1953 and there was a severe shortage of teachers and buildings (Butts & Cremin, 1953). In 1950 an effort was made to generate interest and funds for new schools (Federal Security Office, Office of Education, 1950). Some school boards reassessed the purpose of school buildings and school designs were suggested based on programs. Legislation (Public Law 815, 1950; Public Law, 874, 1950, as excerpted in Bremner, 1974) provided federal funding of construction and operation to school districts affected by the presence of federal employees as a result of wartime industries. This funding was based on the size of the population of the district and the percentage of children whose families were living or working on federal property, with lower percentages required of smaller districts. This legislation aided suburban areas where wartime industrial plants had been built. Most school construction took place in suburban areas during this period. Single-story massive schools or "eggcrates" were the prevalant model. Cities spent only half as much as suburbs, yet they had more dilapidated, overcrowded schools and a higher student-to-teacher ratio (Conant, 1961).

In 1957, the launching of Sputnik solidified the attack on progressive education and changed the support for federal aid.

> What Sputnik did was provide corporate scientists, educators, and politicians with a new context in which to argue for federal aid to education. The cold war generated the arms race, the arms race precipitated the "scientists" or "knowledge" race. (Nasaw, 1979, pp. 188–189)

There was increased criticism of the schools and their "softness." Large amounts of federal money went to the schools through the National Defense Education Act, leading to a "retreat from what had been learned about learning" (Perrone, 1976). During this "skills crisis" (Bremner, 1974), progressive education was criticized as frivolous and described as disregarding the important and demanding aspects of learning. There was an emphasis on identifying youth with mathematical and scientific talent, while the "average or below average student" needed only a "sufficiently broad terminal education to fit him into modern technological society" (Rickover, 1959, as excerpted in Bremner, 1974, p. 1773). New courses in these subjects were created, and accelerated learning and teaching methods became common. "Innovations in support of education by the Federal government were directly tied to the search for national strength" (Bremner, 1974, p. 1577).

By 1960 many of the superficial goals of education had been met. The vast majority of children, about 46 million (Tyack, 1974), were registered in school, including 99.5% of children aged 7–13. The student/teacher ratios had declined and money had been invested in new school construction and new equipment, although the suburbs benefited most. And segregation was illegal even though it continued.

THE 1960s

> On February 1, 1960, four freshman at a Negro college in Greensboro, North Carolina decided to sit at the Woolworth's lunch counter, downtown, where only whites ate. They were refused service, and when they would not leave, the lunch counter closed for the day. The next day they returned, and then, day after day, other Negroes came to sit silently. In the next two weeks, sit-ins spread to 15 cities in five Southern states. There was violence against the sit-inners, but the idea of taking the initiative against segregation took hold. In the next 12 months, more than 50,000 people, mostly Black, and some whites participated in demonstrations of

one kind or another in 100 cities. Over 3,700 people were put in jail. But, by the end of 1960 lunch counters were open to Blacks in Greensboro and many other places. (Zinn, 1984, p. 155)

These sit-ins ushered in an era, from 1960 to the mid-1970s, which Zinn (1984) characterizes as one of "general revolt against oppressive, artificial, previously unquestioned ways of living." He observes that "never in American history had more movements for change been concentrated in so short a span of years" (p. 239).

As television spread into virtually every home in the country, people became witnesses to nonviolent demands by Black communities in the South for an end to segregation and discrimination, and the real implementation of their right to vote. They also witnessed the violent response of Southern segregationists and the murders of Black leaders Medgar Evers in 1963, Malcolm X in 1965, and Martin Luther King, Jr. in 1968. They watched the revolts in poor urban Black neighborhoods in the summers of 1964, 1965, 1966, 1967, and 1968 and the use of extreme force and violence by police and National Guardsmen to control them. They saw the election in 1960 of John F. Kennedy, the first Catholic to be president of the United States, and in 1963 watched his assassination and funeral as well. They heard President Lyndon Johnson promise a Civil Rights Act, declare a "war on poverty," and announce the commitment of American troops to an eight-year undeclared war in Vietnam—and announce that he would not run again. They watched Vietnam battle scenes and saw Americans of all races, classes, and ages demonstrating against that war. And they saw the first American set foot on the moon.

During the first years of the 1960s, however, it was the Southern struggle against segregation that dominated the media. The violent actions of white seg-regationists, including bombings, murders, burning buses, and the use of clubs, tear gas, and attack dogs, did not dissuade non-violent demonstrators. In 1963, 250,000 people, Black and white, gathered in Washington, D.C. to demand jobs and freedom (Zinn, 1984).

When Lyndon Johnson, a part of the Southern voting bloc for many years, took office after the assassination of John Kennedy, he said the time had come to push for civil rights legislation. In January 1964, he declared an "unconditional war on poverty." The Civil Rights Act of 1964 passed Congress in July; it guaranteed the right of Blacks to vote and the government's power to enforce that right. Again, the segregationists responded with violence as 1,000 people took part in Mississippi Summer, an attempt to register Southern Blacks. During 1964 and 1965, the Ku Klux Klan had the largest increase in membership in its history (Manchester, 1973). Nonviolent demonstrations continued as did the violent response of segregationists, but finally in 1965, a federal court banned literacy tests and other means of avoiding the registration of Blacks. After massive demonstrations in Selma, Alabama, a bill passed ensuring the use of *federal* registrars. By 1968, 60% of Southern Blacks were registered to vote, the same percentage as whites (Piven & Cloward, 1979).

By 1962 and 1963, many civil rights activists shifted their focus to economic issues, such as jobs and housing (Piven & Cloward, 1979). The situation of urban Blacks became visible to the rest of the country during the urban revolts of the summer of 1964. In 1963, the rate of unemployment for whites was 4.8%; for people of color it was 12.1%; and one half of the Black population was below the poverty level.

Another attempt to control the rage of urban Blacks was the "war on poverty." Yet the summer of 1965 brought more rioting across the country. In Watts, an area of Los Angeles that was 98% Black, there were 27.3 people per acre compared to 7.4 in the rest of the city. Eventually, 5,000 people were involved in rioting there and 10,000 National Guardsmen were sent in to control them (Manchester, 1973).

In 1966, there were 43 more major outbreaks including those in Washington, D.C., Cleveland, Omaha, Des Moines, and Brooklyn, New York (Manchester, 1973). That summer, the summer of 1967, brought revolts in 114 cities and 32 states (Manchester, 1973).

The Moynihan report, issued in November, 1965, called for "the strengthening of Black families" (Manchester, 1973; Piven & Cloward; Ryan, 1975) as the way to deal with the problems in Black communities.

The Kerner Commission report, published in 1967, blamed the revolts on white racism which had been developing in urban areas since the end of World War II, resulting in the economic deprivation of Blacks. It blamed police for escalating the level of violence, described the restraint of rioters and the focus on looting rather than physical assault, and called for a massive action program to end poverty and racial discrimination, one that included national income supplementation (Allen, 1970; Piven & Cloward, 1979). President Johnson announced legislative proposals to train and hire the hardcore unemployed and to rebuild the cities. Yet, in 1968, Martin Luther King, Jr. was shot in Memphis where he had gone to support a strike of garbage workers, and there were more outbreaks. The Poor People's Encampment he had planned for Washington took place that summer and was broken up by police (Zinn, 1984).

These years of struggles had increased the number of Black voters and of Blacks in elective offices in Southern areas (Manchester, 1973; Piven & Cloward, 1979; Zinn, 1984). Educational opportunity had expanded and the number of Black families getting governmental financial support had risen dramatically. Yet in 1968 the government moved into more conservative hands with the election of Richard Nixon. He vetoed the HEW and Office of Economic Opportunity appropriations bill and it took legal action to release the funds he had impounded. He began dismantling the Office of Economic Opportunity and vetoed the Child

Care Act, claiming it showed fiscal irresponsibility and would break up the family (Bremner, 1974; Ryan, 1975). Between 1960 and 1970, 75% of population growth took place in the suburbs and four out of five new jobs were created there (Kaplan, 1977). Yet by 1970, 85.5% of Black metropolitan families earning less than $4,400 per year were living in the central city (Kaplan, 1977). The unemployment rate of Black youth between 16 and 21 was 30.2% (Bremner, 1974). The percentage of Black families below the poverty level was still higher than for whites and Black women were still the lowest paid workers in the country, with two-thirds living below the poverty level (Ryan, 1974).

The Black civil rights movement became the inspiration and training ground for many of the other activist movements that took place during the 1960s. Students had started the sit-ins, freedom rides, and voter registration activities. In 1964, many civil rights workers became involved in the Free Speech movement at the University of California at Berkeley, protesting the university's attempts to limit students' rights to solicit money for off-campus political activities, such as the civil rights campaigns (O'Brien, 1972). In 1964, as the Gulf of Tonkin resolution gave President Johnson the right to send more American soldiers to Vietnam, draft resistance began as well. The New Left emerged (O'Brien, 1972), and in 1965, with 200,000 American soldiers in Vietnam, demonstrations against the war began.

By October, 1968, the antiwar movement included a broad spectrum of Americans. In that month, 2 million people across the country took part in demonstrations (O'Brien, 1972; Zinn, 1984). College students initially organized teach-ins and did draft resistance counseling but by 1967 and 1968 they picketed government speakers at campuses, protested the existence of ROTC on campus, and blocked campus recruiting by the Army and major corporations doing war-related work. They confronted the universities with their support of war-related research and their involvement in the destruction of Black neighborhoods. And they supported Black students' demands including the creation of Black studies departments (O'Brien, 1972). Between January 1 and June 15, 1968, there were 221 major demonstrations on 101 American campuses (Manchester, 1973).

Johnson decided not to run again under the pressure of these protests. Nixon had promised that, if elected, he would withdraw the troops. He began that process but soon initiated a "Vietnamization" program, using the U.S. military for bombing attacks to support South Vietnamese ground troops. The protests began again in October 1969 with a nationwide moratorium and 250,000 demonstrators marching in Washington (Manchester, 1973). Campus activity continued; between 1969 and 1970 the F.B.I. listed 1,785 students' demonstrations and the occupation of over 313 buildings (Zinn, 1984). Attempts to control these demonstrations were characterized by violence on the part of police and federal troops. Eventually it was revealed that much of it had been instigated by the government (Zinn, 1984). The climax came in Spring 1970, when President

Nixon ordered the invasion of Cambodia. In Mississippi, two Black students were shot during the occupation of a campus building (Zinn, 1984). At Kent State University in Ohio, National Guardsmen fired into a crowd of students gathered to demonstrate against the war, killing four students and paralyzing one for life. Students at over 400 colleges and universities responded with the first general student strike in U.S. history. In 1971, 20,000 people came to Washington to engage in civil disobedience, stopping traffic by blocking the streets, and 14,000 were arrested.

It was clear that the United States could not achieve a military victory and that the Vietnamese War was a liability in terms of the domestic situation. In August 1965, 61% of those interviewed in a national poll said they thought it was right for us to be in Vietnam; by 1971, 63% said it was wrong. The United States began its final withdrawal, and by 1975 active involvement was very low.

The 1960s also witnessed the beginnings of the "sexual revolution," with widespread use of contraception. The Women's Movement, developing during this time, focused on such issues as the legalization of abortion (won in 1973), an equal rights amendment to the United States Constitution, the provision of child care services, and the general issue of sexism in society. These efforts served to make the country conscious about the sexist depiction of women in books, including children's literature, and in advertising; the sexist use of language; and the inability of women to get non-traditional jobs (Koedt, Levine, & Rapone, 1973).

There were several other militant movements during the 1960s. For example, Native Americans organized and fought for control of their land and economic opportunity, and against racist stereotypes in books. In 1969, lesbians and gay males fought the police who violently attacked them at the Stonewall Inn in New York City (Katz, 1976) and began public marches demanding their rights and organizations to secure them. Zinn (1984) states that the general revolt during the 1960s

> touched every aspect of personal life: childbirth, childhood, love, sex, marriage, dress, music, art, sports, language, food, housing, religion, literature, death, schools. (p. 237)

In this period, many of the children of the white middle-class expressed their discontent and alienation from the technocracy of the era by swelling the rank of "hippies" or "flower children" who descended on the Haight-Ashbury district in San Francisco and the East Village in New York. They both reflected and intensified cultural trends to greater sexual freedom, more informal dress, recreational use of drugs such as marijuana and LSD in lieu of alcoholic drinks, alternative family structures, and a rejection of the conventional Protestant work ethic.

Criticism of prevailing social values was also expressed in a growing consumer consciousness. Articles were written about the funeral business, environmental pollution, DDT in our food, the lack of safety in automobiles, and other topics which pointed to the role of corporate interest and the neglect of these problems. Opinion polls showed that by 1970, "trust in government" was low in every segment of the population and there was a pervasive discontent and political alienation (Zinn, 1984). Zinn states that within this context,

> traditional education began to be re-examined. The schools had taught whole generations the values of patriotism, of obeying authority and had perpetuated ignorance, even contempt for people of other nations, races, Native Americans, women. Not just the content of education was challenged, but the style—the formality, the bureaucracy, the insistence on subordination to authority. (Zinn, 1984, p. 239).

The 1960s: The Schools

The 1960s and early 1970s saw projects and proposals for restructuring the educational system; their goals and methods included racial integration, open enrollment, compensatory education, curricular reform, community control, open classrooms, and unstructured learning environments. In the historical context of the early stages of the Civil Rights movement, the major focus was on integration; yet, many of the salient issues surfaced in Northern, Midwestern, and Western urban areas.

In this period migration of Blacks and Hispanics to the cities paralleled that of whites to the suburbs. The result was increased percentages of Black and Hispanic students in the urban schools. Because of residential segregation patterns, most of these students attended segregated schools.

As described earlier, in 1958 the New York City Board of Education began a voluntary transfer plan which allowed Black and Hispanic students access to less crowded schools. Since in 1960, after two years of this program, 327 elementary schools were still predominantly white, an open enrollment plan was instituted. This allowed Black and Hispanic students to leave any racially imbalanced school, overcrowded or not, for designated, predominantly white schools. Similar efforts were occurring elsewhere, for example, in Boston (Green & Hunter, 1978).

Between 1960 and 1962, with the first stirrings of teacher militancy, another factor emerged that eventually would affect the relationship between the school system and urban U.S. minority groups (Rosenthal, 1969). In 1960, 20,000 New York City teachers struck; in 1961, they joined the United Federation of Teachers (UFT); and in 1962 they struck again to obtain salary increases. And while the initial focus for these union efforts was increased benefits and changes in specific schools, teachers eventually did address the structure of the larger educational system and their role (Rosenthal, 1969).

In January 1963, John F. Kennedy sent his message on education to the Congress: to win the cold war would require a "citizenry that understands our principles and problems" and "a scientific effort which demonstrates the superiority of freedom" (Kennedy, 1963, excerpted in Bremner, 1974, p. 1795). His message set the tone for the "culture of poverty" perspective on education, dominant from 1961 to 1965—the educational system was responsible for the ignorance of the poor; their ignorance led to the failure of our social and economic system; and these failures threatened our political system. More and better quality education was the answer to both.

Although it posited a "new kind of poverty" in which families were permanently enmeshed (Meranto, 1967), this analysis harked back to the Progressive Era view of immigrants in its conceptualization of the "cultural deprivation" of the poor, now mostly Black and Hispanic, in terms of a lack of access to white, middle-class culture. In 1963, under the Kennedy administration, experimental programs were started which would reach "educationally disadvantaged" children ages three to five, before they even got to kindergarten.

The struggle against *de facto* segregation in the cities was connected to and affected by the actions and strategies of the Southern-based civil rights movement, for example, the use of a school boycott in Boston in 1963. This boycott protested discrimination against Black teachers, the lack of any Black principals, the large differences in expenditures for Black and white schools, and the overcrowding in six out of the nine Black schools (Green & Hunter, 1978).

The Civil Rights Act of July 1964, passed under pressure from Southern Civil Rights demonstrators, though focused on voting rights, had provisions for an investigation of the "availability of equal educational opportunity." It also called for training teachers to deal with desegregation and provided money for the training. Furthermore, it allowed citizens to bring lawsuits and directed the attorney general to put the weight of the government behind them. In cooperation with Southern Civil Rights demonstrations and those in local urban areas, a nationwide boycott of schools was now planned to protest *de facto* segregation and the resulting poor quality of education for Black students (Manchester, 1973; Meranto, 1967; Piven & Cloward, 1979). These boycotters challenged the explanation that increases in *de facto* segregation were due only to increased numbers of Black and Hispanic children in the city schools.

Boycotters instead cited past gerrymandering of districts by officials; others would point to patterns of residential segregation (U.S. Commission on Civil Rights, 1967a, 1967b). Boycotters said schools for predominantly Black and Hispanic students were overcrowded, old, and dilapidated, lacked educational equipment, and had many substitute teachers. They complained that Boards of Education would not redistrict or take other corrective measures; they felt that schools in their communities would not be upgraded (Meranto, 1967).

Meranto (1967) believes the passage in 1965 of the first U.S. general aid-to-education bill, the Elementary and Secondary School Education Act, was possible in part because the Civil Rights Act of 1964 eliminated segregation of schools as an issue for debate. But it was also an outgrowth, in his view, of the national consciousness about the educational opportunity for Blacks. Black demonstrators had placed pressure on the government to respond or face continued revolt. Yet, ironically, the conceptual framework for the response placed the blame on the victim, citing the culture of poverty as well as Moynihan's (1965) indictment of the Black family.

In his message to Congress when submitting the bill, President Johnson's arguments rested on his assumption that "poverty has many roots but the tap root is ignorance" (Johnson, 1965, reprinted in Bremner, 1974, p. 1801). Like the Progressive Era "childsavers," he located the problem in *particular* urban or rural areas rather than seeing it as systemic. Therefore, federal aid was to be based on the percentage of families in a given area earning under $2,000 per year or receiving welfare.

The bill gave aid to both public and private schools for libraries, materials, remedial education programs, educational research, work/study, and college loans. But its prime focus, and one which revealed its underlying philosophy, was "compensatory" education, what Johnson called "Head Start." It was placed under the Community Action Program of the Office of Economic Opportunity whose philosophy was based on culture-of-poverty arguments and whose long range objective was to "affect a permanent increase in the ability of individuals, groups, and communities afflicted with poverty to improve their own conditions" (U.S. Office of Economic Opportunities 1967, excerpted in Bremner, 1974, p. 1821). The program was intended to make up for the "deprivation" children experienced within their communities before they reached school.

Head Start programs began that summer. Though the program philosophy enshrined condescending assumptions, long familiar to the poor, the placement of Head Start in OEO meant parent involvement in the planning and running of programs, and training and jobs for community residents. By 1966, 45,000 had paraprofessional positions in the program (Shriver, 1966, excerpted in Bremner, 1974).

In 1966 and 1967 there was a transition from the initial emphasis on integration toward an emphasis on community control. Open education emerged as yet another alternative. In Boston some parents had arranged a successful busing plan with suburban schools, and others had created two of their own schools. The majority of students, however, were still in the poor *de facto* segregated public schools. The Coleman report (U.S. Office of Education, 1966) mandated by the Civil Rights Act of 1965, revealed what school activists already knew: that 10 years after desegregation had been ordered with "all deliberate speed," most American children were still in segregated schools. Blacks were the most segregated of all U.S. minority groups. Eighty percent of white pupils attended schools which were 90–100% white. The pattern was the same, though less marked, in the urban North as it was in the Deep South. Coleman redocumented what had been said for years: the schools which were predominantly Black had few facilities related to academic achievement, lacked physics, chemistry, and language laboratories, had fewer books per pupil in the library, fewer textbooks, and teachers with less academic preparation. Yet when socioeconomic background was accounted for, the difference in school accounted only for a fraction of differences in achievement. These findings were a blow for reformers and many criticized his study. Yet one finding of the Coleman report became later justification for community control: children's perception of the extent to which they could affect their own environment and futures had a stronger relationship to achievement than all of the school factors combined. Except for Asian-American children, all other children of color were less likely to believe this compared to white children. Yet those who did hold this belief achieved at a higher level than whites who did not. Coleman found that Black children were more likely to feel they had such control when they were in schools with a large proportion of whites and this could be used as an argument for integration. Others felt that such integration would subordinate Black children to white children (Bremner, 1974) and an equally strong case could be made for creating schools where the program and structure itself would actually give Black children and their parents more control.

In 1966, ideology was shifting from civil rights to Black Power. Spurred on by the construction of a new junior high school on a site where it could not become integrated, parents in the East Harlem section of New York City, a predominantly Puerto Rican community, instituted a move for community control (Gittell, 1972a). IS–201 became one of three community-controlled experimental districts in New York, with funding from foundations as well as the local and federal governments (Rosenthal, 1969). While critics claimed such districts would eliminate integration, supporters pointed out that integration had failed before community control. The community had been excluded from the school system, as parents and as workers, by its centralization, specialization, bureaucratization, and standards (Gittell, 1970). Research eventually showed that in these community-controlled districts, compared to other local districts, parents and community representatives took a greater interest in the schools, and there was higher voter turnout for school elections and high attendance at school meetings. Eighty percent of the students felt they were unhampered in their attempts to get ahead and had a much stronger sense of their own destiny (Gittell, 1972b). When research compared the schools in one of the experimental districts to other urban and surburban school districts, it was found that

> . . . a major social change with far-reaching effects had taken place in the community-controlled schools. This change created a radically different school structure. Despite many problems, the IS 201 schools were doing what the community board wanted

them to do. They were more innovative; the school climate was more intellectual and stimulating; teacher pupil interaction was more positive. Parents made their presence known in the schools; they were frequent visitors for a variety of constructive purposes. Children showed somewhat higher academic achievement. (Gittell, 1972a, p. 17)

Despite such successes, the experimental districts did not survive. They eventually were subsumed into larger districts in the decentralization plan that was finally implemented.

Under this system local boards had no control over personnel. The appointments procedure guaranteed that there would be no Black or Puerto Rican principals appointed for five years and made transfers very difficult; all budget powers were advisory and capital funds were controlled by the city. Parents from the community employed in the district could not serve on the boards; outside funding had to be centrally approved as did curricula; and the procedures for local elections were complex and guaranteed that local political groups, including the UFT, with money and a well established infrastructure, would have control. The result of the decentralization plan was curiously reminiscent of the result of the centralization plan of the Progressive Era "reforms" at the turn of the century: "In 1970, of 269 members of these (local) boards, only 16.8 percent were Black and 10.8 percent were Puerto Rican; in twelve districts in which over 85 percent of the students were Black or Puerto Rican, only half had boards in which a majority of these members were of those ethnic groups" (Tyack, 1974, p. 288).

As conflicts about these districts escalated, pro-integration views were presented in a report which had been requested by President Johnson in 1965 and was published in 1967 (U.S. Commission on Civil Rights, 1967a). This report described the tangible and negative effects of segregation on Black children and also asserted that white children were affected by racism—they developed racial fears, based their self-esteem and assurance on racial superiority, and would be ill-prepared to participate in a pluralistic world. Recognizing the connection between residential segregation and *de facto* school segregation, it did recommend anti-discrimination laws in housing and the careful siting of new housing for low- and moderate-income urban families to guarantee integration. For the short term, recommendations focused on a plan that would desegregate the schools. It called for a standard to eliminate racial imbalance based on New York's plan that schools could not have more than 50% U.S. minority children. Yet it also saw the size, environment, structure, and process of the school as a vehicle which would support integration. The report advocated the creation of larger rather than smaller facilities, using suburban schools as a model, claiming they would draw from many neighborhoods at once and would be cost effective and ensure integration. In addition it advocated flexible open-space classrooms, ungraded classes, and team teaching, claiming these "would allow for greater attention to individual needs and capabilities of students" (U.S. Commission on Civil Rights, excerpted in Bremner, p. 1860). The new structures, they claimed, would also allow the introduction of new technology such as computers.

Whether or not the types of educational environments described would lead to integration, the link was made between large and flexible schools and a better learning experience. This reflected the trends of the 1960s in school design and their connection to open education, a learning process resembling Deweyan learning through activity which would begin to take hold at the end of the decade.

As early as 1960, Educational Facilities Laboratories had been stating the need for "humanized learning environments." In *The Cost of a Schoolhouse* (1960), they described most existing classrooms as a

> glass and masonry box filled with kitchen-like furniture. Its surfaces are hard and cold, with hospital-like floors and plastic desk tops, factory lighting fixtures, painted cinder block. . . . (p. 133)

The emphasis in such schools was on hygiene and indestructibility; they were sterile, unyielding, and institutional.

The publication went on to describe recent attempts at "humanizing education," specifically the new, spacious open-plan school buildings which had no permanent interior partitions. Movable partitions and storage units were used to demarcate spaces, providing a great deal of flexibility. The primary advantage was cost effectiveness, though the schools were also described as allowing the child to take more responsibility for his or her own learning.

A 1965 Educational Facilities Laboratories publication, *Profiles of Significant Schools: Schools Without Walls*, again stressed cost effectiveness—such schools were cheaper to build and they were efficient, as well. Examples of actual schools included one in San Jose, California which had 3,840 square feet for 110 pupils. Claiming that such "space lends itself to innovations in program and schedule" (Educational Facilities Laboratories, 1965, p. 7), the publication described the aim of open-space schools as providing an environment which encouraged greater interaction between the pupil and the teacher and between teacher and teacher. In an attempt to anticipate objections to these schools as too radical an innovation, they explained that self-contained classes could still exist because instruction could take place within self-contained clusters instead of self-contained classrooms. Yet the open-plan school *was* a catalyst for change—it could "create an educational process unbounded by the barriers built into the conventional school house with its rows of standard classrooms" (p. 3).

Between 1967 and 1970, over 50% of all new school construction used open-plan design and, in some states, all new schools were open-plan (George, 1975). In most of these, however, the open architectural style was not accompanied by a change in the educational process. Local school boards adopted them because they were less expensive and symbolized "modern design." Since most new school construction was in newer suburban areas, the link between integration and large, open plan schools did not resurface. The issue in the cities was still community control.

As community control was being replaced by decentralization without community power and the militancy of the Black movement was disappearing or being crushed, the negative evaluations of the Head Start program began to appear. Studies had shown immediate success for children in the program, but no sustained advancement in later grades (Datta, 1969, excerpted in Bremner, 1974). Many educators quickly called the program a failure. Jensen (1968) sparked a fierce controversy when he attributed the failure to the heritability of I.Q. Though critiques of his work appeared immediately, few criticized his underlying assumption that I.Q. determined economic status (Bowles & Gintes, 1976). Indeed, the Head Start program had rested on the same premise. Jencks, on the other hand, argued that it was precisely because educational differences did not account for economic status that efforts should not be put into such programs (1972).

Others took a wait and see attitude. Datta (1969, as excerpted in Bremner, 1974), reviewing the evaluation studies, said that after only four years and five summers, and considering the implementation problems and the need to train community people, it was too early to know what the results meant. Assessing the extreme negative reaction after such a short time, she agreed with McDill and Sprehe (1969):

> People have asked Head Start to do the impossible. No public school system has ever before been abolished because it could not teach children to read and write. (as cited by Datta, excerpted in Bremner, 1974, p. 1827)

However, the negative evaluations gave President Nixon the ammunition he needed in his effort to dismantle the Office of Economic Opportunity and its Community Action programs. These had provided the training for community activists who had organized groups to oppose his policies at home and in Vietnam. Nixon claimed the deprivation of poor children began so early and was so persistent that summer programs were not the answer. He moved Head Start from OEO to the Department of Health, Education and Welfare and created the Office of Child Development to oversee it. He reduced the summer programs and placed emphasis on early intervention with parents and children as well as later remedial help (Nixon, 1969, excerpted in Bremner, 1974). Head Start became a service rendered and administered by professionals for poor children and their parents.

Joseph Featherstone is credited by some educators (Gross & Gross, 1972; Nyquist & Hawes, 1972) with having introduced the concept of open education (also called open classrooms or informal education) into the United States through a series of articles in the *New Republic* in 1967. In those articles, he discussed the *Plowden Report* (Central Advisory Council for Education, England, 1967), just released in England, which extolled the "miracle" of the open-classroom approach of the British primary schools. A few years later he cautioned that

the appearance of new issues—such as the movement for open informal schools— does not cancel out old issues. In fact, open education will be a sham unless those supporting it also address themselves to recurring, fundamental problems, such as the basic inequality and racism in the society . . . Issues like school integration and community control have not disappeared, to be replaced by issues like humane education. . . . (p. 101)

Yet this is exactly what happened in the educational establishment over the next few years.

In 1970 Charles Silberman published the results of a three-and-a-half-year study funded by the Carnegie Corporation. *Crisis in the Classroom* documented the deep trouble in American schools:

What grim joyless places most American schools are, how oppressive and petty are the rules by which they are governed, how intellectually sterile and aesthetically barren the atomosphere, what an appalling lack of civility obtains on the part of teachers and principals, what contempt they unconsciously display for children as children. (p. 10)

His solution was the open classroom.

Yet these criticisms were not new to American education, even within recent years. In 1964, John Holt had published *Why Children Fail*, and in 1968 Jonathan Kozol published *Death at an Early Age*. Both raised criticisms almost identical to Charles Silberman's. In addition his solution sounded surprisingly like John Dewey's "progressive education," to which open educators acknowledged their debt. The question remains: Why were the *Plowden Report* and Silberman's writings the catalysts for the massive implementation of open classrooms in the early 1970s?

In 1968, as massive student demonstrations developed on college campuses, high-school students also fought against the rigidity and authoritarianism of the school structure and process, the irrelevance of the curriculum, and the absence of any acknowledgement of their rights. In Boston, high-school students organized a boycott when a Black student who wore a dashiki was suspended by the principal for violation of the dress code. In Los Angeles, Chicano students struck at five schools; among their demands were bilingual teachers and textbooks that reported Mexican and Mexican-American contributions to the United States. These were not isolated incidents; similar actions were occurring across the country. Demands ranged from the elimination of dress codes to the right to publish student newspapers critical of the schools to the nature of the curriculum and the right not to salute the flag (Bresnick et al., 1978).

These events at the end of the 1960s reflected the impact on young people of the ideas and actions of the civil rights and Black Power movements, the anti-war movement, the women's movement, the Native American movement, and the gay movement, as well as the general social upheaval of the decade. "Free schools" were seen by some more radical educators as a way of attempting to relate to the needs and demands of younger people (see Kozol, 1972). These schools rested on a set of values such as racial and sexual equality and adults and youths as joint partners in learning. Students participated in their operation; the curriculum was not imposed but evolved out of students' inquiry. Free schools did not rely on professional educators, but had staffs of adults from all walks of life who would be supportive of students, treat them with dignity and respect, and help them find their own way to learning. Often they were housed in abandoned industrial buildings, rural farmhouses, or old, large homes. Yet free schools existed mainly outside of the public school system and had a predominantly middle-class white population. Only a few continued to survive into the 1980s.

According to Bowles and Gintes (1976), in the face of the ferment of the 1960s, the pressures created by the failures of compensatory education, and their opposition to real community control, the response of liberal education in the public school systems was the "open classroom." It was perceived "as a means of accommodating the growing anti-authoritarianism of young people and keeping things from getting out of hand" (p. 5) but within the established school structure. Open education was presented as an innovative but rational departure from the traditional learning situation and process. Nyquist and Hawes (1972) described the open classroom in this way:

> Children learn and work at their own individual initiative in activity areas for reading, writing, mathematics, science, nature, art, music, dramatics and crafts. They freely talk and move about in their own room, corridors and other classrooms. Their written, graphed and painted work adorns the wall in profusion. Their teacher sometimes has them all come together for a story or a song, viewing work that they've done, making rules or plans, or setting off on a field trip.
>
> For almost all of their time . . . children engage in activities individually or in small groups, as impelled by their spontaneous interests and as inspired or persuaded by the teachers. Just as their room has no teacher's desk nor rows of pupils' desks, their day has no required periods for studying specific subjects; it is an integrated day in the sense that any and all subjects are integrated in their learning activities. (p. 1)

Open educators described children being treated with respect and trust (Nyquist & Hawes, 1972). In this setting, they said, individuality was possible and each day was different from every other (Gross & Gross, 1972). The layout of the room was supposed to support the program and was described as having no "upfront" (Gross & Gross, 1972). Children could move freely, going to other teachers and rooms. The day had no rigid routine and the teacher was freed from being a timekeeper, a traffic controller, or a policeman (Silberman, 1970). The atmosphere was described as having tolerance and flexibility with regard to time, space, and routine (Nyquist & Hawes, 1972). Learning centered on "hands-on" manipulation of materials and the learning process made use of the environment, both within the school and outside.

Open educators felt required to address the issue of achievement, specifically children's performance on standardized tests (Flurry, 1972; Hazelwood & Norris, 1972; Nyquist & Hawes, 1972). While believing that such testing was not an appropriate measure of the strength of open education they claimed that students in these rooms did as well as everyone else. Most descriptions of open education effusively stressed its positive qualities, but some limitations and reservations were raised. Teachers had to be motivated to do this work. It required a particular attitude and training and should not be imposed if it were to work well (Nyquist & Hawes, 1972). Rogers (1972) raised some potential problems he had observed in British schools, including his sense that the focus on hands-on learning was divorcing the school from the reality of the world around it. He spoke about the need to bring the political and social realities of the times into the classrooms and felt that learning about these areas could not always be done in a "hands-on" way. He also questioned whether every subject was amenable to open-style teaching and learning. Nevertheless, he had great enthusiasm for the possibilities of the method.

The idea of open education spread quickly. By 1971, for example, there were 31 schools in Vermont described as "working toward open education" (State Department of Education, 1972). It was also used as a Follow Through Head Start Program. Armington (1972) claimed that in this case it was not a compensatory education situation. He argued that *all* schools failed in that they dehumanized the educational process. While this was undoubtedly true, the description glossed over the glaring differences that still remained between schools in poor urban areas and those in wealthy suburbs, as well as between poor and well-to-do areas within the cities (Guthrie et al., 1971).

Open educators claimed that in contrast to "free schools" open classrooms were different: they had a scientific basis for their teaching and learning methods, used sophisticated methods that required special training and qualified personnel, and were based on a respect for achievement (Nyquist & Hawes, 1972). Acknowledging the heritage of John Dewey, one educator claimed that "progressive education" failed to have an influence on the public schools because teachers who implemented his ideas did not take authority for organizing and directing learning, a key characteristic of open education (Nyquist, 1972). Furthermore, they claimed that open education was not a "fad" and should be implemented with careful planning and in slow stages.

Open educators were also careful to distinguish open-classroom or informal education from the concept of open-plan schools:

> A building built without walls or with walls knocked out, or with folding doors between certain classrooms may be closed by psychological walls, teacher improvised walls, of bookcases, screens or chalkboards. The most open physical environment can also be closed by formal routines, rigid schedules and curriculum planning which separates subject-matter areas into "periods." (Flurry, 1972, p. 104)

Indeed, since many open-plan schools were built for cost efficiency and not for open education, criticisms began to appear about their inadequacy and caution was urged in matching the school environment to the program (Educational Facilities Laboratories, 1968). In fact, over time there was considerable disillusionment with the open design and gradually many of these schools either reconstructed walls or set up partitions, returning them to more traditional layouts (Ross & Gump, 1978).

Sometimes open education took place within a single classroom in a more traditional school although its implementation was supposed to go beyond the self-contained classroom. There were some innovative approaches suggested for traditional school environments. One was the Open Corridor school introduced by Lillian Weber into the New York schools in 1967. The plan called for creating an open classroom community by utilizing several rooms on the same corridor. The corridor space would be used for a range of activities, including those involving physical movement or those needing larger space. It could also be a quiet area, and was conceived as the information center. Communication between rooms would occur there; teachers could meet one another or parents. Weber suggested that all of the rooms be heterogeneously aged so that children would have some opportunity to work with age peers while benefiting from contacts with older or younger children, as well. By 1971, when we started our work in the New York City schools, there were 12 open corridor schools. For the most part, however, the entire school was not involved in the program. More usually, one or two corridors had open education classes; they were alternative arrangements within otherwise traditional schools. A few schools were completely organized around open education philosophy. In some schools in which we worked we initiated the contact because of our interest in environments for children and the relationship between physical form and program philosophy. In other schools, we were asked to work with teachers, helping them to make the best use of their classroom spaces in their attempt to implement open teaching. We worked in the schools until 1976, in a variety of capacities that will be described in the following chapter.

LATER YEARS

While maintaining formal contact in the intervening years we did not return to the schools on a day-to-day basis until 1980, when we implemented a program called "Children Imaging and Creating Alternative Futures."* We had left the schools at the beginning of the urban fiscal crises of the mid-1970s and returned during the conservative political atmosphere of 1980. Between 1960 and 1981, the gap between white and Black family income had remained essentially unchanged, with Black households earning approximately 56% of whites; the relative unemployment rates were the same with twice as many Blacks as whites unemployed. In 1978, the position of women's earnings relative to men's had dropped from 61% to 57%, the number of single-parent families with women as the source of income had increased dramatically since the mid-seventies, accounting for most of the households below poverty level, and Black women were still the lowest paid workers in the United States (Wolfe, 1981; Zinn, 1984). The ERA had not been adopted and Federal Medicaid funding for abortion had been eliminated.

During the fiscal crisis there had been severe budget cuts and many educational programs had been eliminated. In several cities the depressed economy eventuated in the closing of schools. Thousands of jobs were eliminated and this especially affected Black and Hispanic teachers and paraprofessionals since they were the "last hired." As budgets were cut, working conditions worsened, with larger class sizes and limited materials.

The years between 1976 and 1980 brought an economic depression with the highest unemployment levels since the depression of the thirties, and soaring inflation as well (Zinn, 1984). Homeowners voted against school bonds and increased property taxes, causing further cuts in social services and school budgets (Bowles & Gintes, 1976). In 1973, the Supreme Court ruled that local property taxes did not have to be equally distributed by the state to ensure equality of spending between school districts. They ruled that education was not a fundamental right and that states did not have to provide equal opportunities to rich and poor in the same way they had to provide equal opportunity between Blacks and whites (Bremner, 1974), obviously ignoring the overlap between poverty and race caused by institutional racism.

Traditional right-wing and newer fundamentalist groups allied in support of the election of Ronald Reagan (Petchesky, 1984) and pressured schools to censor books and to teach creationism as an alternative to evolution. There were several attempts to reintroduce prayer into the public schools.

As reading scores continued to decline during the 1970s, performance on the college boards declined as well, the move was "back to basics" and the issue

*Funded by the National Endowment for the Arts. Our colleagues in this project were Carol Baldassari, Sheila Lehman, Raymond Lorenzo and Luciana Lepore.

of "accountability" surfaced—if schools wanted funding and teachers want salary increases they had to demonstrate the effectiveness of their work. This meant that children should be performing well on standardized tests. In New York, children with below-grade reading levels were no longer promoted into their age-level class while being provided with remedial instruction. Instead, examinations were being given in the fourth and seventh grade and students failing were kept back. The likelihood is that this will increase the percentage of high school drop-outs in an economy in which the unemployment rate among teenagers is approximately 15% and for Black youths is 40% (Zinn, 1984).

The concept of magnet schools, first described by Bundy in 1967, had taken hold, especially at the junior high school level. Mini-schools with a special focus—for example, math or art—were created within larger schools in an attempt to provide quality education which was supposed to create an integrated student body. The mini-schools were called "alternative schools," applying the terminology of the 1960s to schools which generally provided traditional educational environments (Bresnick et al., 1978).

In 1976, Bowles and Gintes had written:

> Entrepreneurial capitalism, which brought us the chairs nailed-to-the-floor classroom, has given way to corporate capitalism. It may belatedly usher in the era of open classrooms, minimization of grading and internalized behavior norms contemplated for at least a century by so many educational reformers. (p. 254)

Yet by the time we came back to the New York City schools, open education seemed to have passed as a phenomenon. In some schools there were a few teachers still involved in open education, most in a modified form, and usually within a self-contained classroom. The optimism and spirit of the new forms and ideas of the 1960s and 1970s had receded. Our return to the schools during this period confronted us with the impact of the political and economic situation. We felt compelled to re-examine the actual implementation of open education as we experienced it, to reflect on the reasons open-education attempts had not succeeded in the public schools, and to examine why and how this idea could be eliminated so rapidly. We could see some dramatic differences between our earlier and later experiences, yet we could also see many similarities. This brought us to examine the historical patterns of education in this country.

In the chapter that follows we describe both our earlier and later work and point out the continuities and disparities in the experience and how they relate to the role of the school in the lives of children in our society.

REFERENCES

Adler v. Board of Education (1953). 342 U.S. 485. In R. H. Bremner (Ed.). (1974). *Children and youth in America: A documentary history: Vol. 3. 1933–1973* (pp. 1736–1737; 1745–1747). Cambridge, MA: Harvard University Press.

Allen, F. A. (1952). *The big change: America transforms itself, 1900–1950*. New York: Harper and Row.

Allen, V. L. (Ed.). (1970). Ghetto riots. *Journal of Social Issues, 26*(1), 1–220.

Apteker, B. (1982). *Woman's legacy: Essays on race, sex and class in American history*. Amherst: University of Massachussets Press.

Armington, D. E. (1972). A plan for continuing growth. In E. N. Nyquist & G. R. Hawes (Eds.), *Open education: A sourcebook for parents and teachers* (pp. 55–62). New York: Bantam.

Ashton, P. J. (1978). The political economy of suburban development. In W. K. Tabb & L. Sawers (Eds.), *Marxism and the metropolis*. New York: Oxford University Press.

Bowles, S., & Gintes, H. (1976). *Schooling in capitalist America: Education reform and the contradictions of economic life*. New York: Basic Books.

Brameld, T. (1949). Educational costs. In R. M. MacIver (Ed.). *Discrimination and national welfare*. New York: Institute for Religious and Social Studies. In R. H. Bremner (Ed.). (1974). *Children and youth in America: A documentary history: Vol. 3. 1933–1973* (pp. 1697–1701). Cambridge, MA: Harvard University Press.

Bremner, R. H. (Ed.). (1974). *Children and youth in America: A documentary history: Vol. 3. 1933–1973*. Cambridge, MA: Harvard University Press.

Bresnick, D., Lachman, S., & Polner, M. (1978). *Black, white, green and red: The politics of education in ethnic America*. New York: Longman.

Brown et al. v. Board of Education of Topeka. (1954). 347 U.S. 483. In R. H. Bremner (Ed.). (1974). *Children and youth in America: A documentary history: Vol. 3. 1933–1973* (pp. 1703–1706). Cambridge, MA: Harvard University Press.

Bullock, H. A. (1967). *A history of Negro education in the South: From 1619 to the present*. Cambridge, MA: Harvard University Press.

Butts, F. R. and Cremin, L. A. (1953). *A History of Education in American Culture*. New York: Holt, Rinehart and Winston.

Callahan, R. E. (1962). *Education and the cult of efficiency*. Chicago: University of Chicago Press.

Castaldi, B. (1968). *Creative planning of educational facilities*. Chicago: Rand McNally.

Central Advisory Council for Education (1967). *Children and their primary schools ("The Plowden Report")*. Vol. 1: Report. Vol. 2: Research and Surveys. London: Her Majesty's Stationery Office.

Cox, M. E. (1921). Organization of the elementary school as affecting buildings. In J. J. Donovan (Ed.). *School architecture* (pp. 85–93). New York: Macmillan.

Croley, H. (1909). *The promise of American life*. New York: Capricorn Reprint Edition.

Daniel, P. T. K. (1980). A history of discrimination against Black students in Chicago secondary schools. *History of Education Quarterly, 20*, 147–156.

Datta, L. A. (1969). A report on evaluation studies of Project Head Start. Washington, D.C. In R. H. Bremner (Ed.). (1974). *Children and youth in America: A documentary history: Vol. 3. 1933–1973* (pp. 1825–1830). Cambridge, MA: Harvard University Press.

Davis, A. (1971a). The Black woman's role in the community of slaves. *The Black Scholar*, *3*(4), 1–13.

Davis, A. (1971b). *Women, race and class*. New York: Random House.

Dewey, J. (1966). *Democracy and education*. New York: Macmillan.

Dropkin, R., & Tobier, A. (Eds.). (1976). *Roots of open education in America*. New York: City College Workshop for Open Education.

DuBois, W. E. B. (1935). Does the Negro need separate schools? *The Journal of Negro Education*, 55. In R. H. Bremner (Ed.). (1974). *Children and youth in America: A documentary history: Vol. 3. 1933–1973* (pp. 1686–1692). Cambridge, MA: Harvard University Press.

Educational Facilities Laboratories (1960). *The cost of a schoolhouse*. New York: Educational Facilities Laboratories.

Educational Facilities Laboratories (1965). *Profiles of significant schools: Schools without walls*. New York: Educational Facilities Laboratories.

Educational Facilities Laboratories (1968). *Educational change and architectural consequences*. New York: Educational Facilities Laboratories.

Featherstone, J. (1972). Relevance to the American setting. In E. B. Nyquist & G. R. Hawes (Eds.), *Open education: A sourcebook for parents and teachers* (pp. 92–101). New York: Bantam.

Flurry, R. C. (1972). Open education: What is it? In E. B. Nyquist & G. R. Hawes (Eds.), *Open education: A sourcebook for parents and teachers* (pp. 102–108). New York: Bantam.

Frazier, E. F. (1940). *Negro youth at the crossways*. Washington, D.C.: American Council on Education. In R. H. Bremner (Ed.). (1974). *Children and youth in America: A Documentary History: Vol. 3. 1933–1973* (pp. 1665–1672). Cambridge, MA: Harvard University Press.

George, P. S. (1975). *Ten years of open space schools: A review of research*. Gainesville: Florida Educational Research and Development Council.

Gittell, M. (1970). Urban school politics: Professionalism vs. reform. *Journal of Social Issues*, *26*(3), 69–84.

Gittell, M. (1972a). Children in Harlem's community controlled schools. *Journal of Social Issues*, *28*(4), 1–20.

Gittell, M. (1972b). *Local control in education: Three demonstration school districts in New York City*. New York: Praeger.

Goffman, E. (1961). *Asylums*. Garden City, NY: Doubleday.

Green, J., & Hunter, A. (1978). Racism and busing in Boston. In W. K. Tabb & L. Sawers (Eds.), *Marxism and the metropolis* (pp. 271–296). New York: Oxford University Press.

Greer, C. (1976). *The great school legend*. New York: Penguin.

Griffin v. County School Board of Prince Edward County. (1959). 377 U.S. 218. In R. H. Bremner (Ed.). (1974). *Children and youth in America: A documentary history: Vol. 3. 1933–1973* (pp. 1830–1834). Cambridge, MA: Harvard University Press.

Gross, B., & Gross, R. (1972). A little bit of chaos. In E. B. Nyquist & G. R. Hawes. (Eds.), *Open education: A sourcebook for parents and teachers* (pp. 9–18). New York: Bantam.

Guthrie, J. W., Kleindorfer, G. B., Levin, H. M., & Stout, R. T. (1971). *Schools and inequality*. Cambridge, MA: Harvard University Press.

Hein, G. E. (1975). The social history of open education: Austrian and Soviet schools in the 1920s. *The Urban Review, 8*(2), 96-119.

Holt, J. (1964). *How children fail*. New York: Dell.

Jencks, C. & others. (1972). *Inequality: A reassessment of the effects of family and schooling in America*. New York: Basic Books.

Jensen, A. A. (1968). How much can we boost I.Q. and scholastic achievement? *Harvard Educational Review, 39*(1), 162–170.

Johnson, L. B. (1965). Special message to the Congress toward full educational opportunity. Jan. 12, 1965, *Public Papers of the Presidents, Lyndon B. Johnson*, 1965, Book 1. Washington, D.C. In R. H. Bremner (Ed.). (1974). *Children and youth in America: A documentary history: Vol. 3. 1933–1973* (pp. 1798–1806). Cambridge, MA: Harvard University Press.

Kaplan, S. (1972). *The dream deferred: People, politics and planning in suburbia*. New York: Vintage.

Katz, J. (1976). *Gay American history: Lesbians and gay men in the U.S.A.* New York: Thomas Y. Crowell.

Katz, M. (1971). *Class, bureaucracy and school*. New York: Praeger.

Kearney, N. C. (1953). *Elementary school objectives: A report prepared for the mid-century committee on outcomes in elementary education*. New York: Russell Sage.

Kennedy, J. F. (1963). Special message to the Congress on education, Jan. 29, 1963. *Public Papers of the Presidents, John F. Kennedy*. Washington, D.C. In R. H. Bremner (Ed.). (1974). *Children and youth in America: A documentary history: Vol. 3. 1933–1973* (pp. 1795–1798). Cambridge, MA: Harvard University Press.

Koedt, A., Levine, A., & Rapone, A. (Eds.). (1973). *Radical feminism*. New York: Quadrangle Books.

Kozol, J. (1968). *Death at an early age*. New York: Penguin.

Kozol, J. (1972). *Free schools*. New York: Bantam.

Levine, M., & Levine, A. (1970). The more things change: A case history of child guidance clinics. *Journal of Social Issues, 26*(3), 19–34.

Mackintosh, H. K., & Lewis, G. M. (1965). Headstart for children in slums. *American Educator*, Dec. 1964-Jan. 1965. In R. H. Bremner (Ed.). (1974). *Children and youth in America: A documentary history: Vol. 3. 1933–1973* (pp. 1817–1821). Cambridge, MA: Harvard University Press.

Magaro, P. A., Gripp, R., & McDowell, D. J. (1978). *The mental health industry: A cultural phenomenon*. New York: Wiley.

Manchester, W. (1972). *The glory and the dream: A narrative history of America: 1932–1972*. Boston: Little, Brown.

Marx, G. T. (1970). Civil disorder and the agents of social control. *Journal of Social Issues, 26*(1), 19–58.

Massachussetts Childbearing Rights Alliance (1982). *Staying together: A guide for parents accused of child neglect or abuse.* Boston: Massachussetts Childbearing Rights Alliance.

McClintock, J., & McClintock, R. (1970). *Henry Barnard's school architecture.* New York: Teachers College Press.

Meranto, P. (1967). *The politics of federal aid to education in 1965: A study in political innovation.* Syracuse, NY: Syracuse University Press.

Minersville School District v. Gobitis. (1940). 310 U.S. 586. In R. H. Bremner (Ed.). (1974). *Children and youth in America: A documentary history: Vol. 3. 1933–1973* (pp. 1617–1674). Cambridge, MA: Harvard University Press.

Mohr, J. C. (1978). *Abortion in America.* New York: Oxford University Press.

Mollenkopf, J. H. (1978). The postwar politics of urban development. In W. K. Tabb & L. Sawers (Eds.), *Marxism and the metropolis.* New York: Oxford University Press.

Moynihan, D. P. (1965). *The Negro family: The case for national action.* Washington, D.C.: U.S. Department of Labor.

Nasaw, D. (1979). *Schooled to order: A social history of public schooling in the United States.* New York: Oxford University Press.

New, L. (1969). The failure of national policy: An historical analysis. In U.S. Congress, Senate, Committee on Indian Education, Indian Education: A national tragedy. A national challenge, 91 Cong., 1 Sess., Report No. 91–801. In R. H. Bremner (Ed.). (1974). *Children and youth in America: A documentary history: Vol. 3. 1933–1973* (pp. 152–156). Cambridge, MA: Harvard University Press.

New York City. Board of Aldermen (1902–1937). (1974). Committee on General Welfare. *Preliminary report on the matter of a request of the Conference of Organized Labor relative to education facilities.* New York: Arno Press.

Nixon, R. M. (1969). The president's message to the Congress, with recommendations on the office of economic opportunity and its programs. *Weekly Compilation of Presidential Documents, 5.* In R. H. Bremner (Ed.). (1974). *Children and youth in America: A documentary history: Vol. 3. 1933–1973* (pp. 1823–1825). Cambridge, MA: Harvard University Press.

Nyquist, E. N. (1972). Open education: its philosophy, historical perspectives and implications. In E. N. Nyquist & G. R. Hawes (Eds.). *Open education: A sourcebook for parents and teachers.* New York: Bantam.

Parrish, W. W. (1933). The plight of our school system. *Literary Digest.* 23. In R. H. Bremner (Ed.). (1974). *Children and youth in America: A documentary history: Vol. 3. 1933–1973* (pp. 1580–1581). Cambridge, MA: Harvard University Press.

Perrone, V. (1976). A view of school reform. In R. Dropkin & A. Tobier (Eds.). *Roots of open education in America* (pp. 173–190). New York: City College Workshop for Open Education.

Petchesky, R. P. (1984). *Abortion and woman's choice: The state, sexuality and reproductive freedom*. New York: Longman.

Piven, F. F., & Cloward, R. A. (1979). *Poor people's movements: Why they succeed, how they fail*. New York: Vintage.

Platt, A. M. (1977). *The child savers: The invention of delinquency*. (2nd Ed.). Chicago: University of Chicago Press.

Public Law 815. (1950). An act relating to the construction of school facilities in areas affected by federal activities. In R. H. Bremner (Ed.). (1974). *Children and youth in America: A documentary history: Vol. 3. 1933–1973* (p. 1785). Cambridge, MA: Harvard University Press.

Public Law 874. (1950). An act to provide financial assistance for local educational activities in areas affected by federal activities and for other purposes. . . . In R. H. Bremner (Ed.). (1974). *Children and youth in America: A documentary history: Vol. 3. 1933–1973* (pp. 1785–1786). Cambridge, MA: Harvard University Press.

Rickover, H. G. (1959). *Education and freedom*. New York: E. P. Dutton.

Rogers, V. R. (1972). *An American reaction*. In E. B. Nyquist & G. R. Hawes, *Open education: A sourcebook for parents and teachers*. New York: Bantam.

Rosenthal, A. (1969). *Pedagogues and power: Teacher groups in school politics*. Syracuse, NY: Syracuse University Press.

Ross, E. Q. (1929). *Social control*. London: Macmillan.

Ross, R., & Gump, P. W. (1978). Measurement of designed and modified openness in elementary schools. In S. Weidman & R. Anderson (Eds.), *Priorities for environmental design research* (pp. 243–253). Washington, D.C.: Environmental Design Research Association.

Rothman, D. J. (1971). *The discovery of the asylum: Social order and disorder in the new republic*. Boston: Little, Brown.

Rozak, T. (1968). *The making of a counterculture*. New York: Doubleday.

Ryan, M. P. (1975). *Womanhood in America: From colonial times to the present*. New York: Franklin Watts.

Shriver, S. (1966). Statement in U.S. Congress, Senate, Committee on Labor and Public Welfare, Subcommittee on Employment, Manpower and Poverty, Hearings on S. 3164, Amendment to the Economic Opportunity Act of 1964, 89 Cong., 2 Sess. In R. H. Bremner (Ed.). (1974). *Children and youth in America: A documentary history: Vol. 3. 1933–1973* (pp. 819–821). Cambridge, MA: Harvard University Press.

Shultz, S. (1973). *The culture factory: Boston public schools 1789–1860*. New York: Oxford University Press.

Silberman, C. E. (1970). *Crisis in the classroom: The remaking of American education*. New York: Random House.

Spring, J. H. (1972). *Education and the rise of the corporate state*. Boston: Beacon Press.

State Department of Education (1972). Vermont Design for Education. In E. B. Nyquist & G. R. Hawes. (Eds.), *Open education: A sourcebook for parents.* New York: Bantam.

Stern, E. M. (1937). Jim Crow goes to school in New York. *The Crisis,* 44. In R. H. Bremner (Ed.). (1974). *Children and youth in America: A documentary history: Vol. 3. 1933–1973* (pp. 1683–1685). Cambridge, MA: Harvard University Press.

Stewart, D. (1972). *A short history of East Harlem.* New York: Museum of the City of New York.

Takanishi, R. (1978). Childhood as a social issue: Historical roots of contemporary child advocacy movements. *Journal of Social Issues, 34*(1), 8–28.

Thompson, D. (1966). The new south. *Journal of Social Issues, 22*(1), 7–19.

Tyack, D. B. (Ed.). (1967). *Turning points in educational history.* Waltham, MA: Blaisdell.

Tyack, D. B. (1974). *The one best system: A history of American urban education.* Cambridge, MA: Harvard University Press.

U.S. Commission on Civil Rights. (1967a). *Racial isolation in the public schools,* Washington, D.C. In R. H. Bremner (Ed.). (1974). *Children and youth in America. A documentary history: Vol. 3. 1933–1973* (pp. 1856–1863). Cambridge, MA: Harvard University Press.

U.S. Commission on Civil Rights. (1967b). Southern school desegregation: 1956–1967. Washington, D.C. In R. H. Bremner (Ed.). (1974). *Children and youth in America. A documentary history: Vol. 3. 1933–1973* (pp. 1834–1836). Cambridge, MA: Harvard University Press.

U.S. Congress, House of Representatives, Select Committee to Investigate Indian Affairs (1944). An investigation to determine whether the changed status of the Indian requires a revision of the laws and regulations affecting the American Indian, 78 Cong., 2 Sess., Report No. 2091. In R. H. Bremner (Ed.). (1974). *Children and youth in America: A documentary history: Vol. 3. 1933–1973* (pp. 1717–1720). Cambridge, MA: Harvard University Press.

U.S. Office of Economic Opportunity (1967). *Child development program, a manual of policies and instruction.* Washington D.C.: Office of Economic Opportunity. In R. H. Bremner (Ed.). (1974). *Children and youth in America. A documentary history: Vol. 3. 1933–1973* (pp. 1821–1822). Cambridge, MA: Harvard University Press.

U.S. Office of Education (1966). *Equality of educational opportunity.* Washington, D.C. In R. H. Bremner (Ed.). (1974). *Children and youth in America: A documentary history: Vol. 3. 1933–1973* (pp. 1851–1855). Cambridge, MA: Harvard University Press.

U.S. President's Commission on Higher Education (1947). *Higher education for American democracy.* Washington, D.C. In R. H. Bremner (Ed.). (1974). *Children and youth in America: A documentary history: Vol. 3. 1933–1973* (pp. 1695–1697). Cambridge, MA: Harvard University Press.

Weiman v. Updegraff (1952). 344 U.S. 183. In R. H. Bremner (Ed.). (1974). *Children and youth in America: A documentary history: Vol. 3. 1933–1973* (pp. 1743–1745). Cambridge, MA: Harvard University Press.

West Virginia State Board of Education v. Barnette. (1943). 319 U.S. 624. In R. H. Bremner (Ed.). (1974). *Children and youth in America: A documentary history: Vol. 3. 1933–1973* (pp. 1624–1630). Cambridge, MA: Harvard University Press.

Wishy, B. (1968). *The child and the republic.* Philadelphia: University of Pennsylvania Press.

Wolfe, M. (1981). *Fact sheet on families.* New York: Reproductive Rights National Network.

Wright, G. (1983). *Building the dream: A social history of housing in the United States.* Cambridge, MA: MIT Press.

Zinn, H. (1984). *The twentieth century: A people's history.* New York: Harper and Row.

CHAPTER 6

Settings for Childhood Education: Innovation Versus Tradition

INTRODUCTION TO OUR WORK

The overview of the history of schools has described the criticism of the educational system of the 1960s and 1970s along with the optimism about educational reforms that were being attempted. As in the case of children's mental health services, this history reveals not a slow progression toward enlightenment but rather a variety of educational philosophies, products of the ethos of the times, implemented in buildings that were sometimes relics of the past and sometimes looked toward a future that would never materialize. In the years after World War II, there was both continued use of antiquated buildings, mainly in urban areas, and extensive new school construction, largely in suburban areas.

For environmental psychologists and other social scientists, the study of schools in light of changing educational philosophies can add to the understanding of an experience that informs much of a child's early years. This chapter will consider what we know from this accumulated work with a particular focus on what we learned from our own research.

The studies that form the basis for this chapter were undertaken over a 12-year period in a number of public schools. With the exception of one school located in a midwestern suburban-rural area, these schools were all in New York City, and their students, teachers, programs, and administration reflected the state of education in contemporary times. Some were traditional both in their physical design and educational programs; others were innovative in both of these dimensions; yet others mixed tradition and innovation. Two were considered to be "alternative schools," because they provided alternatives to the usual system for the children. The alternative school concept grew out of changes to schools made in the 1960s. However, its meaning had changed considerably by the time of our studies.

The first alternative school had been initiated by a group of parents and teachers who were interested in providing an open classroom program for the students.

The new school was established in an old, unused school building, and was open to all families in the area.

The second school reflected a very different perspective on an alternative. The site had been selected by the school administration for the instruction of children considered to be ineducable in regular classrooms, because they were judged to have behavior or intellectual problems. These children were removed to a mini-school set up on one floor of an existing junior high school.

Our decision to focus on public education came out of a desire to deal with the form of education that affected the largest population of children. It was not based on any conviction that these were the worst schools. In fact, our consultation work with a number of private schools has indicated that they too have a range of settings, sizes, and philosophies, with some more successful than others. Since the public schools largely accommodated persons with the fewest options, and since their physical form, basic curricula, and staffing—all state mandated— reflected societal goals most directly, they seemed the best settings on which to concentrate.

For the most part, the schools we studied wanted to improve their programs and felt our presence would contribute to this goal. Yet in a decentralized school system, we had to follow a diversity of procedures to gain admittance. These ranged from presentations to the local community at an open board meeting to approval by an individual principal. In all instances, written permission from parents was obtained. Although it was our policy to work only in those classrooms where teachers, not just administrators, agreed to our presence, there were varying degrees of enthusiasm. It is difficult initially to assess the motivations for the cooperation of administrators and teachers. Over time it became clear that some of them were responding to pressure: the teachers from principals, the principals from local school district superintendents. Others were eager to be associated with new projects in the school, or some just saw our work with the children as a way of making the rest of the day more palatable; some were attracted by the idea that added classroom resources would be available in a period of economic cutbacks; and some were genuinely interested in making school a positive place for the growth and development of children. Those teachers most oriented to the children's needs generally wanted feedback about what they were doing and help in reaching their goals.

In these different settings the attempts to improve programs took different forms. During the early 1970s various individualized teaching approaches and open-classroom techniques were used. However, there was only a brief time during which the introduction of open education on a wide scale coincided with an expanding economy. By the mid-1970s, given the constraints of tightening budgets, the loss of personnel, and the demoralization of teachers, many of these programs were in jeopardy. By the late 1970s the schools in which we worked were trying to provide what they considered to be the best education within their means, in an era of even tighter fiscal constraints, growing conservatism, and a "back to basics" philosophy.

All but one of these urban schools were in old buildings, some dating back to the late 1800s and early 1900s. The exception was a new building designed to be structurally open. We will draw on all these places. In some we spent a few years, while in others we conducted briefer studies or environmental workshops with teachers, students, and administrators. The opportunities we had to talk to students, teachers, and parents and to spend time in both formal and informal observations in classrooms have, in conjunction with our reading of history, provided the data for our analysis.

VARIETIES OF ENVIRONMENTS AND PRACTICES

While we have worked in many schools, in order to give a concrete image we will focus on the four involved in the School Setting Study and the Futures Project. Before providing a picture of what they were like physically, it would be useful to know what we were doing in each of them.

The School Setting Study took place over a two-year period in two schools. We were interested in identifying the relationship between the educational philosophies of the teachers, the use of the classroom, and the qualities of the physical environment. A number of different approaches to gathering information were used including observations of the use of the rooms, tracking the behavior of individual children, observations of the location and placement of furniture and equipment, and interviews with principals, teachers, parents, and children. We also worked with teachers and children in environmental workshops aimed at dealing with various problems that they felt existed in their rooms.

The Futures Project, also based in two schools, was a teaching and learning process with adults and children working together to understand environmental change now and in the future. Children were encouraged to see themselves as active participants in change by examining problems related to their own needs and those of their communities. The neighborhood was used as a learning place and resource in the development of images of the future. With the project staff acting as facilitators and technical advisors, the children were given hands-on experiences with the skills and technology useful in dealing with their issues. They were encouraged to tie past and present to the future. The children in each school selected the issues on which they worked. These included housing and landlord problems, difficulties with an empty lot filled with trash, understanding the role of local action groups dealing with neighborhood change, and the assessment of their neighborhood. All of this work was documented by the children, using media skills acquired within the Futures Project.

The Physical Environments of the School Setting Study

This work involved two schools that were studied simultaneously, both of them in buildings constructed around the turn of the century. One school will be identified as the standard borough school, the other, the voluntary alternative. Both were similar in structure, built in a period of grand and elaborate school architecture with facades festooned with gargoyles and turrets.

The voluntary alternative provided another option to parents whose children would normally have attended an overcrowded school nearby. It was in a historic neighborhood that attracted many visitors, including tourists. The narrow, winding streets of the area were lined with a mix of eighteenth-, and nineteenth-, and early twentieth-century buildings which had been converted into modern residences and fashionable, trendy shops and restaurants. The population was largely white, although a minority of Hispanics and Asians lived and worked there.

The antiquated stone school building was in serious need of electrical, plumbing, and structural renovation. Originally it had functioned as a junior high school. Over the years it had been used for a variety of programs and at one time was left vacant. It was now serving 400 kindergarten through fifth-grade students with 16 teachers and a principal. There were five floors in the building, but the top one was not used. The building contained a small basement cafeteria, a gymnasium, an auditorium, and first-floor offices. The rooms varied in size from 595 to 1,035 square feet. On the second through fourth floors were "sub-schools," each with kindergarten through fifth-grade classes variously integrated. The sub-school which was the setting for our study contained interaged classes: a kindergarten–first grade, a second–third grade, a second–third–fourth grade, and a third–fourth grade.

The plans for complete renovation of this school never materialized due to budget cutbacks and other school priorities. Over the years, with parent participation, small changes were made: shelves built, two rooms were opened up into one large space, walls were plastered and painted. Parents were often found working on various building projects in the school.

A multitude of staircases ran off the long corridors, and dim lighting enhanced a feeling of darkness in the building. Rooms were rectangular and traditional in design with wardrobes along one long wall, windows along the others, and closets, shelves and a chalkboard at the front. The furnishings combined standard school tables and chairs with rugs and chairs donated by teachers and parents. Rooms were generally set up informally with interest areas for reading, science, math, and art. Most contained a housekeeping section and a block corner, as well. In three of the rooms we studied the teachers had their own desks; in the fourth the teacher sat on the small-scale tables and chairs as she worked with children.

Students hung their outer clothing in the wardrobe and kept other belongings in small bins or cubbies that were placed on shelves. Although there were movable tables and chairs in the the rooms, none of the children had assigned seats. In one class a few children put their names on chairs and maintained a proprietary interest over them. The walls were heavily decorated with children's work, and in some classes paintings were strung across the rooms on lines that stretched from wall to wall.

The second, the standard borough school, was located in a quiet low-density neighborhood of tree-lined streets with well-maintained, comfortable single-family homes and occasional six-story apartment houses. Some of the children came from this white, middle-class area, but most were bused in from more racially, ethnically, and economically mixed neighboring areas.

The building itself was a rather imposing four-story stone structure, originally built in 1903, with a three-story addition completed in 1954. Unlike the voluntary alternative building, this one was in rather good repair. When our work took place, the school population was 1,250, with over one-quarter Black and Hispanic. (Up to the 1960s the school had been white and middle-class.) The staff included 40 teachers, a principal, and two assistant principals. Some of the classes also had parent aides and paraprofessionals assisting, as well as student teachers from a nearby college.

Lunch facilities were limited. Most of the children who brought their lunches to school had to use the auditorium. About 150 children whose family income was below the poverty line received free lunches in the small school cafeteria. In good weather children played in the schoolyard after finishing their lunches. When the weather was poor they used the gymnasium.

For our research we selected one section of a floor in the school addition containing four classes of first- and second-grade students. The classrooms ranged in size from 864 to 900 square feet. They resembled those in the voluntary alternative although they were arranged in a more orderly fashion, were better structurally, and were kept in good repair. The same pattern prevailed as in the voluntary alternative: wardrobe on one long wall, windows on the other. The furnishings were similar as well, with child-sized tables and chairs, cubbies or bins on shelves, and the children's work mounted on the walls although it was often hung above their line of sight. However, there were some differences between the standard borough school and the voluntary alternative. All of the teachers in the standard school had desks and we found that they used them more than teachers in the voluntary alternative used theirs. Children in two of the four classrooms had assigned seats. The rooms also were quite structured in their arrangement of furniture and equipment and had little of the "found" furniture in the other school.

The Physical Environments of the Futures Project

Like the School Setting Study, the Futures Project focused on two contrasting schools. The first, the Park Hill School, was located in an economically and ethnically heterogeneous neighborhood. The neighborhood bordered on a large park, had good housing stock, and was easily accessible to the urban center. Originally developed in the middle of the eighteenth century as an elegant residential area of brownstones and townhouses, it had come upon hard times during which many structures were converted into rooming houses and apartments for working-class people. Many blocks, especially those farthest from the park, had abandoned buildings. At the time of the Futures Project the area was rapidly becoming gentrified, displacing many long-time tenants and shopkeepers who could not afford the escalating rents. Small grocery stores were closing, only to be replaced by boutiques and expensive restaurants. Although the neighborhood still retained a core of working-class and middle-class Irish and Italian families, including many elderly, it was becoming increasingly upper middle-class. The area also included some blocks occupied mainly by Hispanic and Black families. Some of these people were poor, others working-class or lower middle-class.

The school, located on the edge of this expanding gentrified neighborhood, was an impressive Victorian building which dated back to the 1880s. It had the high ceilings and large doors and windows characteristic of this era and, in the basement, bathrooms and a cafeteria. Small in comparison with the borough school, it served 400 neighborhood children in kindergarten through fifth grade. There were two classes for each grade level except kindergarten. Only one class was needed at this level because many of the local young children were in private nursery schools or all-day child-care centers.

The fifth-graders with which the Futures Project worked had a large, rectangular classroom with tables and chairs placed in the front section of the room. The teacher's desk was set diagonally across one front corner of the room. Although a large, empty space remained in the back, there were no interest areas or equipment in evidence. Despite the fact that the project began in mid-year, the walls were practically bare of children's work or decorations. Seats were assigned and students remained in them most of the day.

The second Futures Project site, the involuntary alternative school for children removed from regular classes was a mini-school of 80 students which occupied half of the fifth floor of a junior high school. It was located in a neighborhood similar in many ways to Park Hill in that it was subject to both abandonment and gentrification. But there were also differences. The area of the involuntary alternative had always been a denser and poorer section and its population was ethnically and economically more homogeneous. During the 1930s large numbers of Puerto Rican migrants had moved into the area, a trend that continued after World War II. With unemployment rates high and increasing, many family incomes were below the poverty level. The neighborhood received poor city services, and there was a great deal of drug traffic and street crime. Older tenement buildings and more recently built high-rise public housing lined the streets. Small factories had also found their way into the area, although at the time of the project most of these had closed. Boarded-up buildings were the relics of their presence. There were also many abandoned residential structures. Green and open spaces were almost nonexistent, except for some rubble-strewn vacant lots.

Recently, renovation of buildings had begun to change one edge of the neighborhood. There were a few expensive shops and cafes and some gentrified housing in this section. However, for the most part the neighborhood shopping streets, social clubs, and lively street life remained intact although there were many concerns for the future. Local community groups had begun to organize around issues of housing, jobs, health care, and schools.

The school building itself was only 30 years old, but its poor physical condition made it appear years older. Because severe budget cuts had limited maintenance, there were signs of disrepair throughout. Children and staff complained of the lack of heat as well as the lack of resources.

The sixth-grade class of 15 students with whom we worked were in a classroom designed for 30 or more. Yet seats were arranged at great distances from each other, rather than clustered together as in the Park Hill school. The room was rather bare, with the teacher's desk up front.

The project was given an unused classroom to use as a resource and meeting space. It was here and in the neighborhood that the work took place.

The Practices

On the top floor of one of the schools that we studied was an unused space, a room with rows of desks and seats bolted to the floor, one behind the other. Up front was the teacher's desk, centered before the blackboard, symbolically the focus of attention and authority. Closets for the teacher and supplies, and a long wardrobe for children's belongings completed the design. This classroom was in a turn-of-the-century building in which other spaces had been modified over time to meet changing educational fashions. For example, in the 1950s most of the fixed desks and seats were removed, replaced by movable tables and chairs. Only this one room had been ignored, to remain as a museum of the past (see Figure 6.1).

In truth, however, the past had survived in other ways, even after desks had been unscrewed and rooms redesigned to add science and math centers, reading corners, and shelves of materials lining the walls. As we observed the rooms in

Figure 6.1.   A view of the past in the present

this school, and in others we studied, we found that although spaces and teaching styles varied somewhat across schools, most did not reflect the modern educational philosophies that teachers said they were trying to implement. In both the alternative schools and the standard ones, there was a great gap between stated aspiration and practice. Teachers talked about the value of individualized programs while they taught group classes. They spoke of the value of manipulation of materials, but little was in evidence. They knew the value of collaborative projects, yet we observed children working alone most of the time. Clearly competing goals were compromising what was happening in these rooms.

Although the desks and seats in the classrooms we studied were no longer bolted to the floor, tables and chairs had replaced the fixed furniture, covering much of the floor space (see Figure 6.2). Our systematic observations, including mapping of the location of furniture and equipment, showed that in most rooms the arrangements set out by the teacher at the beginning of the school year remained until the last day of classes. This was true despite the repeated declarations of staff that their rooms "weren't working" or that they wanted their rooms to reflect their changing programs.

This difference between intentions and reality is both comprehensible and revealing. First, most teachers hold expectations for students which grow out of a cultural system (Rist, 1970) and a school system, not out of their own pedagogical goals. Textbooks are selected by central departments and curricula largely defined

Figure 6.2.   Unmoving, movable tables and chairs covering most of floorspace

by administration. Teachers are assigned to schools by a central administration and budgets are decided centrally as well. Added to this are the various standardized tests administered to all students, some yearly, others at points considered to be crucial to their progression. These test results are carefully scrutinzed by parents, administrators, and the public. Even in the more innovative classrooms we saw that the examinations were a priority for several weeks. We found teachers changing their styles as the testing dates approached, giving children practice time for the exams. This testing reflects the view that the quality of a school can be assessed by reading and math scores. Since the skills developed in open or individualized education are rarely if ever subjected to standardized evaluation, they are largely ignored by school authorities providing little motivation or support for more open approaches on the part of teachers. In fact, since much informal education is based on individual pacing, standardized tests given at specific times contradict the basic philosophy of the individualized approach.

In most cases where classroom teachers were trying to implement open education they were in buildings designed for a very different style of teaching, structured along lines of authority, as reflected in the unused museum room. Such rooms give few environmental messages that support alternatives. In addition, teachers could expect limited inservice training for any new programs and little or nothing for the strategies and methods of open education. For the most part teachers had to locate programs and resources for themselves and set up their rooms without guidance or additional equipment.

There were other difficulties, too, related to the economic and social problems of the times. During the years of our work we saw a gradual increase in the size of classes, a reduction in materials and supplies, and the loss of teachers' aides even for children with reading problems and other academic difficulties. Some teachers provided the resources that they were unable to obtain through school channels by either purchasing materials themselves or soliciting them through parents. Still, it was a period of low morale and disillusionment, however enthusiastic students, parents, or teachers might be about a particular educational philosophy.

The kinds of open-education programs that teachers implemented varied greatly. Not only was flexible use of the furniture ignored but for some teachers "open" merely meant that they would set up interest areas and permit children to use them at specified times.

Observations revealed that children spent most of their days in their seats, getting up only to get materials or go over to the teacher's desk to ask a question or have work checked.

Even in the rooms where teachers were using some innovative, truly "open" approaches, for example, in the voluntary alternative school, there were limits to the departure from traditional school days. Although students planned the sequence of their work themselves and moved about the room more freely, a number of constraints still existed. For example, there was little use of the corridors, a common practice in conducting open education in structurally closed buildings. Teachers admitted that they were unwilling to permit children outside the rooms without supervision: they might "fool around" or disturb other classes. Corridors would be used only when an adult was available to monitor the activity there. In some cases where the corridors were used, there were problems because inconsistent activities were taking place simultaneously. While some teachers used the corridor for activities requiring quiet reading or writing stories, others planned to have noisy activities occur there. The failure of teachers to plan cooperatively undermined the value of this auxiliary space.

There were other constraints as well. Although individualized and open programs are supposed to free teachers from their desks, as we have described, in all but one of the classrooms we studied teachers retained their own desks, usually at the front of the room. The one deskless teacher moved around the room more than other teachers, working with students and becoming involved in the preparation of projects.

An interesting variant concerning movement took place in one of the midwestern elementary schools, where children were in what was called an "innovative" program very much like the Gary Plan of 1912. They had a homeroom but moved from room to room for different subjects, carrying their books and supplies in a small plastic bin. In each class, including their homeroom, they chose their seats each day. Thus the specific place could change each day but they had to remain in their seats for the duration of the class.

The informal arrangements, in many cases a dramatic departure from the bolted-down desks and seats, often embodied a contradiction between the superficial appearance and actual use of the room. A close look at what was happening often uncovered rather formal and set functions for various parts of the space with control over the room's use held by the teacher. Since many of the rooms came out of a standard form for school design, one that had persisted for many years, they supported a hierarchical type of education in which teachers remained at the head of the room overseeing the students and anyone entering or leaving the room. The chalkboard became the center of teaching, the focus, as was the teacher's desk. These silent symbols of an authoritarian teaching style were difficult to overcome however much the rooms were rearranged, especially since all the teachers we observed, the novices and experienced ones, had been educated and trained in the classrooms of the past. In this regard it is interesting to consider the open-space school that we studied.

Figure 6.3a.   Open design school with traditional patterns of use

The faculty and students in this open-space school had been moved from a nearby building constructed at the turn of the century into a setting that was dramatically different in design. The new school was not a well considered outgrowth of the philosophy of the faculty or the administration, but rather based on the Board of Education's desire for a modern-looking school, and their approval of a popular form of construction that was considered to be relatively less expensive than schools with walls.

Observations in the open-design school uncovered patterns common in traditional schools. Teachers did not reflect in their pedagogical styles the open setting in which they worked. In the large, open areas, students clustered around their teachers, who generally positioned themselves in front of the movable chalkboards, which were placed near the windows (see Figure 6.3a). There was little evidence of shared classes or team teaching. Invisible walls existed between classes and eventually arrangements of furniture, bookcases, and equipment defined the territories of each class (see Figure 6.3b). This was a pattern observed in many open schools that we visited; classes shared little beyond the vast open area and high noise level. In many open schools, one class might try to ignore the other groups by facing away from them. Some teachers took more active measures, using whatever equipment or materials that were available to create barriers or

Figure 6.3b.   Open design school with class territories

partitions. Unable or unwilling to follow through on the full implications of openness, which include team teaching and shared resources, they recreated the essence of the traditional rooms.

In the involuntary alternative school we found an educational philosophy of a somewhat different order from those in other schools. Perceiving themselves as offering a last chance for unsuccessful students, the teachers and school administrator were quite open in expressing their views that "these children need structure." Obedience to authority was the prevailing theme and one teacher even served as an "order-keeper." When a teacher anticipated trouble, this bouncer/police officer would be called to remove the offenders from the classroom. The staff expressed commitment to this philosophy of authority and containment. They did not consider their policies to be harsh or repressive but felt that their mixture of structure and support would help their students to learn.

In summary, the schools in which we spent our time ranged in philosophy from traditional to innovative, from structured to open. However, regardless of philosophy there was little reflection on how to implement it given the constraints of the specific contexts or settings. With the exception of those in the involuntary alternative school, few teachers were explicit about their need for structure. Instead, while they gave lip service to a philosophy of openness and individualized programming, many carefully kept their classes in line with techniques that contained and controlled.

WHAT IS A SCHOOL DAY LIKE?

Some of our most revealing school experiences occurred during day-to-day observations when we remained with classes from the time they arrived until dismissal. As in the case of the psychiatric hospital, immersion in the life of a class resulted in detailed information about the teaching program, the use of the room, and the philosophy of the teacher that occasional visits could not provide. The opportunity to hear casual conversations, read memos, go to gym and library with the class, and be present when the teacher interacted with children and staff resulted in a rich picture of the milieu of the classroom. We were also better able to describe and understand the physical arrangements of the room when we could observe the ways in which they changed over the school year. We followed the days of individual children and systematically gathered detailed descriptions of what was happening from the beginning of the semester in September to the end of the school year in June. We will draw on these longitudinal observations for a view of what a school day is like. Although our research took us to many different schools we will focus on those in which we spent the longest periods of time.

The School Setting Study

In this study, all of the teachers in whose rooms we were observing claimed to be using an individualized, open approach to teaching although our observations revealed considerable variability across the classes. However, there was an underlying structure to be found in each of the classrooms.

Generally, the school day began with a class meeting. In one room the teacher conducted the meeting from her desk and children remained seated at their tables. In the others, children sat on the floor in an open space near the teacher. These meetings served a number of purposes. They enabled the teacher to describe the work of the day or week, to conduct a lesson, or plan activities. It was a time when children reported on their assignments. It was also an opportunity for the teacher to give the class "pep talks" or remind students of what was expected of them.

After this initial period, children would move on to the assignments given to them. Most of the time they worked alone, despite the open education rhetoric about the value of group projects. In addition, materials used were largely restricted to paper and pencil with little evidence of other types of projects, again contradicting an educational philosophy that valued the manipulation of varied materials. As the day progressed, children worked on their tasks, pausing to chat with other students and ask questions of the teacher or student teacher, if one was present. When an assignment was completed the child either left it with the teacher or had the teacher check it. Often children waited in a long line for their turn with the teacher.

There were some breaks in the workday—more in the alternative than in the standard school. Children would go to the bathroom, a weekly class in the library, and gym. For some there also were opportunities to water the plants or feed the class pet, play educational games or deliver a message to another classroom. Before lunch a considerable period of time was spent cleaning up the room and putting things away. The lunch break in the standard borough school was sheer chaos, a thunderous roar in the cafeteria or auditorium where the children ate, teachers shouting into bullhorns, and the voices of children trying harder and harder to be heard above the cacophony of sounds.

When weather permitted students would bolt down their lunches and go into the concrete schoolyard where yet another teacher supervised the play, bullhorn in hand. In the voluntary school, lunch was often eaten in the classroom. There was a lively atmosphere and animated sounds of voices, but at a comfortable level. When finished eating, children could go to the play area on the roof of an extension to the building if weather permitted. On some days the students ate in their lunchroom, where mealtime was a noisy contrast to the meals taken in their rooms.

The afternoon program was similar to the morning one although few classes repeated the group meeting. They might begin the afternoon with a lesson or a story read by the teacher, then go on to the various required tasks: reading cards, math assignments, and similar exercises. If these were completed before 3:00 p.m. they were permitted to play one of the educational games available in the room. The end of the day was preceded by another clean-up time with the teacher overseeing as students went about their chores. The days in the voluntary alternative were more varied across classes than in the standard borough school. There was more movement of children, more talking, and more evidence of joint projects complementing individual work assignments.

What was the teacher doing during the day? In addition to conducting group lessons and meetings, most of her time was spent supervising and monitoring, making certain that each child kept busy, scrutinizing the progress of those she felt needed prodding. She also spent a great deal of time answering questions and checking over work. Indeed, waiting in line to see the teacher was a predominant activity in classrooms especially in the standard borough school. A few teachers worked with small groups of children, or even individual students, but this was more common when an aide or student teacher was present in the room.

We traced the uses of various parts of the rooms and the precise locations of teachers and students. The maps prepared from these data showed that in both schools studied the front third of the rooms had the highest density. Other parts were used rarely or not at all, especially in the standard borough school. In three classrooms, two in one school and one in the other, half of the class, that is, 17 students could be found in one-sixth of the total space, comprising an area of about 145 square feet. Most of the time the teacher was located in this same front segment. In fact one teacher (along with a cluster of students) spent 72% of her day in an area that was one-twelfth of the total space. From this position she could oversee the entrance to the room and check on people entering and leaving. She could also monitor the progress of class members who were drawn to this area by various activities—group meetings, lessons, and the distribution of materials that were centered in this part of the room. This convergence within a small portion of the total space persisted in most rooms despite complaints by teachers that they felt crowded and that children were disturbing each other and creating too much noise.

When we suggested distributing class members over the available space we were told that children could not be trusted out of eye view of the teacher or that the back could be used, but only when an adult was present. It became clear that despite interest in open education practices, teachers were not prepared to give children free access to the entire space except in special cases. Children whom they could "trust" were allowed to use the rear alone, but even they had restrictions.

The heavy concentration in the front of the room where behavior could be monitored by the teacher supported and perpetuated traditional forms of teaching and communicated the uneven value and different meanings the teacher attached to various parts of the space. Although each room had a portable chalkboard, these were rarely used. Rather the teachers seemed anchored by the chalkboard on the front wall, even when it was not being used. From this position subtle and direct cues told students that they should remain nearby. Most potent was the teacher's own presence which acted as a magnet for the children, despite the problems that are likely to occur when lively young children are drawn together in close proximity to one another.

It was interesting to observe in a room when the teacher was absent and a substitute took over. In many cases the usual routine of the day would emerge as children gathered for their group meeting, picked up reading and math assignments, and generally followed the structure laid down by their regular teacher despite the fact that she was not there.

Since open education places great value on group projects, we examined the working patterns in classrooms. We found that working alone was the most common form of activity. Little group effort was in evidence. Children might be seated at tables with other children, each one absorbed in the same task, but they were involved in individual rather than group work. Conversation with others at the table constituted an interruption of their work, not an integral part of it.

The detailed observations also identified the specific activities taking place in the rooms. They revealed that of all the school activities we studied, writing and talking were the most commonly seen. Although there were some differences across the schools with more writing and less variety of activities in the standard borough school than in the voluntary alternative one, the similarities were more conspicuous. Both the nature of the work and the materials used were conventional ones. Neither school offered much chance to manipulate materials, although this was an expressed interest of the teachers and a foundation of open education.

Another kind of view can be obtained from observations of individual children. We found that, although the structure of the days was similar for all members of a class, there were significant differences depending on two major factors, the specific environmental style of the child and the teacher's perception of whether that child was to be trusted.

Some excerpts from our written observations can illustrate these points. They describe two children in a class in the standard borough school. It is after lunch in a room in which the teacher identifies her educational philosophy as "open."

Ivy goes over to her cubby and returns some writing materials. She walks around the area near the cubbies looking at the various materials stored there. Then she goes to the reading corner in the front of the room, picks up a reading card from the supply stored on a table, and goes over to the teacher who is standing nearby. After chatting a few minutes Ivy goes over to a table near the front of the room and sits down. Two boys are working on their cards. The teacher calls over to the three with instructions regarding their cards. Ivy works intently. Periodically the teacher gives more instructions. Each time the boys look up from their work. Ivy remains absorbed in what she is doing, paying no attention. The boys have difficulty resuming their work after each interruption and they chat with each other. Ivy continues, completing her work in 15 minutes. She gives her card to the teacher and goes over to the reading corner.

Danny returns from lunch, stopping near the front closet to talk to another boy. He goes to the front center of the room where he picks up a spelling exercise, chatting with a boy nearby. The teacher calls out for him to "get busy." He sits down at a small table where a girl is working. They talk, and then Danny begins to work. After about three minutes the teacher, who is seated at her desk, calls out for Danny to come to her desk. He returns his work to his cubby and goes over to the teacher. She describes a clock that he must make, part of a lesson she had taught that morning. Danny goes to the front shelf and picks up some materials. He returns to ask the teacher a question, waiting three minutes until she finishes talking with another child. He then goes to the front of the room, talks to a boy, goes to his cubby, and takes out some pencils. The teacher calls out, "Start working, Danny!" He goes to a table near the wardrobe and sits down. Two boys and two girls are sitting there working on their clocks. He chats with the boy next to him and the teacher calls out for him to "get to work." He begins and seems absorbed in drawing the face when the teacher tells him to bring his work to her. She seats him in the reading corner where three other children are at work, and again tells him to "get to work."

These two sets of observations document the classroom experiences of two children who were treated quite differently by the same teacher. From the teacher's view Ivy was an achiever, someone who could be trusted. She was given far greater freedom of movement in the room without being challenged by the teacher. Danny, in contrast, often was the object of the teacher's concern as she moved her eyes across the room, spotting children that she felt were wasting time or not attending to assigned tasks. She told us that Danny was a "wanderer" and needed to be watched. Unfortunately for Danny and some others in this room, the teacher's attempts to keep track of students' progress sometimes interrupted them in their work.

The two children clearly differed in their levels of concentration and their work styles. Ivy could persist despite the teacher's voice, very likely because she was aware that she was not the object of criticism. She could work at a table of children who were chatting and remain involved in her work, something that Danny seemed unable to do.

One can only wonder how Danny would have fared in a quiet corner, with less interruption by the teacher's voice. Our feeling was that Ivy would be able to work almost anywhere—and indeed we saw her able to screen out noise and interruptions in a number of instances in order to complete the task at hand. But in this class and most of the others, there was no attention to how children might learn to select work places appropriate to their needs and the task at hand, nor was the freedom to make these judgments usually given.

These observations point up three major factors influencing the flow of activity: the nature of the children involved, the style of the teacher, and the qualities of the setting. The teacher in this class was a monitor anxious to keep close watch on all that was happening. The room was a busy one with much of the class concentrated up front, creating work problems that were not being addressed.

These three factors structure the qualities of days for individual students. However, other forces were operating as well. It was clear from our observations that the teachers treated girls and boys in quite different ways, and some of this is reflected in Danny and Ivy's day. Girls would be given far greater range within the room, taking liberties, albeit small ones for which boys would be challenged. The sex of the child, therefore, in some sense structured the kind of day that child could have.

Among other forces shaping the school lives of children, social class is a powerful one. Belief by the teacher in limits to the potential progress of particular social classes creates constraints on the school days and years of children (Rist, 1970) even more powerful because their underlying basis is concealed.

The Futures Project

In the two schools in which the Futures Project was based the days were somewhat different. The school most like the one already described was the Park Hill School where a fifth-grade class (10- and 11-year-olds) was the focus. Children spent most of their time in their unmoving movable chairs and tables, listening to the teacher's lessons. If they belonged to a school club such as the art group, they were permitted to go out of the room for weekly meetings. The two periods each week during which the Futures Project was held was seen as "enrichment" and this time competed with the few other alternatives, such as the clubs.

Discipline was the primary focus, and order and quiet prevailed throughout the school. In this classroom the teacher used a bell when she wanted the attention of the group. She kept her eyes on the class, scanning the room for anything that she could label misbehavior. One day a girl, caught up in her enthusiasm for what she was doing with the project, tap-danced across the room. She was roundly reprimanded for her exuberance and criticized for disrupting the group. In fact, other children were wrapped up in their own project work and paid no attention to this "outburst."

Some of the teacher's behavior might have been her reaction to the presence of visitors. Or one might suspect that the group was a difficult one. However, the class was a "good" one with reading grades at or above the norm. In addition, we found that this teacher's style was such that her bell and her voice frequently extinguished lively behavior.

Despite the fact this was not a "problem" school, when city-wide tests approached, without any notice to the Futures Project staff, their two periods were taken away for one month and used to give extra drill to the students. The principal explained that they keep reading scores up through "drill and coercion," and that it worked.

In this school the corridors were regularly monitored, and children routinely were challenged by adults about being in them. One example describes the situation that occurred during one Futures Project time period.

Diana and Maria, two Hispanic girls, went out into the hall to put up signs. Although we had met with teachers many times to inform them about the project, while the two girls were hanging up posters they were challenged by a teacher. "What are you doing out in the hall?" they were asked. When Diana tried to explain, the teacher yelled even more loudly, finally saying, "I know you, you're just like your brother, you're all alike—trouble-makers!" Diana came back into the class crying. Her own teacher made her feel even worse by telling her that she was acting like a baby to cry about such a small thing.

In all the time we were in this school, the white students were never reprimanded by anyone no matter where they went.

The involuntary alternative school, which saw itself as "the last chance" for its students, was, as one might expect, even more restrictive. In the class involved in the Futures Project, the children sat in their room all day except during their scheduled art class and gym. The large classrooms, 25 by 40 feet, held no more than 15 students. (There were 13 in the one with which we worked.) The desks were placed as much as 10 feet apart; this was done to prevent "incidents" according to the teacher.

Days were rigidly structured. Each subject area had a given number of minutes. In order to speak students had to raise their hands to be called on and were reprimanded for any spontaneous comments, even if they reflected interest and enthusiasm in the topic. The arbitrary time set for a subject defined the end of a period with military discipline despite the fact that the students might be absorbed in the work. Yet this was a school in which teachers and administrators constantly complained about the students' lack of motivation and interest. The teacher typically came into the Futures Project room five minutes before the period was to end. She would wait, checking her watch, and at the precise minute the allotted time was over she demanded that everyone line up no matter what they were doing or how deeply involved they had become.

Another example of an event in this school, very likely not an uncommon occurrence, gives some idea of the quality of daily life. One day, while working on the project the children were doing different things, going about their tasks, talking, bantering with each other in a light and cheerful way. Their teacher walked into the room and for no reason whatsoever said to one of the boys "Don't let me see you do that again!" The boy asked "What did I do?" The teacher started yelling—"You know what you did!" Within three minutes the argument had escalated to the point where the boy was physically removed from the room by the "bouncer." We never did find out what the boy had done, nor did we think he had done anything at all but by the time he was removed from the room it did not matter because finally he had done something—he yelled at the teacher.

There was persistent reprimanding of students and an expectation that the children were up to no good. This flavored all that occurred in the class, turning the instruction, whatever subject was being taught, into a battle for discipline. The overall message was the anticipation of trouble and the assumption that the children would not and could not learn, hardly optimal conditions for success.

SOME IMPLICATIONS OF SCHOOLS AS INSTITUTIONAL ENVIRONMENTS

Having looked at the schools and their programs, including the school days of students, it is important to know more about the children. As the historical summary revealed, schooling is not a homogeneous process. It is tailored to societal goals and to specific school populations, which are defined along dimensions of social class, race, and ethnicity.

The Children

Over the course of our many years in the schools the student population with whom we worked were economically, culturally, ethnically, and racially varied. Yet with few exceptions the schools were either predominantly white or had mainly Black and Hispanic students, a result of the *de facto* residential segregation that our historical analysis has described. Teachers were generally white, middle-class, and female. The situation was one familiar in many urban public schools in the United States.

In the School Setting Study the voluntary alternative school drew its students from both middle-class and working-class families who lived nearby, but students were predominantly white and middle-class. At the time of our research the standard borough school had a small number of white students, but the predominant groups were Black and Hispanic students that were bused into the school.

The Futures Project also involved two schools. The Park Hill School fifth-grade class with whom we worked included children from the Italian and Irish lower middle-class families that had been in the neighborhood for some years, and those from more recently settled families: middle-class Carribeans and working-class American Black and Hispanic families. Although a few middle-class white children were enrolled in the lower grades, most had transferred to private schools by the fifth grade. In the involuntary alternative school the sixth-grade class with whom we worked was about two-thirds Hispanic, one-third American Black. Children were largely from poor and working-class families.

The students in the schools we studied ranged from below grade level to above, as measured by the standardized tests given to them. However, the characterization of children's abilities and behavior by teachers reflected their own expectations and values more than any "objective" assessment. For example, in the involuntary alternative school for children defined as "difficult," we were told that the students lacked academic skills and were unable to work independently. Yet their self-initiated and self-directed work on the project revealed abilities and interests that had not been recognized. In another school we were told that a class was "average" and that aside from the fact that "some children were rude" there were no other difficulties. In this case several students had rather serious problems that were being ignored.

Goals of Parents, Teachers and Children

Listening to parents, teachers, principals, assistant principals, and children talk about their goals for the school year underscored the overriding direction of the school system. In interviews with parents of children in the voluntary alternative school and the standard one, parents from both schools emphasized academic skills as primary goals. They wanted their children to "do well on the city-wide exam," and to be given more work. ("It seems as if she doesn't have enough work.") The aquisition of social skills was secondary for both groups, and the development of self-reliance, while a concern of the voluntary alternative school parents, was not even raised by the standard school group.

Interviews with teachers, principals, and assistant principals in the voluntary alternative and the standard borough schools again revealed that academic achievement was the primary objective. However, the voluntary alternative school staff was more likely to have a broader set of goals for a particular school year. In addition to emphasizing work on the basic learning skills, they wanted children to develop a greater group sense, explore more, and take on more responsibility.

The involuntary alternative school for "difficult children" was located in an extremely poverty-ridden section of the city, with high rates of unemployment and infant mortality, a large number of families receiving public assistance, and very poor city services. Informal conversations and interviews with administrators and teachers in this school revealed that their goals were to teach children the characteristics required for the kinds of jobs they felt the students were likely to find. The particular qualities emphasized included punctuality, reliability, and being able to follow orders without challenging them.

The children in the standard borough schools and voluntary alternative school were asked somewhat different questions: What would make you happy this school year? What things are most helpful in school? What do you think your teacher would like to have happen this year? Your parents? School achievement was the prevailing theme in their responses, with play, arts, and friends strictly secondary. Academic subjects were considered to be most helpful mainly because they would make it possible to achieve things in life. ("The work will help me grow up and be a science man.") Very few explained their interest in these subjects in terms of the sheer joy of learning; those who did mention enjoyment were almost exclusively from the voluntary alternative school. Attaining social skills was mentioned as helpful for their own personal goals by only voluntary alternative school students. In contrast, only the standard borough schoolchildren mentioned social concerns such as "getting along with other children," and "being good and not starting fights" when talking about the expectations of others (including their teachers and parents) for them. The two groups of children seemed to reflect their different backgrounds in responding to this question, although in general they demonstrated similar goals and attitudes.

In the involuntary alternative school, children's goals were to "get through" and "get a good job." Their attendance was, at best, sporadic and irregular. This was interpreted very negatively by staff who felt that it reflected the students' reluctance to do serious work. We found out the absence from class did not necessarily mean that the student was idle. One boy consistently remained out in order to assist and learn skills from the superintendent of his building. Other children stayed at home to watch younger siblings.

In general, we found school to be viewed in rather narrow terms and as a setting with goals largely predefined by the outside world—and mediated by parents, teachers, and other school officials. Such goals remain fairly conventional, even for those children whose families choose to send them to what they may perceive as a more innovative program. The socialization to a particular image of the functions of a school occurs long before a child even enters school through the books children read, the television programs they watch, and the comments about school which they hear from family members and others.

In a study of children's images of school forms, we found that children who were asked to design a classroom using scaled models, produced conventional forms, generally resembling their own classrooms. Again, in the Futures Project, those school images produced in response to the open-ended request that children draw their "images of the future" were extrapolated from the present rather than discontinuous with it. These images, produced at the very beginning of the

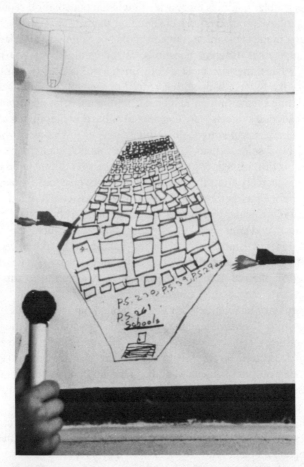

Figure 6.4.   A child's image of the skyscraper school of the future

project, mirrored the growth of bureaucracy and technology. One child drew a picture of a skyscraper school that housed all grades from preschool to high school under one roof (see Figure 6.4). He explained that it would take the entire lunch hour just to reach the cafeteria. Others drew images of robot teachers and computer-based teaching machines located in their homes, where they would study in isolation from other students.

Locked into academic stereotypes by years of subtle messages communicated through both mediated and direct experiences, children find it difficult to imagine any real alternatives to existing forms of schooling, even if they are dissatisfied with them. Our research has shown that socialization to prevailing models of schooling which occurs as early as first grade creates a sharp and enduring image of education. The most available images for children are the settings that surround them and are parts of their everyday lives. They understand, through their experiences in these places, even in the "open" settings, that they have little power to effect change now and cannot imagine a different future. When we asked children in our Futures Project who was responsible for the future world they drew, it was "they"—undefined, unexplained, but obviously in control. This is not to suggest that children are unable to contemplate alternatives, but they need a learning process that stimulates and supports the imaging of alternatives and a sense that they are capable of generating interesting ideas. Neither of these was provided in the schools we saw. Adults were no less narrow in their views. They discussd their attempts to create an alternative, yet they demonstrated behavior and attitudes which were in opposition to change. Movable furniture did not move; the three R's remained the core of the programs; individual academic achievement and control of children to this end was primary. Undoubtedly, the reasons why teachers and parents clung to tradition varied. For some parents, especially those who came from poorer backgrounds and racial groups that continued to experience discrimination, perhaps it was the belief that the traditional approaches had worked for others, would work for their children, and would guarantee economic mobility. When they did disagree with school practices and became involved in innovative programs, it was clear that they had little power in the situation. The history of parental involvement in the schools, reviewed in the previous chapter, provided little to indicate to families that they could have much impact. For other families, only some freedom was acceptable; in many cases the schools reflected parents' definition of its proper boundaries. Teachers had a variety of fears; loss of control in a hierarchical system in which they could control only the students; poor performance by the children on standardized tests for which they could be blamed; or actual responsibility for the children's failure to master academic subjects. They were afraid of the responses of principals or aware of the lack of peer support and even disapproval they received for any innovative attempts. As a result most teachers clung to the safety of traditional approaches.

Social Cooperation, Conformity, and Privacy

Group work, one of the stated innovative goals of open education, is among its heritages from earlier progressive education. In traditional schools, the social cooperation ethic, described earlier, is given great emphasis. When we asked teachers of the early elementary grades in each of these types of settings what schools should be teaching children, they said that one of the main roles of the school is to teach children how to get along with others. They stated that a major function of school is to help make individuals into good citizens. While teachers in both traditional and innovative schools believed that they were accomplishing this, our observations suggest that something else was happening. Conformity to social norms and group behavior defined as appropriate by the authority became the measure of success; group challenges to authority were unacceptable. In effect children were being taught how to accept authority, rather than to define and implement their own group goals.

For example, in the involuntary alternative school teachers complained that students did not listen to or respect one another's ideas and could not get along as a group. In fact, the rationale for separating their desks was the assumption any close physical proximity would result in antagonism and eventually disruption. When teachers sat in on our group discussions with children, they constantly reminded children not to interrupt one another, to listen to each other's ideas. However, the teacher's response to their learning within the Futures Project revealed an underlying focus on conformity and authority rather than on cooperation and sharing of ideas.

The children called a meeting of children, project staff, and teachers, ostensibly to deal with problems with the Futures Project. This student-initiated meeting was a first in the school and indicated to us that the students had coalesced as a group, had been listening to each other, and were sharing their ideas. They initially complained that the school staff had led them to believe that the project was to be "free time" although the project staff had never described it that way. They could not understand why they had "work" to do. Quickly, they moved on to a sharp criticism of the rest of their school day, when they had to sit still in class with little or no time for free play aside from gym. Even gym, they said, was frequently denied to them as punishment for misbehavior.

We saw the initiative demonstrated in this meeting as some measure of the success of the project. The classroom teachers, on the other hand, became extremely defensive. First they challenged the students' perceptions of the situation. Then they blamed the situation on the student. Finally, when the students continued as a group to hold to their position, the teachers said it was not within their power to change anything since it was not their school. Students were referred to a higher authority—the principal. There was no attempt to have a dialogue which might lead to a joint resolution of the problem.

This was not the only instance of lack of real support for group process. There also was little opportunity for a child to retreat with a friend, to share one another's company and confidences. Student-initiated contacts with others in a class frequently were occasions for reprimands and punishment. As we described earlier, even in the open-education classrooms, most work was individual. Groups were arranged by teachers, either as lessons or group meetings. However, despite its prevalence, even individual work did not have supportive physical arrangements. Working alone was common, but not necessarily comfortable.

If you were to ask teachers or school administrators about opportunities for privacy, as we did, most would be surprised at the question, puzzled that we would consider privacy a school issue. Yet, individual privacy needs do not end when children are in school. Moreover, open education classes may, in fact, increase the child's need to withdraw from the on-stage nature of the school day. Privacy needs do vary and some children seem more able to satisfy them than do others, yet this need exists for all.

In a study in which children ranging in ages from 4 to 19 from schools in New York and Wisconsin were interviewed about the meaning of privacy (Wolfe, 1978), privacy was a relevant concept in the school setting for even the youngest age group. This was true for children whether they were in open-space classrooms, traditional classrooms, or what we identified as mobile classrooms, moving from room to room for different classes.

There were interesting differences in the way these privacy needs were played out. At least occasionally some boys attained physical privacy by taking over or creating places in school that were now defined as "private" and defending them against encroachment. Girls found it harder to achieve privacy as physical aloneness in this manner. They were forced to use spaces already normatively defined as "private," such as the bathroom, since their attempts to appropriate other spaces were likely to be obstructed, especially by the boys. As a result of the power difference, girls had less possibility for achieving privacy as physical aloneness within the school building.

In another study, many children expressed their need to withdraw periodically during the school day. We asked what they did at such times, and after we assured them of the confidentiality of their responses, they told us about a variety of private places. Some children hid in the wardrobe, others went to the bathroom, others went to the reading area. One girl went under a table "all the time," a place where her teacher rarely found her. Interestingly, children often took their work with them into these private places, where they could write or study without being watched or escape from high noise levels and confusion in the classroom.

For other children we observed, daydreaming and wandering or hiding offered a form of escape from the routine of the classroom although they could be chastised or criticized for not working or labeled anti-social for such "unfocused" behavior. In addition, while the schools that we studied did not have seclusion rooms, some teachers in both open and traditional classrooms did isolate children whose behavior was not considered acceptable. One might question whether children who repeatedly misbehaved might not be searching for release from required work activity and the pervasive control in the classroom. For some of the children we followed this seemed to be a plausible explanation.

For most children within schools, behavior is controlled and mandated by higher authorities throughout the day with little relief aside from a bathroom break, and the often chaotic lunch and recess periods. This reflects the school's identity as an institution, albeit a partial one. In sum, ordinary classrooms do not support the kind of respite and relief needed periodically by all children, but especially those "distractable"ones who have a hard time concentrating or other special privacy needs.

The struggle to obtain some freedom from surveillance, to find a small haven or refuge is, in fact, as difficult in schools as it is in total institutions. Yet while privacy is consciously withheld in the psychiatric hospitals, in schools it is simply not acknowledged to be necessary or salient. Yet for children in school and their teachers as well, the necessity to be "on stage" for hours at a time is stressful. As we described earlier, even in open classrooms most work was individual, although some groups were formed, for the most part by teachers, either for group lessons or group meetings. Yet individual work was not supported by arrangements that would guarantee privacy, and children at times searched in vain for a refuge in which to pursue their assignments. It was even difficult for us to find places to talk to individual children when privacy was needed, and we had far broader freedom than the children.

There is, however, a specific form of privacy that schools do reinforce: the privacy of personal work. There is a definite effort to teach children to keep their intellectual productions to themselves, especially, but not only, under testing conditions. In fact, there is far more emphasis placed on prohibitions against sharing information than there is on the encouragement of cooperation. Children are often expected to share their possessions, their skills, and their time but rarely to do shared intellectual work. This creates a real dilemma for some children who must learn to understand the fine line between teacher-approved cooperation and cheating or collusion, even though the culture of their home may reinforce quite different categories.

In the end it is *individual* achievement and its assessment that are primary. This tends to divide students, who may perceive other students as interfering with their work. We asked children in one open-education classroom when they preferred to be alone and when they preferred to be with others, and we found they preferred to be alone when doing "work" and wanted to be in groups only to "play." They described the advantage of groups: "you can get help from others," but felt they also meant disturbance, being bothered, and not being able to complete work by which they were being judged.

The Use of the Environment as a Mechanism of Control

Whether consciously acknowledged or not, the classrooms we visited were physically structured to sustain the behavior code and system of pedagogy supported by the school system and the particular teacher in charge. The example of the involuntary alternative school where desks were placed 10 feet apart is a clear expression of the lack of trust in students and the desire to physically discourage contacts among them. And just as rows of seats and desks fixed to the floor, typical of traditional learning settings, acknowledge the authoritarian position of the teacher and reinforce a passive mode of learning, so "movable" tables and chairs which are in reality frozen in position by teacher fiat can do the same. There are many other, more subtle instances of control exerted through use of the setting: for example, the placing of certain equipment or supplies where children cannot have access to them.

Our finding that behavior was concentrated in the small portion of the room most occupied by the teacher is another example of the use of the spacing of students to exert control. In fact one teacher expressed her concern quite openly. "I can't trust kids in the back of the room alone." By drawing children around her, and keeping them within her eyes' view she was able to monitor their actions. However, in her classroom, as in others we observed, some children were given greater freedom than others. The so-called high achievers and teacher's favorites were much less likely to be required to remain up front. They were permitted out of the room more frequently: to go to the bathroom, to act as monitors, or to work in the corridors. These children could be out of the teacher's sight without raising her suspicion, whatever they actually were doing. This pattern was a variant of the old practice of assigning seats to children who were not trusted up front within the teacher's view, or, in some cases to put "smart" children in front rows as a sign of achievement.

We have already referred to a different kind of control over seating, one exerted by the children in one of the open-education classes that we studied. In this instance there were enough chairs and tables for everyone as well as many alternative seating areas. The teacher did not assign anyone to a specific place, but over time the students themselves put their name tags on certain chairs and tables.

In our description of the children's hospital we found lining up to be a powerful tool through which those in charge control the flow of behavior throughout the day. In many schools, too, lining up is an important means of control. Children line up in the schoolyard to enter the building in the morning. They line up to pick up materials and have their work checked by the teacher. They line up in the classroom to go to lunch, walking to the lunchroom in a line. They line up to go to the schoolyard after lunch, and the whole process then is repeated to get back to the classroom. Dismissal at the end of the day is also a lining-up process.

It is reasonable to exert some control over the movement of large numbers of people in confined spaces such as schools in order to assure the safety of the occupants. In fact, many schools define specific staircases as "up" or "down" in an effort to control traffic and to be prepared for emergencies such as fires. However, the degree to which lining up is used in schools and the very young children for whom it is required suggest additional motives. It is a convenient system for teachers which reflects, at least to some degree, a lack of trust in children. The reality that a good portion of the school day is spent in this activity rather than in "learning" is not acknowledged. In fact, lining up has often been described as a way to make transitions more efficient, an idea from the efficiency movement of the 1920s that has become basic and unquestioned school practice.

In the Futures Project based in the Park Hill School, there were other instances of control through the environment. The teacher in the class selected to work on the project had no interest in being involved. However, she remained in the room during the project time, keeping children in line through eye contact and the use of her bell, which she would ring when she felt that the noise level exceeded what she would tolerate. At the first meeting, when we asked children to come to the empty back portion of the room, she added "bring your chairs with you," and it became clear that our preference for more informal arrangements with children seated on the floor was not acceptable to her. When we communicated to children that they could move the desks into different arrangements to support what they were doing, the teacher kept reminding them to return the furniture to the assigned places. When our project time was over at the end of the school day, she required that all the chairs and desks be back in their places and that children return to their seats so that she could send them, one at a time, to retrieve their coats, and then line up to leave the room. Although she declined to participate in the project, in other ways she firmly expressed her desire to accompany the group on its first neighborhood trip. In this instance, she kept telling students to stay close together in a line, established a very rapid pace, and became visibly distraught when they entered stores to speak to people.

In the involuntary alternative school, when we were unpacking the materials with the children, they decided to use the tape recorders to interview others in the school. This, in fact, was one of our expectations. First one child left our project room, walked down the hall with one of us walking behind, and went to the principal's office to interview her. Then a second child followed. At this point the teacher who was serving as staff liaison to the project confronted both children. When we intervened and explained that their activity was part of the project, we were told that when we worked in the school building our project would have to be confined to the room itself. Even the children's movement from their classroom to the project room, 15 feet down the corridor, was controlled. Children lined up inside their classroom and were instructed to proceed, first one, then another, again separated so that each student arrived and entered the room alone.

Thus in subtle and direct ways the physical setting became a partner in a hierarchical control process, with those in highest authority exerting the greatest control over the physical environment. Control over space is power and it was clear that in the classrooms we studied power was in the hands of the teachers. Children we questioned believed that the room "belonged to" the teacher, not them. Clearly, the principal assigned teachers to specific rooms and decided on the allocation of space. However, teachers exerted whatever authority they could to mandate how rooms should be used, where children could go, and who was to have the various spatial privileges that existed.

For the students in the classroom the experience was one of confinement. Although this was certainly not at the level evident in the children's hospital, still there were obvious constraints on their ability to move around, whether to use a library or even to go to the toilet. As we have described, this confinement was greater in some schools and classrooms than in others, and harsher for some students than for others. Certainly, the involuntary alternative school exerted the most powerful limits on the freedom of students; such control was an unquestioned part of the philosophy of its administrators and teachers.

Class schedules represented another kind of confinement, an imposed routine that discourages spontaneity and supports control. This routine was sometimes obscured by a verbal philosophy of openness, but it emerged as we examined the days over time. Obviously some planning is essential, especially where groups of people are involved. However, the institutional routine that we saw in some classes became an end in itself. It interrupted students when they were involved in their work, established inflexible and unquestioned time limits, and in general did not foster learning. Instead, it chilled enthusiasm and discouraged independent investigation.

The right to control time, much as the right to control space, is both a means and a prerogative of power. In schools, time is measured out by authorities who may feel that they are scheduling in the interest of their educational programs. In fact, in many instances their control over time becomes yet another management tool which may serve administrative purposes but hamper intellectual development and growth. Even the very arbitrariness of such control may have its own subtle coercive power.

The Environment as a Mechanism of Socialization

If lining up is a mechanism of control in school, it also is a mechanism of socialization. A major purpose of schooling is socializing students to their roles in life, their places in society, their sex roles, their sense of what is important to learn and what is trivial. The environment and the way it is used contribute in many ways toward producing the kinds of behaviors desired in school and in future years.

The socialization process which takes place in the schools has two major functions. It serves the larger society by producing compliant citizens and productive workers who will be prepared to assume roles considered appropriate to their race, class, and sex. But it also forms individual identities, contributing to people's sense of themselves as worthy or unworthy, productive or unproductive, capable or incapable. School years are formative ones insofar as a person's sense of self is concerned, and experiences in the classroom through early and middle childhood and adolescence as well all help to define individuals to themselves and others. The reactions of a series of teachers and peers reflect back to children what the world thinks of them, in turn defining in large measure what they think of themselves. These experiences also affect aspiration levels and expectations for future training and potential life work.

The school setting is very much part of the process. On the simplest level, the physical appearance of the school, whether it is warm and welcoming or cold and impersonal, whether it is ordered or chaotic, shabby and dilapidated or well-maintained and attractive, all communicate something of what is to go on inside. These qualities also reflect back on the children themselves much as their housing does, providing messages about whether they can expect to have adequate school facilities. Similarly, the qualities of the classrooms they use reinforce these messages.

Environmental messages are received by children in clear and direct ways. As part of the Futures Project in the involuntary alternative school, the students visited the Park Hill School. Park Hill was over 100 years old as compared with their own 30-year-old building. Yet going into Park Hill on a cold, windy day the first words from the visitors were "Wow! They have heat in this building!" Even the teacher commented on the quality of the place and all the equipment she saw, including television sets, pointing out the disparity between her school and Park Hill.

Children spend large portions of their days in school, important parts of their lives. From these hours of exposure to social values, personalities are formed, goals are defined, and directions are set. There is growing evidence from our own research and that of others of the degree to which environmental socialization in the schools has significant later consequences. Rist (1970) observed a kindergarten class of Black students taught by a Black teacher. The children were seated at three tables in the room by the teacher. Those children placed nearest to the teacher in seats where they received most of her instructional time and with the best view of the blackboard were those students who the teacher felt would be rapid learners, children who reflected the teacher's middle-class values. The judgment was made on the basis of information obtained by the teacher *prior* to the beginning of school, information drawn from pre-registration forms (e.g., whether the child's family had a telephone, and whether the child had been in preschool), from public welfare lists, from interviews with the children and their mothers during registration, and from the teacher's experiences with the child's older siblings. This information, which had little or no relationship to the child's learning potential, ultimately determined the amount and quality of attention each child received. When Rist followed the course of these children's school careers in first and second grades, in almost every case, the tracks defined for children by their kindergarten teacher persisted through second grade.

We might like to think of this study as reflecting an extreme example of the self-fulfilling prophecy, but our own observations in classrooms verify the kinds of limits placed on children defined as poor learners or troublemakers. The descriptions of Danny and Ivy, cited earlier, demonstrate this same attribution process, with the teacher's differing expectations for the students leading to quite different reactions to their behavior. This phenomenon is even more pronounced in looking at the two alternative schools, the voluntary and involuntary ones. In the voluntary alternative school, children were given greater leeway than in any of the other schools studied. The middle-class teachers' values matched those of the parents and a greater attitude of trust was present than in the other schools. Children could use the corridors with much more freedom than in other schools, they could work on their own projects with teachers checking up less frequently. More time could be spent on arts and crafts ("frill subjects" from the perspective of the other schools). This freedom was offered because teachers had confidence in the ability of their students to do well on standardized tests and to complete the work that was laid out for the class and, we might add, to be trained for the kinds of jobs that were open to them.

In the case of the involuntary alternative school precisely the opposite was true. Teachers expected trouble, misbehavior, and lack of achievement. Not only was the class physically arranged in anticipation of misbehavior from the teacher's view, but the general attitude of the school authorities was that these children were likely to fail. The emphasis was placed on serious subjects and all but the basics were considered expendable. Yet there was little expectation that the students would accomplish much or rise above what was perceived to be the "low" level of their families and their neighborhood. Most important, all of this was communicated to the children in direct and indirect ways.

For example, when we began working with the involuntary alternative class we explained that we had worked in another school with other children. Frequently, over the year, they would compare themselves with the Park Hill group, with comments such as "I bet the Park Hill kids were better than us." It was only after meeting the Park Hill children that these comments ceased.

Work on the Futures Project at the involuntary alternative school was seen as a frill by school personnel, not as a substantive learning experience, despite evidence to the contrary. The accomplishments of the group at the end of the year were minimized. There was resistance on the part of the teachers to acknowledge that the group could present a skilled and worthy final product. When planning the final presentations, the school administrator rejected the idea of inviting families. Instead she wanted it confined to the room in which we worked. Some classes were permitted to attend but the administrator felt that the children could not sit for any length of time without creating a disturbance. In fact all 40 students who came were enrapt most of the time, and there were no problems.

When the presentation ended the administrator left without any mention of the fine decorum.

In this school, specific traits were emphasized: being prompt, remaining seated, talking when given permission, not questioning authorities; traits that are essential to the low-level, low-skilled jobs into which they were supposed to move. The Futures Project encouraged thinking, creative use of resources, free movement into the neighborhood, and exploration of community problems. These were neither valued by the institutional system nor seen as contributing to the students' progress. The school, its staff, and program had a very different set of goals for the particular students in this school.

The reinforcement by the schools of the race and class structure continues to be accompanied by a similar reinforcement of sex-role stereotypes, even though such constraints are currently being challenged within the mainstream culture. The environment is used in direct and indirect ways to support role-appropriate behaviors and discourage inappropriate ones.

Our observations in classrooms have revealed a great deal of sex segregation of both activities and use of specific parts of the room. In classes where children had some options in the use of different areas, we observed either boys or girls favoring a given location. This pattern was often reinforced by the equipment and materials available. The housekeeping area typically used by girls was one such sex-typed location.

There is also evidence that classrooms, like other spaces, may be perceived in different ways by males and females. Some of this was reflected in conceptions of privacy, discussed earlier. When students in schools in the suburban–rural community in Wisconsin were interviewed as part of the study of privacy mentioned earlier, whether they were in open-space, traditional, or mobile classrooms girls were more likely to say that they had their own classrooms than boys. Boys responded in terms of technical ownership of a room, so that shared space was not seen as "owned." Girls saw the space in personal terms; it could be their own whether or not it was shared with others. This was not only true for the question regarding classrooms but also was reflected in the responses to the question about a place of their own in school. Girls felt they had a place wherever it might be, while boys were careful to point out the proprietary rights and joint tenancy of others. Their patterns mirror the sex-role stereotypes in our culture, where women are supposed to be available physically and socially and are less likely to have a room of their own.

In the same study, when we asked children to describe how they knew when members of their family wanted privacy they described their mothers as saying "I have a headache" or "I have work to do." Mothers, with limited physical privacy, closed themselves off in the bedroom or used the kitchen, a space in which they were still accessible to others. Fathers were described as sitting in their chair, going to the garage, study, or basement, or leaving the house.

From the late 1960s on, researchers influenced by the women's movement produced a great deal of literature about sex-role stereotyping of young children and how school experiences helped to create or reinforce these differences (Harrison, 1973). Open-classroom teachers, especially, had material on this subject in their rooms. Yet teachers continued to participate in the stereotyping process in subtle and direct ways. Boys could take over areas such as the block corner and defend it as theirs with a minimum of teacher intervention. Girls would then have to use the blocks during lunch hour when boys were playing outside. In general, our observations in classrooms identified many more male than female territories. Although boys might not define these spaces as theirs in technical terms, their domination of specific sections of the rooms and the schoolyards limited their use by others. Such findings concerning sex differences underline the extent to which school experiences and school settings contribute to the socialization process.

Responsibility for care of space might also be unequally apportioned; we observed girls seemed to participate more actively in the domestic and cleaning chores in the open rooms than boys. Such activity may enhance a sense of attachment to place, a positive outcome, while at the same time perpetuating the female stereotype. It is possible that the open classroom may allow increased opportunities for stereotyping because it constrains the flow of activities less.

The school day is filled with silent and not-so-silent messages about what good behavior and good people should be like. Simple requirements such as lining up, working on one's own products, cooperation with others when it makes the teacher's work easier, not sharing work during tests, all lay out the normative base of the society and the place of each person within it by sex, class, and race. This does not mean that there is no rebellion. As our historical analysis has shown, opposition exists on many levels. The long-term influence of student uprisings in the United States and abroad indicates that some very basic norms can be challenged. In our own school experiences, however, there were only minor uprisings, and these were mainly at the involuntary alternative site. The predominant picture was one of the school as a successful socializaing agent, with little evidence of any questioning of its goals.

CONTRADICATIONS BETWEEN INNOVATION AND TRADITION

Challenging the Institutional System

One of the characteristics of an institutional system is its strong resistance to change. Within such a system, just as teachers and administrators resist altering their impressions of children whom they define as "achievers" or "nonachievers," "good children" or "troublemakers," it is difficult for them to conceive of alternative ways of running an educational program or arranging a classroom or organizing a school. In too many cases we found that school staff expressed an interest in change, but were reluctant to alter any of their underlying goals or basic notions of what a school experience should be. Strong evidence in favor of a different view did not change this situation.

Nevertheless, changes did occur. For example, in one of the rooms we studied a loft structure suddenly appeared in the classroom one day. It was a free-standing, two-level wood piece made for the teacher by a group that specialized in creating new school furniture. No warning had been given that new furniture would be coming into the room, nor was there any prior discussion with students of how the loft could be used or what function it could serve. In fact, an interesting environmental learning experience was overlooked and the loft was presented as a *fait accompli*. It was something the teacher valued, but there was no explanation of why.

As one might expect, there was great excitement and competition for use of the loft space. The chaos this created angered the teacher, who decided that children would have to sign up for the upper or lower space, one at a time, for a maximum of 20 minutes. If the privilege of using the loft was abused, it would become off-limits for that child. In fact, after the initial burst of enthusiasm, the loft's popularity declined. The teacher finally moved the film strip projector into the space under the loft since it afforded a quiet and protected place in which to listen and work.

To some degree this was change for change's sake with little attention to the impact it would have on the classroom, the students, and the educational program. Most critically, the teacher missed an opportunity to discuss an immediate and personal environmental issue, but clearly that was not a priority for her. The manner in which she introduced the loft verified her control over the classroom and her proprietary interest concerning the disposition of furniture and equipment.

In the case of the Futures Project there was initial staff enthusiasm. Nevertheless, there also was a great deal of resistance to the process used in the project, the independence given to students, and the Project's challenge to the assumption that all learning must happen within the school walls. In the involuntary alternative school, the administration wanted to continue the project after we left, creating a social studies curriculum focusing on neighborhoods. But it would be "taught" to the students rather than created by them. We were told clearly that the "content" was fine but the "process" would have to be changed so that control would remain firmly in the hands of the staff. In the Park Hill School, even the Project's content worried the teacher when it involved "potentially touchy" issues. Littering was thought more appropriate for investigation than landlord–tenant relationships; it became the focus of a mini-project conducted after we left the school.

In the course of our work in the schools, we have seen some instances of positive changes made by teachers and by students although, sadly, not in concert with each other. When we observed the eight classrooms of the School Setting Study, our findings ended up as computer printouts for each room. Data on the observation sheets were arranged to show the use patterns of specific sections of the room. A member of the research team who had extensive experience in elementary schools discussed the findings for their classes with each of the teachers. The teachers had no difficulty understanding the printouts and raised interesting questions about the data. In the display of activities by location they recognized the concentration of use in the area, and some expressed disappointment that the specialty areas were not being used more. Most recognized their role in the process and some were determined to make changes. A few were resistant to any changes, expressing satisfaction with existing patterns of use.

In the case of the teachers desiring change we saw two kinds of impacts. In five of the eight rooms small changes were made immediately. In one a table holding reading and math exercises was moved out of a traffic lane. In others pillows and partitions were added to the reading corner to attract greater use. In another class the teacher placed a low table in the math corner in the back of the room. This teacher was willing to increase the use of the rear but only under conditions where she could monitor what was happening. After considering mounting mirrors on the back wall to facilitate such surveillance, she decided on the table strategy and reported its success.

There also were instances of change projects that involved students. In the standard borough school and the voluntary alternative, we found that a simple series of workshops enabled the participants to come up with creative solutions to problems in their classrooms. In one school, working with a group of second-grade students, we began with a short course on the design process, with exercises on awareness of the qualities of a setting: scale, color, form, textures. After students described environment problems in their rooms they were asked to think about ways to improve the setting. They prepared scaled models of the elements that they felt would deal with the problems. The final phase was construction of these elements. Although the projects that the workshop participants selected were modest, all were conceived, designed, and implemented by the children. Workshop staff members were available as resource persons, offering suggestions and assistance where needed. The final products—low tables for work, partitions, and bookcases—were moved into the classrooms when completed. In the following year, a number of teachers copied these elements for their own rooms.

These workshops had many of the qualities of the Red Room designs described in Chapter 4, suggesting that children are capable of seeing alternatives when given the opportunity. However, most school experiences present children with programs and settings defined by authorities with little possibility that any component could be changed.

Despite these changes we did observe, the overall prospects for change in the schools, environmental change included, are not promising.

In considering alternatives to the various school systems we have detailed, one must address the ethos of contemporary times along with the history of schools. The prevailing mood has all but eliminated the willingness of public schools to experiment with new forms be they educational or physical ones. The current pressure for attention to basics reflects, in many ways, a move toward conservative and traditional schooling, bypassing many of the experiments of the past.

It is difficult to feel optimistic about the future of schools in light of these trends. They have become in many ways more institutional in form, reflecting little of the optimism and innovation of the progressive-school period or the brief romance with open education. The traditional symbols of the past have persisted, many of them reflected in the form of the school building itself. But it is difficult to imagine that experimentation and change will occur in a place and a time when reading and arithmetic scores are priorities and when school budgets are being cut.

If anything offers some prospects for improvement it is recognition that there is a storehouse of creativity waiting to be released. Our confidence in the young people with whom we have worked ignites a small spark of hope. At least for the moment, changes must be made in individual classrooms by courageous teachers willing to take risks, to share control with students, to challenge the restrictions of the institutional system, and to both see and create alternatives.

REFERENCES

Harrison, B. G. (1973). *Unlearning the lie: Sexism in school.* New York: Liveright.

Rist, R. (1970). Student social class and teacher expectations: The self-fulfilling prophecy in ghetto education. *Harvard Educational Review, 40,* 411–451.

Wolfe, M. (1978). Childhood and privacy. In I. Altman & J. F. Wohlwill (Eds.), *Children and the environment.* New York: Plenum.

CHAPTER 7

Settings for Nurturance: A Future Institution?

Our analysis of history and the review of our work in both children's psychiatric facilities and schools point out that they cannot be considered entities independent of the social system. The discrepancy between the rhetoric and reality, in fact, reflects the constraints placed on their form and functioning by that system. In every institutional setting in which we have worked there has been an enormous gap between the stated goals of administrators and staff and what happens on a day-to-day basis. We have seen a psychiatric hospital expressing a community philosophy of treatment isolate their residents; we have seen open-classroom teachers restrict students to their seats.

One could argue that the discrepancy is occurring on a subtle level. Yet oftentimes people have not been aware of what seem to us to be glaring contradictions between what they say they are doing and what we see them doing. We have heard people define their programs and physical environments as innovative while reinforcing all of the traditional values that they have purportedly rejected. The psychiatric hospital claimed to be implementing a "milieu" or therapeutic community philosophy but functioned in a manner historically associated with the most restrictive of institutional settings. The involuntary alternative school claimed that its approach to education for the types of students they had would succeed where standard school practices had failed. However, its small size did not mask its continuity with schools of the past, emphasizing military drill and discipline for the comparable group of the era. In each of these settings, tradition triumphed over innovation. It is important to understand how these institutions prevent all children from developing their potential while at the same time understanding the particular ways they affect different children.

INSTITUTIONAL QUALITIES

All of the settings shared a set of institutional qualities, manifested in their principles, practices, and physical environments, reflecting an underlying set of assumptions not necessarily derived from the nature of the settings. These were the barriers to innovation.

Structure and Routine

What impressed us in each of these settings is the incredible routinization of the day, the absence of variety and change in the physical qualities and activities. Although there have been differences in the types of children, the nature of the neighborhood, and the purposes of the facilities, day-by-day life has been a repeated series of events taking place in a repeated series of similar spaces orchestrated by an unvarying time schedule, all defined by an outside power.

There is structure in all aspects of daily life including the physical setting, the activities, and the time frame within which they occur. The children's psychiatric hospital is the most obvious example of the value placed on the need for structure in the lives of children. Children are required to wake up, eat meals, and go to sleep at set times each day all week whether or not the scheduling meets their needs. Punishments and sanctions, ranging from the denial of privileges to the administration of medications and confinement in the isolation room, are used in an attempt to force compliance. Yet the environment of the involuntary alternative school was not so different. In fact, it was the only alternative to an institution for these young people, and they were informed of that fact time and time again. For the other schools we studied the structure was less obvious but nevertheless present, with subjects slotted into specific times of the day and a defined range of acceptable activities. The sanctions and punishments were often milder although not always, varying according to the race, class, and sex of the child. Others have described the use of drugs in public school situations, most notably for children considered to be "hyperactive" (Brown & Bing, 1976).

The overriding goals of these institutions preclude the treatment of children as people. Within the psychiatric institution, "therapy" predominates, and special spaces and specially trained personnel are used to carry out the mandate. Within schools, education is the prevailing theme all of the day. The child is a "student," despite lip service to the concept of the whole child. In the end only the three R's count.

In all of these settings little space or time belongs to the child. When time is called "free," limits on movement and resources circumscribe what can be done. Even this limited freedom is granted as a privilege. The use of the environment, its aesthetics, and its accessibility are controlled by the adults.

The structuring of the day, the routinization of time and activities, and the narrow definition of goals provide children with little opportunity for serendipity. Signs of spontaneity are cause for concern and are considered to be impulsivity, disruptive to ongoing plans. There is a fear of loss of control.

It is commonplace to describe environments as more or less "restrictive." This terminology, now applied to any environment, developed out of the "normalization principle" (Wolfensberger, 1972), which courts have mandated in the institutional placement of children. In that context, it requires that children be placed in the "least restrictive" environment in which they can function. The implicit assumption is that some restriction is necessary. The necessity is unexplained and the nature of the restriction is undefined but includes such criteria as the range of freedom of movement, access to resources and spaces, and the amount of supervision. There is no mandate to provide the most liberating environment, a perspective that would accept disabilities as within rather than outside the range of normality and provide the necessary support systems, both physical and social, for this to be realized.

Within the school context, restrictiveness is also assumed to be necessary. The idea that "kids need structure" was expressed not only by the psychiatric hospital personnel but by the staff in every school in which we worked. In the involuntary alternative school as well as in Park Hill, the principle was clearly stated and enforced; the difference between them was the harshness of application, probably the result of the categorization of the students. In the voluntary alternative and standard borough schools, the open-education philosophy led to an attempt to teach students to internalize the structure. Authoritarian methods were less evident but differences in its application to boys and girls were clear. Yet the structure created by the routinization of the day and the lack of variety were there nevertheless. In all of these situations adults were in control and wanted to remain in that position. In this sense, while these settings might be described as more or less restrictive, it is doubtful that any could be called more "liberating."

Control and Authority

Throughout the history of institutions in the United States, control and authority have been prevalent themes. Issues of control and authority have been central in defining the relationship between children's institutions and the rest of the society. They also have organized much of the debate over what happens within the walls of buildings or rooms. At some points in time, control and authority are explicit and overriding aspects of policy or educational philosophy. At other times, they are less obvious but powerful nevertheless. The centralization of school boards in the Progressive Era and decentralization of school boards during the 1960s, as well as the long debate over federal aid to education revolved around these themes. The primacy of order and obedience as parts of programmatic philosophy and physical design for schools and psychiatric institutions for children were clearly stated in Lancasterian schools and Houses of Refuge. As our work has shown, however, remnants of these approaches are ingrained in present-day institutions, forming an unquestioned assumptive base through which they continue to have an impact on the physical and organizational aspects of these settings and the lives of children within them.

The emphasis on orderly movement of bodies from one area to another led to elaborate rituals concerning the use of corridors, which perhaps more than any other physical feature describes the physical environment of children's institutions. Long and circuitous routes rationalize the curtailment of children's freedom of movement and reveal the suspicion and distrust of the kind of behavior that would emerge if there were no surveillance. The elaborate procedures for dealing with the movement of children ranged from passes for using the bathroom in a school to privilege systems based on distance in the children's hospital. The fear of children being in the corridors in the involuntary alternative school had its counterpart in some schools using traditional environments for open education. Corridors, initially viewed as ancillary learning spaces, often were used only when a staff person was present, even though they were directly adjacent to the rooms. The system for deciding which children could be trusted outside of direct control not only reflected the existing stereotypes of children but reinforced them as well.

Less obvious but equally reflective of the need to control were the spatial patterns created by the physical location of the teachers in open classrooms, often unrelated to the position of their desks. In these rooms children were discouraged and sometimes prevented from using the spaces outside the teacher's view. Immobile movable furniture and lining-up rituals are further examples of the ways control remained in the hands of the teachers.

The persistent use of policies of containment is consistent throughout the course of children's experience in and between these settings. To guarantee compliance, procedures are used that define the authority of the adult and demand obedience of the child, often under conditions that are patently arbitrary. We have seen children told to do individual work requiring concentration when the only spaces were tables shared by others. We have observed children expected to line up or clean up within a specified and brief number of minutes with no access to watches or clocks. Each of these instances led to reprimands and punishments when children failed to adhere to an impossible standard in a physical environment providing no support for the behavior that was required. Children in schools were ordered to stand or sit in corners facing the wall; in psychiatric facilities placement in seclusion rooms and confinement to bedrooms were usual procedures. These were not unusual events in exceptionally harsh institutions, but methods for disciplining children that most staff thought reasonable and necessary.

The underlying assumption in all of these institutions was that if authority were not exercised and if obedience were not required, children would be totally out of control. This was most obvious in the psychiatric facility where the labeling of children created expectations of imminent volatile outbursts. But it was under the surface in many schools, couched in terms of "behavior problems" even at very young ages. Our work supports Rist's (1970) findings that these expectations are connected, by the adults in the setting, to characteristics of children such as race, sex, and class and, as we have seen in the involuntary alternative school, are self-fulfilling. One of the clearest ways to insure obedience to authority and to exercise control was through surveillance of children.

Public Versus Private Experience

Whether we are dealing with institutions categorized as "partial" or "total," life in these settings is public. What is learned about privacy has more to do with the purpose of the institution than the development of the child. The monitoring of children's behavior occurs whether stated as a goal or not, as our descriptions of open classrooms have revealed. Teachers openly verbalized their need for surveillance and their lack of trust in the children. There also were numerous explanations given for the absence of opportunities for physical aloneness. Children's welfare was cited as the primary excuse for surveillance and may be a valid concern under particular circumstances. In functional terms it is often unnecessary or is largely related to legal issues of liability.

The accountability of children's institutions to the public and, specifically, to the parents, is necessary especially in light of past and present horror stories of the abuse of children in such places. Yet the impact of the political and social context on the institution eventually defines the quality of children's experiences in unintended ways. Furthermore, whether there is real accountability is as questionable as whether liability is a real concern or a rationalization. In the children's psychiatric facility the measures to prevent children from using their bedrooms as places to be alone were often described in terms that implied concern for the children's well-being and the responsibility of the institution. However, issues of safety and liability were never expressed when children were placed in concrete-walled seclusion rooms. Later, safety and liability rationalized the proliferation of seclusion rooms, which were then built with carpeted walls and floors. Surveillance was the concern in both instances and, althouth its form varied, its intent remained the same.

For the open schools, in comparison to the more traditional ones, the messages concerning privacy were more contradictory. The goal of sociability was contradicted by the need to show evidence of individual achievement, both on standardized tests (over which the individual teacher had no control) but also by the continued use of other forms of testing initiated by the teacher. The amount and range of work each child accomplished was checked by the teacher with specific standards being applied.

What is learned about public life is also related to institutional needs. In open schools, groups occurred infrequently and usually were orchestrated by the teacher.

In the involuntary alternative school, group cohesion was not supported and in some cases was directly negated. In none of the schools was there any support for a real sense of community. Schools and classes are given labels and numbers, are identified as entities. The identity of the child during the school year comes from being a member of that class or school. But this is an illusion of "groupness." Much behavior that would be seen as social outside the school environment was generally discouraged within it. Even in the open classroom little of the work involved collective effort and, in fact, a good deal of sharing was prohibited, especially the sharing of academic information. In this sense it is similar to traditional schools except that the distinction between what can and cannot be shared is less clear. In the psychiatric facility the choice was between enforced group situations under the eye of a staff person or imposed isolation.

Children in all of these settings attempted to achieve some kind of privacy, sometimes in extreme ways such as feigning emotional upset in order to be placed in the quiet room or daydreaming or pretending to be absorbed in work. Yet their minimal power in these situations led staff to view such attempts in negative ways. Cohesive groups were even more rare, generally taking place outside the school building. When occurring inside, they were often construed as rowdiness.

Independence and Conformity

We have described the lack of real independence that children have in any of these settings, since control is in the hands of others. The day is structured, ordered, and routinized and life is public with few opportunities for privacy. Yet most children's institutions cite as their goal the development of independence, albeit in the context of children being social. How are they defining independence?

Independence means taking responsibility for one's own behavior and performance, whether this involves being on time, doing homework, keeping a shared room neat, eating in an orderly fashion or, if not doing these properly, admitting one's fault in the situation. In the open-education setting the philosophy claims that children should also take responsibility for organizing their work, planning their time, acquiring the necessary materials, and finding the appropriate space in which to carry out the work. This gives them responsibility without any real control. In fact, in most open-education settings that we have observed, the opportunities are very limited, with independence narrowly defined as the choice among preselected options.

The limited possibilities for independence in all of these settings, such as some freedom of movement and some options for choosing what to do, are given to those children who demonstrate overall conformity to the goals of the setting, a privilege for those who obey. What is described as independent behavior is freedom offered to children when the authorities are fairly certain that they will not deviate from what is expected of them.

Whereas in the past "individualized" teaching was a codeword for differentiated schooling, in the present "individualized" teaching and "individualized" treatment are meant to imply that children are not simply cogs in a wheel, that their needs vary, and arbitrary norms should not be used to judge their behavior or structure their experience. Yet if children express their individual needs by questioning authority or deciding not to obey, there will be negative repercussions. Programmed independence hides conformity from view and fosters the idea that individuals are responsible for all of their behavior.

WHAT ARE CHILDREN LEARNING IN INSTITUTIONS?

Bowles and Gintes (1976) state that liberal school reformers at different times have claimed that the changes they were making would (1) integrate youth into their roles as workers, citizens, family members—roles required by a changing economy—as a means of ensuring the social continuity of life; (2) equalize the extremes of poverty and wealth by allowing equal educational opportunity; and (3) promote moral and psychological development, and, as a result, personal fulfillment. Overall their efforts did not have a very profound impact on public education. Education has not led to economic mobility, and differences in the incomes of groups based on race, class, and sex have not been eliminated (Bowles & Gintes, 1976; U.S. Bureau of the Census, 1980). Nor have schools promoted personal fulfillment or psychological development for the majority of the students attending (Glascotte et al., 1972). Schools have raised the general level of literacy. Our own work also has demonstrated that the integrative function of education continues to predominate.

Reforms in settings for the care of "deviant" children also have claimed varying goals over time. These have included improving children's morality, removing them from evil influences, rehabilitating and educating them to become productive citizens, punishing them or dissuading them from engaging in deviant behavior, and protecting society from their influence. Punishment and protection of society have been paramount. When children have demonstrated their unwillingness to engage in appropriate behavior they have been removed from society and many remain in the institution for long periods, moving from one to another over the years.

Both today and in the past, institutions for children have had embedded in them a set of dominant values which define appropriate and inappropriate patterns of behavior. They are teaching and judging children using criteria that maintain the status quo. This can be seen in the organization and quality of time and space as well as in such mundane things as the food available in the cafeteria.

There are differences in what is considered appropriate behavior for children, since their assigned role in the society will vary, depending on race, class, and sex. But there is also an overriding set of lessons that all children will confront in public institutions.

They will be taught that the purpose of daily settings is functional—places to learn, places to play, places to receive therapy. The purposes describe the appropriate behavior for each of these settings and the physical qualities that they should possess. In them, a series of planned and timed events define human needs rather than respond to them. Rewards are given for individualism rather than individuality; for conformity rather than community. Children may not always be consciously aware of this; the message they get is that it is paramount to behave properly, and someone else defines what is proper.

What is proper is then different for particular groups of children. Some will be taught to be the planners and others to follow their plans; some will be taught to think and others will be taught to do. For children from families or communities whose values are similar to those of the institution, who value propriety and define it in ways that are similar to the institution, compliance will be easier. Other children, from families and communities who do not value propriety and/ or define what is proper in ways that are different from the institution, will be taught that relying on families and communities will result in behavior that is inappropriate and unacceptable (Silverstein & Krate, 1975). Initially this may create confusion, but most children eventually internalize the institutional values and use them to judge themselves, their families, and their communities.

In these institutions most of the children who are rewarded are those who comply and do not openly challenge the system. In effect, children are taught to be passive rather than active in the creation of life and experience.

While institutions attempt to socialize children to dominant values and to their appropriate place in the social system, they are not universally successful. Giroux (1983) has pointed out that some children attempt to resist the imposition of institutional definitions on their lives. We have seen children in schools and hospitals resist and maintain a sense of themselves despite pressure to do otherwise. Some understand the basis of their resistance and can protect themselves and their interests. Others resist out of frustration rather than out of a clear image of the institution or of themselves. These children often challenge authority alone, without the support of their peers or adults, and are likely to find themselves punished with no further recourse. Their punishment stands as an example to other children of what might be their fate under similar circumstances. Most children in institutional settings neither question nor are aware of the nature of the system and are passive and compliant in the face of the power of others.

The institutional goals which we describe are not an occurrence of the past. While we tend to believe that we have progressed, that our institutions are less oppressive and offer more possibilities to children, that educators and administrators are more enlightened as we approach the twenty-first century than they were approaching the twentieth, there is ample evidence to prove otherwise. Some years ago governmental agencies were interested in research that demonstrated how institutions could be made more humane; now they fund studies of vandalism to find ways of designing institutions impervious to the assaults of people who find them inhumane. Research about the social, political, and economic factors that relate to learning or the development of "deviance" is being replaced with research that seeks the genetic or biological bases for behavior. Some of the values and attitudes we presume to be antiquated still exist and can be seen in newspaper reports of what is happening today. In the July 5, 1983 *New York Times*, an article describing plans for all-day kindergartens in New York City public schools quoted a principal from a school in a predominantly Black neighborhood, although one with different economic groups:

> "There is going to be even more emphasis on formal instruction in our all-day kindergarten," said David A. Brown, the principal at P.S. 305. "We believe in structure. Even at the possibility of damaging a student's spontaneity, we think structure is important. We intend for the child to recognize school as serious business." He said this was particularly important in neighborhoods such as Bedford-Stuyvesant. "Many of our youngsters come from unstructured home backgrounds, so school is the only place for them to get any structure." (Purnick, 1983, p. B1)

Thus while institutions appear to be flexible they are in fact very resistant to change, subject to the conditions existing outside them that set the criteria by which they are administered and judged.

The kindergarten as a public institution has a relatively short history in the United States. As late as 1965 only half the school districts in the United States provided kindergarten classes (Johnson, 1965). Even today, many states do not require a child to attend kindergarten before the first grade. However, the reality is that over the years what was conceived of as an optional year in school, with half-day classes, is slowly moving into standard practice covering a total day with programs formerly seen as appropriate to the first grade. Although still optional, for some it will undoubtedly be perceived as a requirement.

Over the last 150 years, the major change in children's lives has been that more and more of their time, their days, and years are spent in institutional environments. These institutions, as we have seen, have acted mainly as interventions into the lives of low-income families and communities. The intrusion lessened parental and community control with a progression of laws and professionals having access to children in places away from the home and community. Yet it did not lessen parental responsibility. A few years ago, it appeared that day-care centers would become the next extrafamilial community setting in which children would be spending time, especially poor children. However, today this is far less clear. The historical development of day care in this country has had more to do with the relationship of women to the paid work force than with the needs of children, and the barriers to its expansion may be connected to this fact.

SETTINGS FOR NURTURANCE: A HISTORICAL PERSPECTIVE ON DAY CARE

The most consistent attitude toward day care has been that it is a substitute for the "ideal" form of care—by a mother within the nuclear family—and that it is the last alternative and appropriate only for the poorest families. It is significant that day care has been viewed separately from nursery school although the ages of the children served are roughly the same. Day care is seen as preventative and remedial and supportive, while nursery school is seen as enriching. It is also clear that the extent and quality of publicly supported child care has been and still is based largely on governmental and industrial needs rather than on the needs of children or their caretakers (Ryan, 1975). Despite the fact that over 42.7% of children under one year of age have their caretakers working outside the home (Brozan, 1983) and that one out of five children in the United States is being raised in a single-parent household (U.S. Bureau of the Census, 1980), these attitudes persist and have severely limited the conception and growth of viable child-care alternatives.

These attitudes can be traced to the early day care of the 1880s, modeled after the British Infant schools. While progressive in that it rejected placing the children of working caretakers in orphanages, it also was based on the notion that these children should be separated from their parents at an early age, so that they would not learn from bad examples (Nasaw, 1979). The children ranged in age from 18 months to six years and, through activities performed in unison including marching in processions, they were taught that being obedient and well-mannered were signs of good moral character (Steinfels, 1973; Nasaw, 1979).

The large-scale development of day nurseries occurred between 1870 and 1912, spurred on by such reformers as Charles Brace and groups such as Children's Aid Societies. By 1910, New York City had 85 day nurseries serving 5,000 children daily. There were 450 centers nationwide and a National Federation of Day Nurseries (Steinfels, 1973).

Around 1860 the introduction of the kindergarten movement to the United States provided the model for preschools for the children of the well-to-do. Early public day nurseries were formed mainly to educate the children of poor immigrants to "proper habits," and these were modeled on the French crèche. The nurseries focused on hygiene and nutrition. Each day, children were bathed, their clothing aired and disinfected. Infants slept and stayed in cribs while preschoolers played. Children were taught that "the clock helps us to be good" as well as patriotic

American songs (Rothman, 1980). The environment and programs were custodial. In 1915 a nursery on the Lower East Side in New York City was described as located in a gloomy building with little light, gray walls, and so many cribs that there was little room left on the floor for preschoolers to play. Food was served in shifts with children waiting in line for their turn. The emphasis was on cleanliness and order and it was rare to find toys lying around (Steinfels, 1973). Despite the condescending attitudes toward the families of the poor, those who fought for day nurseries at this time still accepted the reality of the mother who had to work outside the home. Day nurseries provided such services as infant and toddler care and emergency night service and focused on job training and finding jobs for the mother, though in the lowest paying and least skilled work (Rothman, 1980).

Corporations supported the creation of day nurseries, especially in the growing numbers of company towns. These were part of the welfare principles, the "business paternalism" developed as an attempt to prevent unionization and as a way to allow both parents to work. For example, after a child had been burned to death while both parents were working, the Dean River Power and Manufacturing Co. of Danville, Virginia provided a day nursery, citing the danger of unattended children as the reason (Spring, 1972). The Kellogg Company of Battle Creek, Michigan had a nursery school with two shifts—one from 7 A.M. to 3 P.M., the other from 3 P.M. to 11 P.M.

There always was opposition to day nurseries and with the decline of the Reform Movement after World War I, this element gained control. Day care was categorized as undesirable and not appropriate for "normal" families. During the 1920s and into the Depression, day nurseries became increasingly narrower in conception. In the 1920s social work professionals took over the cause of day care, bringing with them the attitude that the day nursery was a temporary social service for so-called problem families. This definition made many families hesitant to use day nurseries. The immigration laws of 1921 stopped the flow of the people who used the nurseries most and by 1924 waiting lists had declined. Philanthropists and other sources of support cut back on their funding. By the end of the 1920s, the day nursery was underfinanced, understaffed, and provided marginal care services for those families labeled "pathological."

During the Depression the creation of jobs was the first federal government support of early child care (Pidgeon, 1953, excerpted in Bremner, 1974). In 1933, 80,000 schoolteachers were unemployed and thousands of schools across the country were closing (Parrish, 1933, reprinted in Bremner, 1970). Day-care centers, funded under WPA, required that staff be recruited from teachers on relief despite the fact that they had no professional experiences with very young children. Another requirement was that centers be housed in buildings owned by or loaned to the public school system, which was given control of administering them (Kelly, 1936, excerpted in Bremner, 1974). Many centers ended up in elementary schools. These constraints shifted the emphasis toward educational goals, and centers no longer accepted children younger than two and one-half years of age (Pidgeon, 1953, excerpted in Bremner, 1974; Fein & Clarke-Stewart, 1973; Steinfels, 1973).

Attendance at WPA centers was limited to "underprivileged" children. In 1934/35 there were 1,900 centers with 75,000 children attending. Yet as defense preparations buoyed up the economy, many families became ineligible under income guidelines. By 1941, when the Children's Bureau sponsored a conference on day care and working mothers, there were only 1,300 centers serving 37,000 children (Pidgeon, 1953, excerpted in Bremner, 1974).

As large numbers of women entered the workforce at the beginning of the war years, requests for funding for day care were being sent to the government by employers and chambers of commerce. Existing WPA centers were inadequate in number and understaffed, using parents and high-school students as volunteers (Langdon, 1942, reprinted in Bremner, 1974). More centers were requested in order to protect children from being left alone. It was also claimed that centers would "maintain top efficiency on the assembly line" (Close, 1943, excerpted in Bremner, 1974, p. 684).

An amendment to the Lanham Act, originally passed in 1941 to provide funding for schools and other community facilities in areas with rapid population growth due to the location of war-related industries, allowed the use of federal funds for day-care centers. But the money was slow in coming, due to complex bureaucratic procedures and a requirement that communities provide half of the funding. Many communities did not want to apply and others did not know how. In 1943, WPA nurseries were transferred to Lanham Act funding, forcing 550 of the 1,700 to close and others to have their locations changed because they were not in areas affected by defense industries (Close, 1943, excerpted in Bremner, 1974). It was a grant of only $400,000 from the Office of Defense and Health Services that eventually allowed some centers to open. This funding did not cover operating expenses. Rather, it provided money for planning and coordinating day-care programs and was used to hire staff who helped communities through the red tape of Lanham Act procedures (Close, 1943, excerpted in Bremner, 1974).

Many describe this period as one of great expansion of day care (see, for example, Grotberg, 1969). In fact, the federal and local programs served only 10% of mothers who needed child care, and only one in ten war production centers had any facilities (Ryan, 1975). In 1942, under the Lanham Act, there was approval for 3,700 centers. Yet by August 1943 there were only 1,726 centers serving 49,197 children, about the same number served by the WPA in 1937. At its peak in July 1944 there were 3,102 units with 129,357 children and by November 1944 the number of centers had dropped to 2,828. California had the greatest number—302. Washington State had 103 and New York had only 84 (Pidgeon, 1953, excerpted in Bremner, 1974). Most centers charged fees for service to meet the requirement of matching funds. Close (1943, excerpted in Bremner, 1974) contends that need surveys were not accurate because many women, coming out of depression-year experiences, fearful that they would not obtain jobs, did not reveal that they had any children. All states except California placed day-care programs under Departments of Public Welfare, which also discouraged many women from using them (Grotberg, 1969). California placed their centers under the Department of Education. Centers were limited to providing care during the day, yet many women were forced to work night shifts because they had little seniority. There were hardly any after-school programs (Close, 1943, reprinted in Bremner, 1974).

When the war was over the centers in almost all areas disappeared rapidly. All federal funding was ended in February 1946, and very few states continued funding centers on their own. California was one, although parents had to pay one-third of the cost and eligibility was limited to low-income households. As propaganda was claiming that mothers should now stay at home, studies such as those by Spitz (1945) were used to discredit group day care for young infants (Grotberg, 1969). Many states passed legislation prohibiting group care for infants and this attitude generalized to any day-care services (Grotberg, 1969).

Under the Housing Act of 1948, public housing projects were designed with spaces for day-care centers. Yet there was no public money forthcoming with which to implement and operate them. In 1950, as a result of the Korean War, federal money was once again available for community facilities in defense-impacted areas. Although day-care centers were listed as one possible facility, no appropriations under this act were used for day-care centers (U.S. Interdepartmental Committee on Children and Youth, 1953, excerpted in Bremner, 1974).

In 1953 only three states provided any funding for child care. In California and Massachusetts these were operated under the Department of Education; in New York there was a limited amount of money available for the childcare of migrant workers, a carryover from wartime projects. These were described as giving children "good care, good food and training in health habits," and parents "also were helped to learn about the care of children" (U.S. Interdepartmental Committee on Children and Youth, 1953, excerpted in Bremner, 1974, p. 694).

In 1955, Judith Cauman, a day-care consultant for the Child Welfare League of America, described most existing day-care programs as "historic relics" (Cauman, 1956, excerpted in Bremner, 1974, p. 697). She said that what was not happening was significant. The pre-school-age population had increased greatly, a result of the baby boom. Many more mothers were working outside the home despite the myth that they were not. Yet day care was not being expanded. It was still a limited service focused on low-income working mothers. She distinguished between nursery school, which she saw as mainly an educational experience for a narrow age range of children, and day care, which was a "service to supplement the family's care of the child for part of his day outside his own home" (Cauman, 1956, excerpted in Bremner, 1974, p. 698) which was necessary for older as well as younger children.

Between 1940 and 1958, there had been a 27% increase of women in the paid labor force and approximately 35% were married women with children. Compared to 1948, 80% more of these women workers had children under 18. Most of these children were taken care of in their own homes by parents or relatives and only 2.3% of children under the age of 12 were in group day care (Lajewski, 1958, excerpted in Bremner, 1974).

Despite the activism of the early 1960s there was a limited focus on day care. Some attitudes had changed, especially the idea that difficulties in families were only to be found among low-income groups. At a conference on working mothers and child care, the president of the National Committee for the Day Care of Children and of the Day Care Council of New York City saw day care as the way to strengthen family life. She said it was a myth that most parents love their children. Day care in her view could give a child "the strength he needs to withstand the pressures of home without good relationships and/or help change the home and attitudes of the parents" (Guggenheimer, 1960, as summarized in Bremner, 1974, p. 765). She ascribed the ambivalence about women working to attitudes in the society that focused on status defined by material possessions and also looked down upon women on public assistance. From her perspective, whether for the economically advantaged or disadvantaged, day care could reach children before crises occurred in their families and would also help them do better in school and get along better with other children.

Yet the federal funding earmarked for day care in 1962 came under the Social Security Administration as part of public welfare programs. While the Great Society programs were providing for the expansion of many community programs, day care received a minor allocation which was then removed in 1965 (Ruderman, 1968, excerpted in Bremner, 1974). The emphasis on the need for day care for children of mothers working outside the home, particularly poverty-level mothers, continued. Some money was channeled through Head Start programs, but day-care supporters saw this mainly as competition for qualified staff, especially preschool teachers. They continued to distinguish between day care, described as family-centered and as a supplement to family life, and compensatory education (Close, 1965, excerpted in Bremner, 1974).

Beginning in 1967, there was a movement toward the community control of existing day-care centers. In New York, demonstrations and sit-ins resulted in many programs being turned over to community groups and control of day care by the community. Funding for it received broad support because it

also appealed to the poverty warriors. . . . the idealist among them saw day care as a vital service, liberating to the parents, with vast potential for community development. . . . steely-eyed realists who controlled the poverty program nationally saw day care as highly desirable because it was safe. To put it crudely, three-year-olds don't riot. Educators and social workers thought they would cure poverty through education—so what better place to begin than in the day-care centers. The women's movement, growing explosively, made day care one of its key demands. Even fiscal conservatives, at least grudgingly, conceded that day care would allow people to work, would "reduce dependency"—magic words. (Ward, 1979, p. 12)

The 1967 Amendment to the Social Security Act, which provided funds for child care, had two aspects which greatly aided the expansion of centers and the shift away from day care as a service only for the poor. It provided almost unlimited funding in the sense that it would match dollar for dollar any amount of money which individual states spent on day care. Those eligible could be "past, present, and potential" welfare recipients. The word "potential" was used to create programs with economically diverse populations.

This idea of day care for *all* children, regardless of economic background, was advocated by the women's movement as well, based on the concept that a working mother was not the concern for social workers. Indeed, by 1970, the work-force participation of women had increased dramatically, espcially among women with young children. It was becoming the norm. Despite this particular shift in attitude, the basic premise was still that day care was a supplemental program for women working outside the home. In arguments for day care, little was said about women's work in the home and the need for a respite from it. Furthermore, while there were some who raised issues about the benefits for all children of day care that was economically and racially/ethnically integrated, the prime focus was on the working woman. And, despite increases in funding, in 1969, 90% of all child-care centers were privately owned and run for profit (Grotberg, 1969).

In New York, many of the community-based programs and community-controlled programs were open to a wide range of families and sought models for day care based on the needs of the child and the needs of the local community (Ward, 1979):

Publicly funded centers in New York City increased from 105 to 455, the number of children from 10 to 55 thousand, and program styles proliferated. . . . In many centers children learned Swahili or Spanish and centers experimented with 24 hour care, drop-in care, infant care, mixed age grouping and anything else that seemed needed. . . . It was a hectic and intense period when day care programs approached the ideal of the community model and program quality ranged from abysmal to very good, and occasionally superlative. (Ward, 1979, p. 13)

A specific aspect of day care in New York brought about our involvement in day-care centers. As these centers were proliferating they were using a variety of spaces—old store fronts, church basements, old houses. The City of New York had granted funding to these groups on an "interim" basis, allowing them to function in these spaces but requiring that they be brought up to code and licensing regulations within a given period of time. As a result many centers were threatened with being closed. Neither the city nor the state seemed to be able to find the money for construction of centers, although at the time, many large-scale building projects were underway with government money, including the World Trade Center.

The city developed the idea of direct-lease arrangements, so-called because they were contracts directly between the city and landlords rather than between the community groups and the landlords. The city guaranteed private landlords a substantial rent for 20 years out of day-care funds if they would build day-care facilities. Ward (1979) contends that this was not a bad idea, but eventually it became a nightmare.

> Buildings were slapped together out of shoddy materials or cheaply renovated from abandoned garages and supermarkets. Rents were enormous (averaging $89,000 per year) while the city paid heat, gas, lighting, repairs, water and sewer rates, and even its own real estate taxes on the buildings, all out of day care funds. By 1973, the city had signed over 177 of these leases. (p. 13)

Day-care groups, struggling along in found spaces, were excited about the prospect of new spaces. Some were also concerned, however, that city-defined standards would create sterile environments in contrast with the variety that existed at the time. These standards mandated that one playroom be 525 square feet for 20 children. The ideal center would have 95 children. One writer, describing one such center said, "it could be a small elementary school, for all the eye can tell from the outside" (Gupte, 1972). The description lauded the seven large playrooms clustered around a multipurpose space, the playground on the roof with rubberized floor covering, traditional playground equipment, and high wire fences and "the spacious kitchen which can accommodate 100 children. At 8 A.M. the other day, near 90 were fed a breakfast of milk, hot cereal and fruit" (Gupte, 1972). Yet most centers were being housed in older buildings, many of them former schools.

THE CONTEXT OF OUR WORK

In 1971, at their request, we began a series of discussions with ARCH, a group of Harlem-based architects and urban planners. They were unhappy with the city-wide standards for day-care centers in Harlem and wanted information about child development and children's environments on which they could develop alternatives, along with strong arguments with which to confront officials. We decided to visit as many of the existing day-care centers as we could within the limited time frame available. We wanted some sense of the issues as understood by day-care staff and parents—the programmatic and physical environmental advantages and disadvantages of their present spaces. We also wanted a firsthand look at what was being experienced on a day-to-day level by the children and staff.

We visited approximately 50 of the day-care centers functioning in New York City at the time in three out of five boroughs. Most were public, interim-funded centers; some were newly renovated public centers involved in the direct-lease program; others were private centers. We would agree with Ward's (1979) description, mentioned earlier, as to the range of settings and their quality, except that we found none we could call superlative.

Most were located in the types of interim sites we have described—storefronts, church basements, old houses. Several of the direct-lease centers were in renovated supermarkets. One of the private centers was probably the most dreadful place we have ever seen. There were 50 or more children in an old church with no materials and hardly any furniture except chairs, in which children were forced to sit. This was custodial care at its worst. Yet this center was providing a much-needed service that was not available elsewhere—it was open 24 hours each day—and it was heavily used. In the community-controlled centers the spaces often were inadequate in size and quite shabby. In some, parents and staff had worked together, building lofts and shelves, in an attempt to solve the space problem. Yet, despite problems, the morale was high and the children moved about easily and with energy. There was an informal, comfortable quality to most of these physical spaces. They often included cast-off couches and chairs, cushions on the floor, and had a warm, soft appearance. In many, the food was at least partly prepared by parents, different ones each day. The children also helped with some cooking and with setting and clearing the table as well. Of the direct-lease centers, one particularly comes to mind. It had a tunnel entrance through which children crawled, which could be used instead of the door. Once inside, however, the brightly colored walls could not mask the elementary school quality created by the typical tables and chairs, the large bare spaces, and the unlived-in look.

In the discussion which followed with members of ARCH, a number of themes emerged concerning the city guidelines. The scale of the rooms and the number of rooms proposed seemed too large. The smaller centers seemed to have an intimate quality and children had a sense of connection to the staff that differed from the larger, more school-like centers. The city had proposed that flexible walls and movable partitions and furniture could be used to create more intimate settings when needed. Yet our experience had revealed that movable partitions rarely moved and furniture and equipment was locked in place as though bolted to the floor. The variety that was evident in the interim centers was missing from the larger centers that were conforming to city guidelines.

It was clear from our visits that the location of the kitchen and the integration of eating and meal preparations into the children's day greatly influenced the quality of a center. In general, when the kitchen was hidden far away from the rooms, where access to it was limited to the kitchen personnel, the institutional preparation and distribution of food isolated the children from an important domain of life that we felt should be available. This aspect of the care of young children is more than nourishment; it is an important realm for learning and development. When smells of food cooking are absent, not only does a nurturance signal disappear but the setting itself loses part of its vitality, taking on a bland, neutral quality, giving the institutional odors of disinfectant and soap a chance to predominate. This was true for many of the centers conforming to city guidelines, with kitchens in basements, usually off limits to children.

Access to play areas was another issue. The city guidelines required a play area and because of the size and cost of existing city sites many new centers had put a play area on the roof. This placement created difficulties in use. It also kept children within the center environment for the entire day. Many of the interim centers, on the other hand, used local play areas; children were out in their communities for at least part of the day. Yet the farther these areas were from the center itself, the less frequently they were used. We tried to develop some guidelines that would encourage the design and development of sites as close to existing outdoor play spaces as possible.

We discussed what we felt to be another important attribute of day-care centers, the quality of the entrance to the building and what it communicated to children and their parents as they arrived each day. We looked at the entrances of centers we were visiting and the messages they conveyed. Some were intimidating, others confusing, still others inviting or cheery, too many shabby and worn. Many of the entrances to renovated city centers were anonymous and somewhat frightening—two steel doors leading into a large windowless building. In centers conforming to city guidelines the spaces inside the entrance were narrow and crowded with children arriving and leaving. The message seemed to be that parents should leave as quickly as possible. There was no space for them to linger or to chat with staff or other children, and the importance of leavetaking was not acknowledged. At the very least, the issue of entrances seemed a critical one to consider in the design of sites.

A major effort went into what seemed to be a rather simple question: What should day-care sleeping arrangements be like? We observed that napping was a major day-care activity, in fact, one that had specific regulations regarding the distances between cots. In almost every center we visited staff complained about nap time—with problems concerning the storage of cots, arranging them in the rooms, and dealing with restless children (see Figure 7.1). It was apparent that

Figure 7.1.   Preparation for naptime

any designs for day care had to consider this central activity. We undertook a study of nap times, with members of our group observing dozens of centers.

Napping was considered to be an essential part of the day. Its necessity for all children was unquestioned by staff even though they were dealing with an age group that, under other conditions, might not have slept during the day at all, and certainly not for the length of time evident in the centers. It was difficult for many children to fall asleep, especially in a room that had wall-to-wall cots with sometimes two children sharing a cot as well as a blanket. For many children it was a frustrating time. But it was also clear that napping served some important institutional needs rather than individual ones. First, it provided a respite for staff, not unimportant when dealing with young, lively children. It gave teachers a chance for a break since a single teacher could supervise a large group, releasing some of the staff. However, napping as a part of institutional routine obscures children's individuality, treating them in ways that deny their right to nap or not, eat or not, depending on their needs. Setting nap time as a fixed part of a day for a defined period of time, two or more hours in most centers, structures a child's basic needs. Few centers had places where non-sleepers could go. Most said, and we saw that it was true, that all children could learn to nap. We might question what this did to a child's sleep patterns, and whether some children might have great difficulties falling asleep at night. But, more than that, nap time, taking up so much of the day, ignored individual differences and needs and became one of the times when the teacher's authority was clearly exercised. Children had to sleep, whether they wanted to or not. The teacher on duty mainly functioned as a disciplinarian over this issue. She would tell children to lie still or to be quiet, over and over. In the end most acquired the napping habit, whatever the consequences. With ARCH, we discussed possibilities for sleeping arrangements that would provide alternative activity areas for the non-nappers and more private spaces for the nappers. If the environment had some options for teachers, they might be more willing to consider the possibility of a less rigid arrangement for naps, a less stringent structure for this central part of the day.

Growing out of this work with ARCH we became interested in day-care environments. We applied for and received a grant to do more systematic research and consultation. At that point, in 1971, the Comprehensive Child Care Act was introduced into Congress. It was also the year that the KLH Corporation began providing on-site day care for their employees, claiming it would "help prevent competition for workers that pushes up wage rates, promotes inflation and causes production bottlenecks" (Ryan, 1975, p. 409). It also would support women's entry into the paid work force.

The Child Care Act was based on a model of child care as a service for all families. It required the federal government to establish and expand existing programs and to allow community control with the full involvement of parents and other individuals and organizations in the community. This bill, passed by both Houses of Congress, was vetoed by President Nixon, and the Congress did not override the veto. President Nixon's message about the veto in one sense accurately gauged the impact of such legislation: "I must share the view of those of its supporters who proclaim this to be the most radical piece of legislation to emerge from the Ninety-second Congress" (Nixon, 1971, excerpted in Bremner, 1974, p. 718). He claimed that there was need for a national debate on such a controversial issue and asserted that since programs for children of the disadvantaged already existed to help parents off the welfare rolls, there did not seem to be justification for such a large expenditure. However, the main reason for his veto was his view of the family and its role in child development. Describing the objective of his welfare "reform" program as "bringing the family together," he said that this legislation would go in the opposite direction:

> . . . it would lead toward altering the family relationship . . . diminish both parental authority and parental involvement with children—particularly in those decisive early years when social attitudes and a social conscience are formed, and religious and moral principles are first inculcated . . . it would commit the vast moral authority of the National Government to the side of communal approaches to child rearing over and against the family centered approach. (Nixon, 1971, excerpted in Bremner, 1974, p. 719)

Clearly, this statement did not reflect the reality of the lives of most families, given the number of single parents and the number of families in which both parents were working. It was an ideological statement, claiming that the economic situation which required most women to remain in the workforce would somehow be swept aside by the denial of support of their situation. During this period, President Nixon also impounded funds appropriated by Congress to the Department of Health, Education and Welfare and OEO. It required a court order in 1973 for these funds to be released, among them the funding for our research.

By the time we started our formal work in day-care centers in 1973, the urban fiscal crisis was beginning. The day-care budget in New York City was cut by $49 million in 1975 (Brozan, 1976), continuing the already tenuous financial situation of most centers. In the first six months of 1976, the last year in which we worked formally in day-care centers, 78 programs in New York were closed completely, others lost groups or components of their programs. Staff was drastically reduced and budgets for equipment and maintenance were severely cut.

In 1975, funding of day care by the federal government was transferred to Title XX of the Social Security Act. Title XX had elaborate regulations, defining eligibility in the usual narrow terms, and put a ceiling on expenditures. Programs in states such as New York, which had spent a large amount of state money based on unlimited matching funds, were immediately affected. Even if the city's fiscal crisis had not occurred, these regulations alone would have devastated day care.

Day care became professionalized and removed from the community as the intake procedure became centralized. Parents were required to travel to a city office, fill out an application, be interviewed by someone unfamiliar with the local day-care center and then get assigned to a center, not necessarily of their own choosing. In 1975, maximum income levels were set and these were kept the same over the next few years, despite inflation. Fees were charged as a percentage of income. Eligibility requirements and income maximums, along with fees for service, led to largely segregated centers where 42% of the parents were on welfare. Only a small number of centers had a racially and ethnically mixed population. By 1975, private for-profit day-care centers were being hailed as the better alternative.

During the period of our research, the public centers we were in were being subjected to the pressures created by these budget cuts and changes in requirements. The level of staffing, the resources available, the maintenance of their buildings, and services were being seriously jeopardized. In some cases this meant that hours were restricted, that teachers had to be fired and that basic equipment and materials could not be purchased. Since funding became based on the number of children in attendance each day, despite cuts in staff, centers were forced to overenroll children to ensure that on any given day there would be enough children to guarantee a stable level of funding. Staff also complained that the new, centralized intake procedures meant that they did not have any relationship to new registrants until they appeared for their first day. This was affecting the quality of the program as was the constant shift in population as families became ineligible. Morale was low as people faced the unpredictable threats to their futures. It was a difficult time to be in these settings, yet we felt it was important to recognize the tensions and concerns and try to look at the impact they had on life in the centers.

This situation, one in which political and economic factors outside the settings were creating the framework within which they could operate, while tense for the people involved, was a usual event when considered in a historical context. From a historical perspective, in fact, the years during which centers were left to their own devices were the more unusual situation.

In addition to wanting to understand this aspect of the day-care environment, our work with ARCH had raised many questions that we wanted to address. Most basic was the question of the models that day-care programs have taken for their form and the impact this has on the children's lives. We considered these issues through an intensive, comparative study of day-care centers. Before examining the qualities of children's lives we should first look at some of the places we studied.

DAY-CARE ENVIRONMENTS AND THEIR IMPLICATIONS FOR CHILDREN

The Day-Care Settings

Our comparative study took place in three different publicly funded day-care centers selected because they presented some contrasts in physical form and size. All three had similar programs aimed at the development of cognitive and social skills. All serviced working-class and poor families, predominantly Black and Hispanic.

All of the centers were located in the same general area but in different neighborhoods, all of which were mixed business and residential. There was a variety of housing, some of it substantial but markedly old, some abandoned, with a few public housing projects as well. All centers had full-time directors, a secretary, and minimal kitchen and janitorial staff. In addition to full-time teachers, some part-time aides and student teachers were occasionally available. All the centers had groups for three-, four- and five-year-old children.

The first center, the Roofplay Center, was in a five-story building with a roof play area. It accommodated about 70 children and had eight full-time teachers. The kitchen was in the basement. The second, Project Center, occupied the ground floor of a large public housing project, with direct access to two playgrounds immediately outside. It was a smaller place with 55 children and six full-time teachers. The center had three large rectangular rooms, each accommodating one of the age groups served. A small kitchen faced the classrooms. Park Center, the third site in which we worked, was located in a double brownstone building but moved in the second year of our study to a small building nearby, formerly a parochial school. In its first site they had 55 children and eight full-time teachers. In the larger quarters they increased the number of children to 65, although no additional staff was provided. In both sites this center used a nearby park for play. Unlike the other centers studied, this one had variously shaped rooms in both locations. The kitchen was located in the basement in both of their sites. Classrooms were considerably smaller in physical dimensions in the second site. Meals were served in the classroom in the first site, but the size of classrooms in the second necessitated the use of a lunchroom, which operated on two shifts.

In describing these places we have used the term teacher for staff members because that term was used in all the centers. All were licensed preschool teachers assisted by aides with various degrees of training. All centers had some form of inservice training and, in fact, we presented our findings to each of them as part of their inservice programs.

After three years of intensive study, much like the School Setting Study, we had extensive observations of what was happening in each of the centers. We had interviews with staff about their programs and philosophies as well as records of how rooms were being used, including the physical changes that were made in the arrangement of furniture and equipment. Through our presence over such a long period we had many informal conversations with staff and children.

Qualities of Day-Care Life

Despite the contrasts in setting, life for children in the centers was remarkably similar. Much as we found in the case of the schools, these three day-care centers had similar appearances in their rooms, similar activities in their programs, and days that reflected a relatively unchanging series of activities. There also was similarity across ages with three-, four-, and five-year-olds doing much the same things.

The rooms looked remarkably like classrooms (see Figure 7.2a,b,c. In fact, since we were conducting research in schools at the same time, it was important for us to label slides, photographs, and data lest we confuse the two study sites. Although the day-care furniture was smaller in scale, the rooms contained many tables and chairs, bookcases, housekeeping and block areas, class pets (fish, gerbils, and the like), and various student productions hung around, usually well

Figure 7.2a,b,c. Daycare "classrooms"

out of the eye-level of children. All of the centers called their rooms "classrooms" and that is what they were like. They had chalkboards, teacher's desks, and many of the trappings of school life. The rooms also functioned like classrooms, even for the three-year-old children. Although there was much time for play, some of it free play as compared with directed activities, our observations identified a great deal of routine in all of the centers, whatever their form.

The outdoor play was one factor shaping the schedule. In the case of the Roofplay Center, the small play area on the roof made it essential to limit the numbers of children there. Only two classes could be there at any one time. Play, therefore, had to be carefully orchestrated, fit into the day with equal opportunities for all. In the two play areas of Project Center, the large spaces could well accommodate all the children. However, teachers preferred the playground with equipment scaled for young children, again a constraint that resulted in scheduling use. For the Park Center, it was usual for two classes to go to the park together, also requiring planning, leading to a set time for each class. In all these cases, outdoor play became a programmed activity not only affecting that time but along with mealtime and nap-time, structuring the entire day.

For the center with the kitchen adjacent to the rooms, meals were more flexibly scheduled. In the case of the Park Center we were told that they had to keep a tight schedule in order to get to their meals in time especially for the first shift, since getting to and from the lunchroom was a major effort. For the Roofplay Center, dumbwaiters carried meals from the basement to each floor, mysteriously appearing with no connection at all to the children or their lives. The Project Center was the only site in which food could be smelled and seen while being prepared. The kitchen staff in this center was very much a part of the program. They allowed children to watch meal preparation, made special treats, and functioned in ways quite different from other places we studied and visited where kitchens were buried out of sight.

Nap time had what must be seen as the strongest impact on the children's day. As we had realized in our work with ARCH the nap period flavored much of the afternoon in all centers. Whether or not the children were sleepy, napping took place after lunch and could last as long as three hours when preparation was included. In all three centers cots were stored in closets and setting them up was a lengthy ritual. None of the teachers questioned the need for naps and few rooms provided other options for children unable to sleep. As in the case of our ARCH observations there was institutional napping.

Aside from meals and napping the pattern of activities in the centers not only were similar across centers but across ages as well. The predominant behaviors, after napping, were preparation for activities and transitions from one activity to another, behaviors such as waiting.

One activity children spent time waiting for was the use of the bathroom. This occurred at specific times and children lined up, with a few at a time permitted to use the room. Reading and teaching/learning covered as much as 40% of all activity. All of the classes had some form of daily group meeting.

The general similarities in programs apparently transcended different personal qualities and personalities of individual teachers as well as the pronounced physical differences in center architecture, exerting a powerful homogenizing effect on the behavior of all the children and teachers. Acceptance of the school model for day care apparently shaped the program whether for three-year-olds or older children.

We also found other patterns reminiscent of the schools. Space within the variously shaped rooms was used very unevenly with convergence of the children around the area most used by teachers, generally a segment of the room close to the doors. This concentrated use of a limited portion of the room occurred despite complaints from teachers that they needed more space. When we raised this issue with staff, teachers recognized their role in clustering children and acknowledged their need to control movement in the class, their conscious decision to monitor the door and their basic lack of trust of children. They did try to consider alternative strategies and, indeed, some changes were tried.

Also similar to our school findings, rooms remained set over the course of the year with few changes in the classroom arrangements. Those changes that did occur were slight shifts in small pieces of furniture such as tables. Again, as in the school, teachers were not happy with their rooms but nevertheless rarely altered their form. The use of the room by boys and girls also paralleled our earlier findings in schools. Much of the activity was sex segregated and some areas of the rooms, the block corner and housekeeping area, had sex-stereotyped patterns of use.

For all the centers, the predominant type of behavior was children working or playing alone, covering at least 63% of all activities observed. This finding is similar to one in the schools. Recognizing the fact that young children do engage in considerable parallel play, the impact of institutional life must also be offered for part of the explanation.

Although the children in day care were younger than those in the elementary schools we studied, it was clear that privacy and aloneness were issues here as well. It was especially evident in the use of the cubbies. For many children their cubbies adjacent to their rooms were home bases. Over the course of a day children would go to their cubbies to touch their possessions, to suck their fingers, to obtain some kind of release from the activity of their rooms. They spent eight or more hours in shared spaces, in classes of 15 to 20. Even if much of their activity was working or playing alone, the presence of many others, the noise level and movement of children could very well cause a child to look for relief. The cubbies seemed to offer a respite or haven to which children could retreat.

THE FUTURE IN LIGHT OF THE PAST AND THE PRESENT

What is the picture of day care today, eight years after we completed our initial work? In 1983, there were 223,500 New York City children younger than six whose mothers were working outside the home and only 77,400 places available in public and private day care. There were 995 licensed preschool facilities in New York; 325 were group centers much like the kind we studied; 158 were Head Start programs; the remainder were private facilities. There were 41,000 children in publicly subsidized facilities. The most typical user of group day care is a single-parent family with three children (Brozan, 1983).

While there is considerable discussion about "choice" of day-care settings, with tax deductions being substituted for public funding, publicly funded day care is the only alternative for most single-parent families. Almost all of them are supported by women and likely to be below poverty level. This is most true for families maintained by Black and Hispanic women. In 1980, the median earnings for women working outside the home (full-time and year round) were $11,703 for white women; $10,915 for Black women; and $9,887 for women of Spanish origin (U.S. Bureau of the Census, 1980). In New York City, the private centers charge between $4,500 and $9,800 per year for children below three years of age and from $3,360 to $5,700 per year for children aged three to five (Brozan, 1983). Continued budget cuts are placing the publicly funded centers in a precarious financial position and the city has expressed an interest in attracting more full-fee-paying families, those who would be charged $80 per week, but the income limit of $21,000 for a single parent with three children is considered a barrier. The city is also encouraging employers to buy slots in centers for use by their employees. Each of these suggestions is aimed at making centers as self-supporting as possible—but they may also push low-income children out.

Based on research showing inadequacies of large, publicly funded day-care centers (Hoffereth, 1979; Ruopp, 1979), there have been advocates for creating alternatives. One is the "for-profit" system of day care, located near places of work. There are questions as to whether "for-profit" or franchise settings can provide quality care. Employers have not been eager to commit the necessary funds, even though the limited numbers providing on-site care have claimed that it has led to a decline in turnover, lowered absenteeism, and improved recruitment because it lessens the need for women to change jobs because of child-care demands or costs. The less than enthusiastic response by employers is attributed by some to research findings showing that on-site care is the least preferred by women workers. It creates the need to transport children long distances, locks women into a rigid routine after work hours, and ties them to a particular job. Probably more salient is the economic situation of the mid 1980s. Judy Fountain, chairperson of the National Coalition for Campus Child Care, said: "I've heard corporate employers saying that for every female employee who they might lose because of a lack of day care, there are six more waiting for the job" (Brooks, 1983, p.C10). Some employers are providing on-site child care as an optional benefit, paid for by the worker. The on-site plans have basically shifted economic responsibility to the caretaker. Other employees are suggesting "flexi-time" as the most suitable option. Rather than provide any form of child care, they will allow workers to take needed time off and to make it up at other hours. But most flexi-time plans assume a two-parent family in which child care is shared. This is not the situation for most households and certainly not for the people who need child-care most.

Some people have advocated family day care, the care of several children in the home of one woman. In New York City in 1983, there were 2,100 licensed family day-care providers with a maximum of six children per provider allowed. These arrangements are somewhat less expensive than group centers costing between $2,160 and $6,700 per year (Brozan, 1983). Some of these places are subsidized by the city for low-income families. While family care has always been an alternative used by low-income families because such care was inexpensive and close to home, it is not always a positive situation for children (Emecheta, 1975). Arguments in favor of this type of care are based on the untested assusmption that the healthiest environment for a young child is in a home with one caretaker (usually the mother). Family day care is considered to be good because it mirrors this "homelike" situation. Arguments backed by researach (Ruopp, 1971) claim that this is the most frequently used and "preferred" care, but the research has failed to explain why this is so and to consider the alternatives against which it is being judged. It is questionable whether such care is best either for children or for the child-care worker who is isolated from other adults and often burdened with too many children to provide a variety of experiences. One can wonder how a single woman with six charges can plan outdoor trips and play experiences. In effect this form replaces one woman with another but leaves the basic situation unchanged.

When we began our review of the history of day care we pointed out that its availability was related more to the relationship between women and the work force than to the needs of children. It is clear that contemporary day-care settings embody institutional qualities in their programs and their physical forms. Children in day care are having institutional experiences. Yet, day care itself has not been allowed to take on the role of a major institution, one that affects the lives of a majority of children. The possibility that day care will become a major public institution for children remains questionable.The failure of day care to expand to meet need seems related to the efforts of groups within the system to maintain the myth of the family. While statistics show that the number of two-parent families with children, where the woman remains at home while the man works outside the home, accounts for only 17% of U.S. households, arguments are made for limiting day care so that the mythical family remains intact. The myth of the family rationalizes paying women workers less on the assumptions that they are not the major breadwinner and their work is a temporary phenomenon rather than a long-term economic necessity. There are two factors which we believe could cause day care to expand. One is that it becomes structurally essential within the economic system. The second is that it become essential for the socialization of all children.

If the economic and socialization functions of day care become pivotal, leading to its expansion, we will be faced with the problem of how to create non-institutional alternatives. Discussions of day-care alternatives, largely focused on the need for women working outside the home, have failed to examine the socialization of children within day care and the qualities that would make it a positive experience. Publicly funded group day care modeled after school environments is being used as a mechanism for socialization with negative implications. Despite our agreement that these settings are creating an institutional experience for children which we do not support, this has not led us to abandon the concept of publicly funded group day care. Our early visits to the interim-funded community-controlled centers convinced us that there could be variety, that places could function without restrictive routines, that programs could address the individual and community needs of children in a way that retains the spontaneity and curiosity of childhood. It was not that these programs or places were perfect, but they did have possibilities we have not seen in the centers that replaced them.

The focus on educational models in these places is not unrelated to the fact that the centers are no longer community controlled and that standards modeled after school environments have been imposed on their form and functioning. Eligibility requirements in public day care make it a service for the "disadvantaged," and without community control the ideology of cultural deprivation remains. Despite claims to the contrary, most public day-care settings are operated as compensatory education and assimilation experiences. It was clear in our work that a major goal of the centers was preparing children for their next institutional entry, that of the school. In fact, staff members verbalized these attitudes to us.

Yet day-care can be seen as an experience in and of itself, appropriate to the needs of children as children rather than as potential students. Instead of being another institution with the goal of social control, we can envision day-care providing a range of experiences in a variety of environments that would broaden all children's potentials without imposing a rigid concept of appropriate development. We believe that these alternatives are possible—and essential.

REFERENCES

Bowles, S., & Gintes, H. (1976). *Schooling in capitalist America: Educational reform and the contradictions of economic life*. New York: Basic Books.

Brooks, A. (1983, July 21). Corporate ambivalence on day care. *New York Times*, pp. C1, C10.

Brown, J. L., & Bing, S. E. (1976). Drugging children: Child abuse by professionals. In G. P. Koocher (Ed.), *Children's rights and the mental health professions*. New York: Wiley.

Brozan, N. (1983, July 20). Day care in New York: A growing need. *New York Times*, p. C1.

Cauman, J. (1956). What is happening in day care—new concepts, current practice and trends. *Child Welfare, 35*. In R. H. Bremner (Ed.). (1974). *Children and youth in America: A documentary history: Vol. 3. 1933–1973* (pp. 696–701). Cambridge, MA: Harvard University Press.

Close, K. (1943). Day care up to now. *Survey Midmonthly, 79*. In R. H. Bremner (Ed.). (1974). *Children and youth in America: A documentary history: Vol. 3 1933–1973*, (pp. 684–690). Cambridge, MA: Harvard University Press.

Close, K. (1965). Day care as a service for all who need it. *Children, 12*. In R. H. Bremner (Ed.). (1974). *Children and youth in America: A documentary history: Vol. 3. 1933–1973* (pp. 707–711). Cambridge, MA: Harvard University Press.

Emecheta, B. (1975). *Second class citizen*. New York: George Braziller.

Fein, G. G. & Clark-Stewart, A. (1973). *Day care in context*. New York: Wiley.

Giroux, H. A. (1983). Theories of reproduction and resistance in the new sociology of education: A critical analysis. *Harvard Educational Review, 53*, 257–293.

Glasscote, R. M., Fishman, M. E., & Sonis, M. (1972). *Children and mental health centers: Programs, problems, prospects*. Washington, D.C.: The Joint Information Service of the American Psychiatric Association and the National Association for Mental Health.

Grotberg, E. H. (Ed.). (1969). *Day care: Resources for decisions*. Washington, D.C.: Day Care and Child Development Council of America.

Guggenheimer, R. (1960). *Day Care Services: Form and substance, a report of a conference, Nov. 17–18*. Washington, D.C.: Children's Bureau, Pub. No. 393. In R. H. Bremner (Ed.). (1974). *Children and youth in America: A documentary history: Vol. 3. 1933–1973* (pp. 704–706). Cambridge, MA: Harvard University Press.

Gupte, P. (1972, Oct. 15). Day-care unit nears the "ideal." *New York Times*, Section 8, p. 1.

Hofferth, S. L. (1979). *Day care in the next decade: 1980–1990*. Urban Institute Reprint. Washington, D.C.: The Urban Institute.

Johnson, L. B. (1965). Special message to the Congress toward full educational opportunity. Jan. 12, 1965, *Public Papers of the Presidents, Lyndon B. Johnson*, 1965, Book 1. Washington, D.C. In R. H. Bremner (Ed.). (1974). *Children and youth in America: A documentary history: Vol. 3. 1933–1973* (pp. 1798-1806). Cambridge, MA: Harvard University Press.

Kelly, E. E. (1936, March). Uncle Sam's nursery schools. *Parents Magazine*. In R. H. Bremner (Ed.). (1974). *Children and youth in America: A documentary history: Vol. 3. 1933-1973* (pp. 679–680). Cambridge, MA: Harvard University Press.

Lajewske, H. C. (1958). *Child care of full-time working mothers*. Washington, D.C.: U.S. Children's Bureau, Pub. No. 378. In R. H. Bremner (Ed.). (1974). *Children and youth in America: A documentary history: Vol. 3. 1933–1973* (pp. 701–704). Cambridge, MA: Harvard University Press.

Langdon, G. (1942). The program of the Works Progress Administration in U.S. Children's Bureau. *Proceedings of the Conference on Day Care of Children of Working Mothers*, Pub. No. 281, Washington, D.C. In R. H. Bremner (Ed.). (1974). *Children and youth in America: A documentary history: Vol. 3. 1933–1973* (pp. 681–684). Cambridge, MA: Harvard University Press.

Nasaw, D. (1979). *Schooled to order: A social history of public schooling in the United States*. New York: Oxford University Press.

Parrish, W. (1933). The plight of our school system. *Literary Digest*, 23. In R. H. Bremner (Ed.). (1974). *Children and youth in America: A documentary history: Vol. 3. 1933–1973* (pp. 1580–1581). Cambridge, MA: Harvard University Press.

Pidgeon, M. (1953). *Employed mothers and child care*. Washington, D.C.: Women's Bureau Bulletin, No. 246, In R. H. Bremner (Ed.). (1974). *Children and youth in America: A documentary history: Vol. 3. 1933–1973* (pp. 677-679; 690–692). Cambridge, MA: Harvard University Press.

Purnick, J. (1983, July 5). How to teach kindergarten: The debate is on. *New York Times*, p. B1.

Rist, R. C. (1970). Student social class and teacher expectations: The self-fulfilling prophecy in ghetto education. *Haravard Educational Review, 40* (3), 411-451.

Rothman, D. J. (1980). *From conscience to convenience: The asylum and its alternatives in progressive America*. Boston: Little, Brown.

Ruderman, F. A. (1968). *Child care and working mothers: A study of arrangements made for daytime care of children*. New York: Child Welfare League of America, Inc. In R. H. Bremner (Ed.). (1974). *Children and youth in America: A documentary history. Vol. 3. 1933–1973* (pp. 711-715). Cambridge, MA: Harvard University Press.

Ruopp, R. (1979). *Children at the center: Final report on the national day care study*. Cambridge, MA: Abt Books.

Ryan, M. P. (1975). *Womanhood in America: From colonial times to the present*. New York: Franklin Watts.

Silverstein, B., & Krate, R. (1975). *Children of the dark ghetto: A developmental psychology*. New York: Praeger.

Spitz, R. A. (1945). Hospitalism; an inquiry into the genesis of psychiatric conditions in early childhood. *Psychoanalytic study of the child. I*, 53–74. New York: International Universities Press.

Spring, J. H. (1972). *Education and the rise of the corporate state*. Boston: Beacon Press.

Steinfels, M. O. (1973). *Who's minding the children? A history of day care in America*. New York: Simon and Shuster.

U.S. Bureau of Census. (1980, March). Household and family characteristics. *Current Population Reports*. Series P-20, 366.

U.S. Interdepartmental Committee on Children and Youth. (1953). *Planning services for children of employed mothers*. Washington, D.C. In R. H. Bremner (Ed.). (1974). *Children and youth in America: A documentary history: Vol 3. 1933–1973)* (pp. 694–696). Cambridge, MA: Harvard University Press.

Ward, A. (1979, Feb.). The political economy of day care. *WIN*, 8–15.

Wolfensberger, W. (1972). The origin and nature of our institutional models. In R. B. Kugel & W. Wolfensberger, *Changing patterns in residential services for the mentally retarded*. Presidential Committee on Mental Retardation. Washington, D.C.: U.S. Department of Health, Education and Welfare, Social and Rehabilitative Services Administration, Division of Development Disabilities.

Postscript

The process of writing this book has given us the opportunity to reflect on our experiences in these settings and to think about their meaning to us and significance for our future work. We support public education but we do not think that present-day schools are the answer to children's thirst for learning. We can envision places for learning that respect children as people and provide the support necessary for them to grow and change in ways that are positive for them. Similarly, we do not deny that there are troubled children who need places and people to go to for help. We can envision a world in which so many children would not need help. We can also envision a world where help giving and receiving is an integrating experience rather than an isolating one, building on children's strengths, rather than stressing their weaknesses.

Over the years of our work in these settings we were changed more by our experiences than they were changed by our presence. As environmental psychologists, one of the things we learned over time was how easy it was for our work to be co-opted. Administrators could and did take our evaluation efforts and the physical changes we helped to implement and used them as signs that the lives of the children were being improved when it was clear to us that this was not the case. In effect, the physical changes were covering up the real nature of what was happening. Insignificant physical changes had symbolic power far beyond their material impacts. While this supports the view with which we began our work, we learned through our work that it was important to have a perspective on environmental change—that attempts at change revealed more about the institution than change itself.

As we think about all of the work we did, in hospitals, schools, and day-care settings, the part that seems most satisfying and promising was our work with the children themselves. From our various contacts, which included participatory workshops, ongoing projects, informal discussions, and the like, we began to recognize the potential that children had to envision alternatives if they were given the support to do so. Whether it was working in the hospital with the children who created the Red Room, in the schools with the children who developed portable desks and other items useful to their daily lives, or in the Futures Project with the children who could create for their neighborhoods alternative futures that reflected a vision of a just and humane society, we know the potential exists. This was in marked contrast to the adults in the situation who were far more limited in their visions, were unwilling to take risks, and hardly ever questioned their assumptions about children.

Our perspective is not based on a romantic picture of children but on what we have seen them capable of doing when the environment gives them a sense that they can have an effect on their world and can have some control over their futures. Perhaps this is best expressed by one of the boys in a future group who, several months after the project was over, described a decision he made to attend an anti-nuclear demonstration he had heard about:

> I was going down there, I thought I could change my future. I could stop them, at least one more hand could help stop the war. So I went on the walk.

Name Index

Subject Index

Psychotherapy: An Eclectic Approach
  by Sol L. Garfield

Handbook of Minimal Brain Dysfunctions
  edited by Herbert E. Rie and Ellen D. Rie

Handbook of Behavioral Interventions: A Clinical Guide
  edited by Alan Goldstein and Edna B. Foa

Art Psychotherapy
  by Harriet Wadeson

Handbook of Adolescent Psychology
  edited by Joseph Adelson

Psychotherapy Supervision: Theory, Research and Practice
  edited by Allen K. Hess

Psychology and Psychiatry in Courts and Corrections: Controversy and Change
  by Ellsworth A. Fersch, Jr.

Restricted Environmental Stimulation: Research and Clinical Applications
  by Peter Suedfeld

Personal Construct Psychology: Psychotherapy and Personality
  edited by Alvin W. Landfield and Larry M. Leitner

Mothers, Grandmothers, and Daughters: Personality and Child Care in Three-Generation Families
  by Bertram J. Cohler and Henry U. Grunebaum

Further Explorations in Personality
  edited by A. I. Rabin, Joel Aronoff, Andrew M. Barclay, and Robert A. Zucker

Hypnosis and Relaxation: Modern Verification of an Old Equation
  by William E. Edmonston, Jr.

Handbook of Clinical Behavior Therapy
  edited by Samuel M. Turner, Karen S. Calhoun, and Henry E. Adams

Handbook of Clinical Neuropsychology
  edited by Susan B. Filskov and Thomas J. Boll

The Course of Alcoholism: Four Years After Treatment
  by J. Michael Polich, David J. Armor, and Harriet B. Braiker

Handbook of Innovative Psychotherapies
  edited by Raymond J. Corsini

The Role of the Father in Child Development (Second Edition)
  edited by Michael E. Lamb

Behavioral Medicine: Clinical Applications
  by Susan S. Pinkerton, Howard Hughes, and W. W. Wenrich

Handbook for the Practice of Pediatric Psychology
  edited by June M. Tuma

Change Through Interaction: Social Psychological Processes of Counseling and Psychotherapy
  by Stanley R. Strong and Charles D. Claiborn

Drugs and Behavior (Second Edition)
  by Fred Leavitt

Handbook of Research Methods in Clinical Psychology
  edited by Philip C. Kendall and James N. Butcher

A Social Psychology of Developing Adults
  by Thomas O. Blank

Women in the Middle Years: Current Knowledge and Directions for Research and Policy
  edited by Janet Zollinger Giele

Loneliness: A Sourcebook of Current Theory, Research and Therapy
  edited by Letitia Anne Peplau and Daniel Perlman

Hyperactivity: Current Issues, Research, and Theory (Second Edition)
  by Dorothea M. Ross and Sheila A. Ross